Charging Communication Networks

From Theory to Practice

Charging Communication Networks

From Theory to Practice

Edited by

D.J. Songhurst
Lyndewode Research Limited,
Cambridge, U.K.

1999
Elsevier
Amsterdam - Lausanne - New York - Oxford - Shannon - Singapore - Tokyo

ELSEVIER SCIENCE B.V.
Sara Burgerhartstraat 25
P.O. Box 211, 1000 AE Amsterdam, The Netherlands

First edition 1999

Library of Congress Cataloging in Publication Data
A catalog record from the Library of Congress has been applied for.

ISBN: 0.444.50275.0

∞ The paper used in this publication meets the requirements of ANSI/NISO Z39.48-1992 (Permanence of Paper).
Printed in The Netherlands.

Contents

Acknowledgements

This book is based on work done in the ACTS project CA$hMAN (Charging and Accounting Schemes in Multiservice ATM Networks). The participants of CA$hMAN (listed in Appendix C) have all contributed, in one way or another, to the work presented here, but I would like to acknowledge the influence of three people in particular:

- Costas Courcoubetis, who was the main driving force in initiating project CA$hMAN and who led the project as Technical Manager in its later stages.

- Frank Kelly, whose work and ideas appear in very much of what is presented here.

- Marion Schreinemachers, who, as Technical Manager in the earlier part of the project, brought a much-needed business-like approach, and who represented the project so well to the outside world.

Particular acknowledgement should be made to the following CA$hMAN members for their contribution to this book:

Chapter 1: Charging in communication networks

Vasilios Siris, David Songhurst, George Stamoulis, Marion Schreinemachers, Costas Courcoubetis.

Chapter 2: The abc scheme

David Songhurst, Frank Kelly.

Chapter 3: Design and implementation concepts
Chapter 4: The CA$hMAN Charging and Accounting System

Sub-Editor for chapters 3 and 4: Vangelis Baltatzis.
Other contributors: Karim Traore, Stelios Sartzetakis, Snorre Corneliussen, Kevin Kliland, Nicky van Foreest, Jan Gerard Snip, George Memenios.

Chapter 5: Agents

George Stamoulis, Ragnar Andreassen, Mechthild Stoer.

Chapter 6: Open issues

David Songhurst, Jeroen van Lierop, Nicky van Foreest, Michel Mandjes, Frank Kelly, Richard Gibbens.

Appendix A: Pricing for guaranteed services

Frank Kelly, Richard Weber, Vasilios Siris, George Stamoulis, Costas Courcoubetis.

Appendix B: Pricing for elastic services

Frank Kelly, George Stamoulis, Vasilios Siris.

Most of the chapters include excerpts from material that has been published elsewhere, or has been submitted for publication. This material is referenced at the appropriate places. Acknowledgement is made to the Institution of Electrical Engineers for permission to publish excerpts from IEE Colloquium papers [26, 112].

David Songhurst
February 1999

Introduction

This book proposes that usage-based charging schemes are essential to generate the incentives necessary for efficient operation of multiservice networks. The rapid development of network technology is enabling sophisticated new services and applications which demand new charging models. The same technology provides the means to operate the right charging schemes. We present here some of the work done in the European collaborative project CA$hMAN (Charging and Accounting Schemes in Multiservice ATM Networks). This project combined performance and economic models of network resource usage and customer utility to construct simple but effective charging schemes which were implemented and trialled in an advanced management platform.

Charging for telephony has traditionally been on the basis of call duration. There have been some exceptions, such as local call access in the US where flat-rate charging is the accepted norm, but elsewhere usage-based charging is generally accepted. In the old environment of national monopoly telecommunication companies there was no pressure for charges to mirror costs, but this pressure has been growing with the impact of competition. This can be seen for example in the reducing cost of long-distance bandwidth, allowing new companies to compete in international and inter-city markets. However it would be fair to say that, despite the increasingly competitive environment, price structures owe more to the power of marketing and customer expectations than they do to any correspondence with cost structure.

In contrast to telephony, packet-switched data networks (for example, based on the X.25 protocol) have typically used per-packet pricing, so that communications are charged according to the amount of data sent. In some cases different priorities of transmission might be available, with appropriately differentiated pricing. However the growth of the Internet has stimulated the popularity of flat-rate pricing, where there are no usage charges but subscription charges are dependent on the speed of the customer's access link. The Internet has developed from a non-commercial network linking academic and government institutions, which is one reason why the facilities for usage charging were never developed. Flat-rate pricing has proved to be a major stimulant to traffic growth and the development of new Internet services which make maximum use of available bandwidth.

The telecommunications vision of a broadband multiservice network has long been centred around the development of asynchronous transfer mode (ATM) switching. Current standards for ATM include a number of different transfer capabilities which provide for a range of different traffic and quality of service characteristics and can thus support a full range of high-level services and user applications. A key issue for ATM implementation is to define suitable charging schemes for these transfer capabilities.

The issues surrounding charging in multiservice networks can be described independently of the underlying technology. It is helpful at first to polarise the issues into a simple argument: usage-based versus flat-rate charging.

In support of usage-based charging

- User has incentive to constrain traffic demands.

- Network provider's revenue is related to resource usage.

- Fairness - users pay for what they use.

- A range of differentiated services can be provided - suitably defined charges encourage users to use the service best suited to their requirements for each connection.

In support of flat-rate charging

- Cheap to implement and operate.

- User bills and network provider's revenue are predictable.

- Generally popular with users - stimulates traffic growth.

The use of flat-rate pricing in the Internet illustrates both sides of this argument. With its simplicity, low cost, and attractiveness to users it has helped to stimulate the enormous growth of the Internet. However congestion has been an ever-present problem, and with no quality-of-service differentiation there is no way for users to obtain an assured level of service. There are currently proposals for enhancing the Internet protocol to provide different levels of service, but it is not yet clear how these would be charged. A case for simple flat-rate pricing in broadband telecommunications was expounded by Anania and Solomon ([24], based on an article first appearing in 1987).

CA$hMAN (Charging and Accounting Schemes in Multiservice ATM Networks) was a collaborative project within the European ACTS programme (Advanced Communication Technologies and Services). It ran for three years from September 1995 and aimed to develop and evaluate potential charging schemes. It was a multidisciplinary project involving mathematical models for usage-sensitive charging schemes, implementation of an experimental platform using specially developed measurement hardware and management software, and carrying out user trials. CA$hMAN used mathematical models aimed at finding simple functional approximations for resource usage, and studied charging schemes derived from these models. This book is based on the work done in CA$hMAN.

Structure of the book

This book necessarily covers a number of specialist fields, and has contributions from authors who are expert in these differing areas. Although the mathematical development of charging models was fundamental to CA$hMAN's charging schemes, the exposition of this work is placed in two Appendices as it is mostly specialist material. The main section of the book aims to introduce the issues relevant to charging, and then provide a short overview of the mathematical development of charging models, leading to a description of the unified charging approach used in CA$hMAN. We then describe the architectural issues related to charging functionality in multiservice networks, and present the experimental platform that was used for user trials in the CA$hMAN project. CA$hMAN experiments with intelligent user agents are described, and the final chapter discusses some open issues surrounding the future of usage-sensitive charging schemes.

In chapter 1 we give an introduction to the issues of charging in communication networks, starting with a general discussion of usage-based charging in multiservice networks, then a review of the current status of charging in the Internet and in ATM networks, and a discussion of the requirements to be met by charging schemes. Chapter 1 concludes with an overview of the CA$hMAN project.

Chapter 2 presents a simple and unified charging mechanism, with charges that are linear in measured duration and volume, that is applicable to both guaranteed services and elastic services (i.e. services for applications that are able to modify their data rates in response to the network). This charging scheme, motivated by the results of Appendices A and B, was the basis for a large part of the work in the CA$hMAN project. We illustrate this general mechanism with numerical examples, and discuss how network operators can use the mechanism as the basis for a full range of practical charging policies. Several other practical charging issues are also discussed here - these are issues which motivated much of the experimental work in CA$hMAN.

The mathematical work underlying the development of CA$hMAN pricing models is presented in Appendices A and B, dealing with guaranteed services and elastic services respectively. This work is fundamental to everything that was done in CA$hMAN and that is presented in this book. Section 2 of chapter 2 provides a short overview of this work.

Appendix A presents a concise view of the mathematical theory underlying usage-based charging for guaranteed services. These are services, such as the deterministic bit-rate (DBR) and statistical bit-rate (SBR) transport capabilities in ATM, which provide strong delay guarantees and hence require bandwidth to be reserved for each connection. This work is based on the theory of effective bandwidth, which is explained briefly here. Some charging mechanisms based on effective bandwidth are presented, followed by discussion of fairness issues and the relationship between charging and connection acceptance control.

In Appendix B we present the mathematical development of charging for elastic services. These are services in which the user is able to adapt the rate of the connection in response to signals by the network. Examples include the available bit-rate (ABR) service in ATM, and the TCP/IP protocol used in the Internet. The theory of proportional fairness is presented, which is important in determining the relationship between charging and rate control. Several approaches to charging for elastic services are discussed.

Implementation of usage-based charging in broadband multiservice networks requires tight integration of charging and accounting management with service provision mechanisms. The architectural design and implementation requirements to achieve this are discussed in chapter 3. This chapter describes how the charging and billing functions are designed as part of the overall network and service architecture. It also presents the requirements for interfaces between end-users, service providers and network operators, and discusses the use of intelligent agents to support charging interfaces.

Chapter 4 provides an overview of the charging platform that was developed for use in the CA\$hMAN project. This platform development adopted an architectural framework based on TINA principles (Telecommunications Information Network Architecture). The platform was required to provide the infrastructure for CA\$hMAN user trials, and its implementation aimed also to validate the charging architecture design with CA\$hMAN charging schemes. This chapter also presents the equipment used to collect measurements for charging in the CA\$hMAN trials, and the interfaces that were developed, and describes how the platform was used for user trials.

Chapter 5 describes some of the experiments and user trials that were carried out within CA\$hMAN to investigate the use of user agents. Several examples of such agents were developed, including an agent for automated renegotiation of DBR or SBR tariffs and an agent for dynamic renegotiation of ABR connections. Such agents are able to use analytical or heuristic algorithms, combined with observation of user preferences, to make optimal selections of tariff and traffic contracts on the user's behalf. The main purpose of implementing such agents within CA\$hMAN was to demonstrate that CA\$hMAN charging schemes, with a simple user/network interface, could provide suitable incentive signals for user applications to operate at high efficiency.

Finally in chapter 6 we discuss some of the open issues that must be solved in the process of implementing usage-based charging in broadband multiservice networks, and we consider how these issues might be addressed for CA\$hMAN charging schemes. Such issues include the design of charging schemes for higher-level services and for interconnection between networks, and the standardisation activities necessary to enable suitable ATM charging schemes to be implemented. We also present some proposals for how CA\$hMAN charging ideas might be implemented within IP networks.

Chapter 1

Charging in communication networks

Charging, accounting and billing are crucial features of telecommunication services. How should the network provider design tariffs for the range of services offered? This is partly a marketing decision - tariffs must be attractive to customers - but network providers are also concerned with efficiency and cost-recovery. Charging schemes should encourage efficient use of the network and should generate revenue in a fair way according to the relative usage of customers.

The development of multiservice networks poses new challenges to the design of charging schemes. Section 1 of this chapter sets out these issues in general terms. In section 2 we discuss the Internet, and in particular we review research into possible Internet pricing schemes. Section 3 provides a short overview of ATM standards for transfer capabilities and quality of service classes, upon which ATM charging schemes must be based. In section 4 we discuss the requirements to be met by multiservice charging schemes from the viewpoint of customers, network providers, and other interested parties. Finally in section 5 we introduce the CA$hMAN project, whose work forms the basis for the remainder of this book.

1.1 Multiservice networks

In multiservice networks, tariffs might depend on a number of parameters defining the traffic and quality of service characteristics of a connection, in order that charges should reflect network resource usage. The way that a customer uses the network depends on the tariffs and also on how the customer values each type of connection (the customer's *utility*, in the language of economics). This interplay between tariffs, network resource usage, and customer incentives is a fertile area for economic and mathematical models.

Multiservice networks need to include facilities for charging, accounting, and billing. In this context, *charging* designates the calculation of a charge for a connection. This is calculated based on some characteristics of the connection, according to a *charging scheme*, which in turn is part of a tariffing policy. *Accounting* involves gathering the information necessary so that total charges can be itemised against tariffs and usage measurements. *Billing* involves collecting charge information over a given period and communicating this to the customer in the form of a bill. Another important concept is *advice of charge*, where a customer can be given on request the charge for a specified call (whether intended, ongoing, or just completed).

A tariffing policy may include both connection charges and subscription charges. We will say that charging is *usage-based* when connection charges are included. Usage-based charges may also include subscription charges that are not related to usage (some authors have used the specific term *usage-sensitive* to refer to charges which could have both components).

Paying for what you get, and getting what you need

The role of charging is not only to cover the costs of service provision and generate income for the service provider, but also to influence the way that customers use network services. This happens as each individual customer reacts to tariffs and seeks to minimise charges. The tariff structure should provide the right incentives for users to use network resources efficiently. This is the key idea of *incentive compatibility*. Tariffs should guide customers to select services and use the network in ways that are good for overall network performance.

Tariffs which are not incentive compatible give wrong signals and lead users to use the network in very inefficient ways. One example of this is the Internet which faces intense congestion problems due to its ineffective pricing structure, which is based primarily on flat-rate pricing. Under flat-rate pricing, charges depend only on the rate of the access pipe which connects customers to Internet service providers. Such a pricing scheme provides no incentives for users to use less bandwidth than the rate of their access pipe. Furthermore, flat-rate pricing does not enable users to adequately reveal their preferences for network usage. All users are treated the same, even though different users might place different values on the same service. Both of these limitations result in a congested network where resources are not used according to the actual needs of users.

Usage-based charging is necessary for incentive compatibility, and economic theory suggests that usage-based charging will be employed where there is perfect competition. This is important in view of the worldwide process of deregulation which is increasing the competitive nature of the telecommunications market. However charging schemes will also be determined by marketing and strategic decisions, customer preferences, and the cost and complexity of implementing and operating these schemes.

The difficulty of charging in multiservice networks

Traffic characteristics and user behaviour in telephone networks have been widely studied. An important feature of telephone networks has been that once a user is granted a connection, the resources associated with the connection remain reserved throughout its duration. Furthermore the quality of service for each connection is the same. Unlike such networks, in broadband multiservice networks the full bandwidth does not need to be reserved for the whole duration of the connection, but is used on-demand. Since in broadband networks there will be a large number of connections carrying bursty traffic which share network resources (link bandwidth and buffer space), there are significant gains in statistically multiplexing such connections (i.e. sharing the bandwidth between them without having to reserve the full peak bandwidth for each). Multiservice networks are intended to carry traffic with different characteristics, which may vary in time, and support connections with different quality of service (QoS), expressed in terms of loss probability and delay. In order to offer QoS guarantees the network must generally reserve resources for connections. Charges for connections should reflect the resources required.

The amount of network resources used by a connection and the QoS experienced by the user also depend on the statistical properties of the traffic generated by the connection. Within the telecommunications and computer industries it is possible to discern two extreme approaches to this issue. One (impractical) approach is to expect the user to provide the network with a full statistical characterisation of traffic, in advance, which is then policed by the network. Another approach stresses the difficulty for a user of providing any information on traffic characteristics, and expects the network to cope nevertheless. The correct balance will necessarily involve trade-offs between the user's uncertainty about traffic characteristics and the network's ability to statistically multiplex connections in an efficient manner. A desirable property of a charging scheme would be to encourage the cooperative sharing of information and characterisation effort between the user and the network. This can be realised if tariffs encourage cost-minimising users to make a more accurate characterisation of some statistical properties of their traffic. This information can then be used by the network to multiplex user connections more efficiently.

The cost of charging

An important requirement of a charging scheme is that it is efficiently implementable. By this we mean that the information required by the charging scheme should be easy to obtain and to manipulate. It is well known that accounting and billing are major parts of the total cost of telephone networks. Hence, a prerequisite for a realistic charging scheme is low cost of implementation and operation. Current technology allows sophisticated traffic measurements to be done in hardware, which greatly expands the spectrum of charging functions which are feasible to implement. However detailed statistics are costly to manipulate and store, hence there is a trade-off between the amount of statistical information gathered (which would allow more accurate characterisation of a user's traffic) and the cost of gathering, storing, and manipulating such information.

Services

Multiservice networks will, in general, offer two types of basic services which differ in the performance guarantees offered by the network: guaranteed services and elastic services.

With guaranteed services the network provides some form of quality of service (QoS) guarantees in terms of loss probability and delay. A key concept for such services is the *traffic contract* between the user and the network. From the part of the user, this contract specifies the constraints that the traffic must satisfy. These constraints are expressed in terms of filters (usually in the form of leaky bucket constraints), placed at the entrance to the network, which are used to police the user's traffic. From the part of the network, the traffic contract specifies the QoS the network must guarantee.

Guaranteed services are subject to connection acceptance control (CAC) whereby a user sends a connection request to the network specifying desired QoS and a traffic description. The network uses this traffic contract information to check if it has enough resources to satisfy the request. Once a connection is accepted, the network will need to reserve some amount of resources in order to satisfy the connection's QoS requirements. Such network control is also known as open loop control. Examples of such services include the Constant Bit Rate (CBR) and Variable Bit Rate (VBR) services defined by the ATM Forum. These services are very close to the Deterministic Bit Rate (DBR) and Statistical Bit Rate (SBR) services defined by the ITU-T for Broadband Integrated Services Digital Networks (B-ISDN). The guaranteed service and controlled-load service defined by the IETF for the Internet's integrated services architecture are also examples of services providing some performance guarantees.

If charges are to reflect resource usage, it is clear that tariffs must take into account the QoS and traffic description of connections, since the amount of resources the network needs to reserve depends on both. However the traffic contract parameters alone will not accurately determine resource usage. This is because the contract only confines the user traffic to lie within specific ranges determined by the traffic description. Since the user will not in general need to produce the worst case input allowed within the contract, charging according to this worst case traffic would not give the right incentives. From the above discussion it becomes clear that in order to create tariffs with the right incentive properties we need to combine traffic contract parameters with actual measurements. How this is done is closely related to the statistical multiplexing capability of broadband multiservice networks.

Unlike guaranteed services, elastic services do not have specific performance guarantees. As a result, performance during overload periods deteriorates. Such services are intended for applications that can adapt their sending rate to varying network conditions. To support this, elastic services employ closed loop congestion control which provides feedback signals to the user throughout the duration of a connection. These feedback signals provide an indication of the congestion inside the network. In the presence of congestion the user's traffic rate must decrease, whereas in the absence of congestion the traffic rate is allowed to increase. Examples of elastic services are the traditional TCP/IP service in the Internet and the Available Bit Rate service (ABR) in ATM networks.

The design of charging schemes for elastic services should take into account the feedback control mechanisms of such services, and address issues of network optimality and convergence. In this direction, it is important to identify a key role of charging, namely to lead the network to stable operation and economically efficient utilisation of network resources. This implies that charging should be closely integrated with congestion control, whose role is to minimise the extent and spread of overload conditions which lead to information loss.

Service-level and content charging

Multiservice networks should have the capability to offer higher-level services that utilise the basic transport-level services. In ATM networks the transport-level services are provided by ATM Layer Transfer Capabilities such as DBR, SBR, and ABR. Services such as real-time video, Internet access, etc, may be provided over transport-level services by Service Provider organisations. These service providers must consider how to charge for higher-level services, and in particular how their charges relate to charges for transport-level services.

For some types of service (such as video on demand) the service provider also wishes to charge for content. Connection charges may be bundled in with content charges so that they cannot be distinguished by the customer.

This book is primarily concerned with charging at the transport level, and in fact the CA$hMAN project was aimed mainly at charging schemes for ATM Layer Transfer Capabilities. However we will also discuss (in chapters 2 and 6) how service-level and content charging might be implemented over CA$hMAN charging schemes.

1.2   Internet

The Internet started in the late 1960s as a United States Department of Defense ARPA (Advanced Research Project Agency[1]) funded project, initially called ARPANET [86]. In the early 1980s a new family of protocols were specified for the ARPANET and associated networks; these are commonly referred to using the names of the two basic protocols TCP/IP (TCP:Transmission Control Protocol, IP: Internet Protocol). In 1987 the U.S. National Science Foundation (NSF) funded a network connecting the six U.S. national supercomputer centers. This network was called NSFNET and served the research and

---

[1]ARPA is now called DARPA (Defense Advanced Research Projects Agency).

academic community. At the same time initiatives in Europe and worldwide developed networks based on the TCP/IP protocol suite. Today the Internet has grown to become a ubiquitous network used as a communication and information tool for researchers, students, teachers, business and the general public.

The remarkable success and growth of the Internet has convinced many agencies, organisations and researchers that it will play an important role (but perhaps not in its present form) in the evolving broadband network infrastructure. Even today, network operators are offering both Internet and ATM services. Both services are bit transport services, hence their pricing models are not independent. Work is underway in the IETF (Internet Engineering Task Force) to enhance the Internet's current best-effort only service with real-time services [45, 37]. The IETF's service model is very close to the ATM Forum's service model, suggesting that the two pricing models will share many commonalities. The changing nature of the Internet [106] and the problems of congestion have made it clear that its economic model (in which flat-rate pricing, where tariffs depend on the customer's access pipe, is the most common) needs to evolve. This has prompted numerous related studies and workshops (cf. [46, 29, 99, 101]), which have shown, among other things, the importance and need for usage-based pricing. Because of its widespread use and availability the Internet provides a valuable testbed for testing pricing models in order to understand their practical implications in large scale, real-world environments, and the users' response to various pricing models [55].

We begin by describing the aspects of Internet technology that affect pricing, identifying the areas where it differs from ATM. Next we describe some proposals for pricing Internet services. Our objective is to present the underlying key ideas and understand their relation with the networking technology.

Internet technology and costs

The Internet's success can be attributed to the effectiveness of statistical sharing of network resources (e.g. communication lines, routers), the positive network externalities from being connected to the network (i.e. the ability to effectively communicate with a large number of users), and the openness of the underlying communication protocols (namely TCP, UDP/IP) along with the interoperability of the different implementations. Specifically, the Transmission Control Protocol (TCP) deals with end-to-end issues (e.g. message segmentation and reassembly, flow control, retransmissions) while the Internet Protocol (IP) is responsible for routing packets to their destinations. Each packet contains all the necessary information for routing (source and destination addresses), and is routed independently. This forms the basis of IP's connectionless communication paradigm. This characteristic, which is the cornerstone of the Internet's success, is what makes accounting difficult: since all packets are independent at the IP level, how can a source be accounted for the amount of resources it uses? By contrast, accounting is simpler in connection-oriented architectures such as ATM and the telephone network. Due to its connectionless nature, the Internet's transport service resembles the postal service. However, this analogy cannot be extended to the economic aspects. In the Internet, the cost of sending an extra packet is essentially zero (when there is no congestion), which is not the case with the postal service where labour forms the largest percentage of the total cost.

In more detail, the cost of the Internet consists of the following [90]:

- The incremental cost of sending an extra packet. In the absence of congestion this is essentially zero.

- The congestion costs, or social costs of delaying other users' packets. As above, this cost is zero when there is no congestion.

- The fixed costs of the network infrastructure (e.g. routers, communication lines), maintenance, and management.

- The incremental costs of connecting to the network. This involves the cost of the access lines and customer premises equipment needed to connect to the network. This cost represents the largest portion of the total cost for an organisation to connect to the Internet [101].

- The cost of expanding the capacity of the network.

Fixed costs constitute the major percentage of the total costs. On the other hand, the marginal or incremental costs are non-zero only in the presence of network congestion. This observation leads to the proposition that under normal (i.e. uncongested) operation, network charges should include only fixed charges. However, in the presence of congestion, charges should also include a non-zero usage charge which depends on the level of congestion and the magnitude of the users' contribution to it. The effect of congestion on prices can be expressed either with dynamically adjusted prices or time-of-day sensitive prices.

From the previous discussion, one understands that congestion is tightly related to pricing. In fact, many believe that usage-sensitive pricing provides the only practical way of tackling the problem. The current Internet offers a single best-effort service where all packets are treated the same. However, this can be unfair since a user can obtain an increasing share of capacity by sending a continuously increasing number of packets, while ignoring packet losses, at the expense of conforming TCP connections. Some proposals for Internet pricing provide a way to differentiate packets, providing different service to different packets. Furthermore, this service differentiation translates to monetary value: packets receiving better service are charged more than packets receiving lower quality service.

Besides charging, there are other methods for controlling congestion. One approach involves overprovisioning the network. However, experience has shown that the demand for bandwidth has always been ahead of the supply. In addition, router technology advances at the same rate as the technology used by the end-systems. This suggests that demand will continue to overtake supply in the future. Another approach for controlling congestion involves engineering solutions such as priority queueing. However such solutions fail to give users the incentive to use the offered services rationally. This incentive problem can be solved with pricing.

Internet integrated services architecture

Work within the Internet Engineering Task Force (IETF) has focused on enhancing the Internet's best-effort service model in order to support services with some guarantees [45, 37]. This work has led to the development of two new service types: guaranteed service [108] and controlled load service [120]. With the guaranteed service type the network provides a deterministic delay guarantee, whereas with controlled load service type the network provides service close to that provided by a best-effort network under lightly loaded conditions. Hence the controlled load service offers a bandwidth guarantee but not a hard delay guarantee. It is important to note that for both the guaranteed service and controlled-load service types the user traffic is described using a leaky bucket, which is also used for traffic description in ATM networks. This traffic description is part of the traffic contract between the user and the network. Because of these similarities (traffic contract, leaky bucket characterisation) the same pricing structure used for guaranteed services in ATM networks can potentially be used for both guaranteed services and controlled-load services in the Internet.

Internet pricing: current status

The most common model for Internet pricing is to charge a flat rate which depends on the size of the customer's access pipe. Many believe that such a model is suboptimal and unable to tackle the problems of congestion. What flat-rate pricing lacks is the ability to give users the incentive to use network capacity rationally. Under flat-rate pricing, a low volume user, who occasionally uses up to the peak bandwidth that his access pipe allows, is charged the same as a high volume user who continuously has his access line working at a high utilisation. With usage-based pricing, customers with high-capacity access are not charged the same, rather their charge depends on the level of usage. In this way, a provider can offer more flexible and competitive tariffs. Interestingly enough, some Internet Service Providers have started to offer usage-based pricing for high capacity access pipes. Flat-rate pricing is not without advantages. Predictable network charges and essentially zero accounting overhead are among the most important.

Work on Internet pricing

Bohn et al [32] present a scheme to differentiate user traffic based on the precedence field in the IPv4 header. Specifically, end users set the precedence field depending on the level of service they require. Intermediate routers maintain more than one queue for packets with different precedence values and implement a priority service discipline rather than simple first-in-first-out (FIFO). Packets with a higher precedence are placed in a queue with higher priority, hence experience better service (lower delay) in periods of congestion. A quota system can be used to discourage users from always selecting a high precedence. If quotas are related to monetary units the resulting scheme generates charges based on (precedence) priority level *independently* of the level of congestion. An advantage of this proposal is that it can be gradually implemented in the parts of the Internet where congestion is a problem.

MacKie-Mason and Varian [90] propose a "smart market" approach to pricing. According to this approach, each packet contains a "bid" which indicates how much a user is willing to pay for the transmission of the packet. Routers queue packets in the order of decreasing bids, hence packets with a higher bid experience less delay. All end users whose packets were transmitted pay the cutoff price which is the value of the bid of the last packet the router served. Advantages of the scheme are that optimal prices can be computed as soon as packets, with their respective bids, arrive at the switch. In addition, users do not have any advantage in mis-representing their valuations, hence their best strategy is to truthfully declare their bids. The disadvantages of the scheme include the additional overhead in the packet header, and most importantly the complexity of the service discipline in the switches which has now become tightly interconnected with the pricing scheme.

Gupta et al [72] model the Internet as a collection of servers (e.g. providing entertainment, news, database services) offering a number of priority classes. Servers post prices and expected waiting times for each priority class they offer. Based on these values, clients (users) are free to select the priority class that maximises their benefit. The aggregate user demand depends on the prices, hence the server can control it (hence the average delays) through the posted prices. It is proved that there exists a unique welfare-maximising allocation of resources, and with simulation it is demonstrated that approximately optimal prices can be computed using a decentralised algorithm. The algorithm is motivated by the classic tatonnement process where the price is increased when the delays at a priority queue are excessive and vice-versa. A user selects the priority class that maximises his benefit, and the network adjusts prices using exponential averaging. The price updates use online measurement of the average flows and time-average estimates of expected waiting times, and do not require knowledge of the demand functions.

Both the scheme of [90] and [72] present methods to obtain (or at least approximate) optimal prices. The optimal prices depend on the level of congestion, and provide necessary feedback required for network administrators to decide whether investment for capacity expansion is justified. In [90], optimal prices are computed as soon as packets with their respective bids reach the router. On the other hand, in [72], an iterative approach was used to obtain optimal prices. In this case the convergence time of the algorithm is important. This time tends to be large for high latency networks. Neither of these schemes takes account of interconnection of networks, which is a predominant characteristic of the Internet.

Odlyzko [100] presents an approach to pricing the Internet called Paris Metro Pricing (PMP), due to its resemblance to the pricing structure of the Paris Metro. The basic idea is to partition the Internet into several logical networks, each with separate and nonsharable resources. The (fixed) price of bandwidth would be different for each logical network, and the expectation would be that higher priced networks would be less congested than lower priced networks. Hence, the scheme allows a user who requires better performance to switch to a higher priced, and less congested logical network.

Clark [44, 43] takes a different approach to pricing the Internet. The main objective of the approach is to discriminate users at times of congestion. The scheme allows different users to obtain a different share of capacity at times of congestion, by purchasing a profile or *expected capacity*. One possible way to express user profiles is the two parameters of a leaky bucket. Packets are marked as *in* or *out* depending on whether they are within the user's profile or in excess of it. In the absence of congestion all packets (both those marked *in* and those marked *out*) receive the same service. On the other hand, in the presence of congestion, routers preferentially drop packets marked *out* since those packets have exceeded the profile purchased by the user. A user's *expected capacity* is not a guarantee from the network to the user. In fact, even under overload conditions, the network does not guarantee this capacity. The *expected capacity* represents the capacity a user *expects* to be available to him, and provides a method of allowing users to obtain different shares of network capacity during periods of congestion. An important advantage of the scheme is that internally the network switches are required to implement a simple scheme where, in periods of congestion, packets marked *out* are preferentially dropped. Buying expected capacity rather than peak rate of the access link allows a customer to vary his profile depending on his demand without changing or upgrading his access link. At the same time, the network provider can better dimension its resources based on the expected capacity that it sells, rather than on the sum of the peak rates of the customers' access links. The author does not present specific methods or approaches to how this can be achieved. Similarly to the scheme in [32], prices do not depend on the state of congestion. Finally, the author does not address the issue of how user profiles (*expected capacities*) are assigned a price value.

Related to the above is the Premium Service Model of Nichols et al [98]. This scheme guarantees that a user's contracted capacity is there when he needs it. When the capacity is not used, it may be used by best-effort traffic. At the entrance of the network, traffic belonging to premium service is marked with the premium service bit set. Inside the network there is a separate queue, with higher priority, for premium service data and for normal best-effort data (which has the premium service bit cleared). The IETF Working Group on Differential Service for the Internet [69] is investigating the policy and architectural issues for supporting differentiated services, based on servicing packets with different priority or with different dropping preferences.

Rather than present a specific pricing scheme, Shenker et al [107] focus on structural and architectural issues such as the local control of pricing policies, multicast charging, and receiver charging. In the proposed architecture, charges are determined locally at the access point, hence the name *edge pricing*. This is important because more detailed pricing schemes can be implemented and tested at the edge of the network, while maintaining a simple and generic network core. Rather than try to compute the congestion costs, which the authors argue are inherently inaccessible, they propose to approximate them with prices that depend on the quality of service (QoS), the time-of-day, and the expected path from the source to the destination. In the case of multicast traffic, there is a potentially large and varying group of destination users. One approach for accumulating accounting information to the source would be to have receivers periodically send *accounting messages*. While traveling to the source, each node (router) would add the cost of its downstream link to the accounting message. Branching nodes would add the sum of the costs of all downstream links. Hence, when the accounting packets reach the source they will contain the accounting information for the whole multicast tree. In the case of receiver charging, charges can be computed at the "exit" point (the receiver's access point). For multicast connections each receiver can be assigned a fraction of the total charge. Policies for assigning these fractions are discussed by Herzog et al [75].

The problem of pricing the best-effort Internet does not have a single solution. Practical evidence supports this claim: in New Zealand, usage-sensitive pricing has been successfully used to finance the high cost link to the Internet [38]. On the other hand, usage-based pricing was unsuccessful in Chile [28], and when the U.S. Department of Defense attempted to implement it in its inter-agency Defense Data Network [77, 29]. Furthermore, a usage-based pricing scheme was too complex to be implemented for New Zealand's Internet Frame Relay network. This experimental evidence suggests that there is no single solution for pricing best-effort services, and methods to be adopted will necessarily depend on factors such as the relative cost of the link, the topology (e.g. single high capacity link or meshed network), and the nature of the customers (commercial organisations, academic sites, residential users).

Consider finally that we are in a new technological and commercial environment brought about by the deregulation of the telecommunications industry, the growing integration of services, and the ability to successfully use best-effort services for the transmission of voice, audio and videoconferencing (e.g. using MBONE). In this environment the problems of pricing Internet services, pricing ATM services, and pricing telephony can no longer be approached independently.

The Internet Demand Experiment (INDEX)

Whereas for networks offering a limited range of services, such as telephone networks, a large amount of empirical data exists, this is not the case for networks that have the ability to offer a wide range of service qualities. Such data is particularly important in order to identify the market structure for network services. The Internet Demand Experiment (INDEX) [114] at the University of California at Berkeley aims to answer exactly this question, namely to understand the structure of user demand for Internet access for different price/quality combinations. Among the objectives of the INDEX project are

- to measure user demand for Internet access as a function of quality of service, pricing structure, and application

- to demonstrate an end-to-end system that provides access to a diverse group of users at attractive price-quality combinations

- to develop a prototype system that can be scaled to serve the demand for remote network access from a whole community of a large university.

Internet settlements

A different but related problem to that of charges by Internet providers to end users and organisations is that of inter-carrier financial settlements [39]. A settlement agreement is an agreement between two or more service providers which specifies an agreed set of metrics and the corresponding charges. It is current practice that competing carriers usually exchange traffic free of charge. It is expected (and even inevitable) that this situation will change in the future. Carpenter [39] attempts to stimulate a discussion on Internet settlement metrics. Metrics identified include the access capacity, connect time, total traffic, peak traffic, number of announced routes, mean RTT (round trip time), mean loss rate, and others. The author identifies the need for developing measurements of these metrics and collection of results.

Related to this is the lack of existence of metrics to quantify the quality of best-effort service and methods to measure it [70]. Such metrics necessarily involve the cooperation of service providers, and are required if customers want to know what kind of service to expect for the prices they are charged by their providers. Paxson [102] provides a general framework for the particular metrics to be developed by the IETF.

1.3   ATM

Asynchronous Transfer Mode (ATM) has been under development for a number of years as the technology to support Broadband Integrated Services Digital Networks (B-ISDN). ATM is designed to combine the benefits of packet switching with connection-oriented transport, in order to offer integrated services with appropriate quality of service guarantees and efficient use of bandwidth. Standards for ATM, defined by the ATM Forum and by ITU-T, are approaching a mature and stable state.

ATM is designed to provide shared capacity for multiple traffic classes having different traffic characteristics and quality of service requirements. Several key features of ATM enable this to be achieved efficiently:

- The use of packet switching to enable statistical multiplexing at the cell and burst levels.

- Connection-oriented operation with connection acceptance control to ensure quality of service guarantees.

- Rate control protocols which allow elastic traffic services to use spare capacity efficiently.

Standards

The ITU standard for the B-ISDN protocol reference model [3] defines three layers:

1. The ATM Adaptation Layer (AAL) assembles data from user connections into ATM cells for transportation and reassembly at their destination.

2. The ATM Layer is responsible for the end-to-end transfer of user cell streams, including functions such as flow control, cell routing and switching.

3. The Physical Layer transfers cells between ATM switching nodes. This layer will typically use Synchronous Digital Hierarchy (SDH).

The ITU has defined several ATM Layer Transfer Capabilities (ATCs) [13, 20]. These are tailored to distinct demands of likely application groups. The ATC used by a connection should fulfil the general requirements of that connection, for example whether bandwidth varies over time at the initiative of the network, and what actions the network may take if cell rates are exceeded by the source. Detailed characteristics of the ATC are captured in the associated traffic contract, and in the QoS class for the connection. The defined ATCs are:

- Deterministic Bit Rate (DBR): throughput at the peak cell rate (PCR) is guaranteed throughout the connection. DBR is intended for constant bit rate traffic with strong delay requirements. Examples could include voice and videoconferencing.

- Statistical Bit Rate (SBR): throughput at the sustainable cell rate (SCR) is guaranteed as a long term average, with bursts at up to the PCR for periods constrained by the maximum burst size (MBS). Sub-categories of SBR vary in how they treat the Cell Loss Priority (CLP) indication in each cell, depending on the quality of service class explained below. SBR is intended for variable bit rate sources. Delay guarantees can be provided for real-time applications. A typical application would be video with variable rate encoding.

- Available Bit Rate (ABR): the network uses a rate control protocol to signal changes in the allowed rate of each connection; the rate may vary up to the PCR, and there may also be an agreed minimum cell rate (MCR). ABR is intended for sources which are able to adapt their rate according to network conditions but have low cell loss requirements. Examples include Web browsing and file transfer.

- ATM Block Transfer (ABT) allows transfer characteristics to be negotiated for ATM blocks (groups of cells).

The ATM Forum has specified service capabilities analogous to the ITU specifications for DBR, SBR and ABR, with one addition [60]:

- Unspecified Bit Rate (UBR): there are no throughput or quality of service guarantees. A typical application might be email.

Ensuring quality of service

The network aims to achieve maximum efficiency by multiplexing many connections with varying bit rates. However if utilisation is high then statistical fluctuation in the overall cell rate can cause cell losses. This is controlled in several ways:

- Buffering is used to store cells until links or switches are free to handle them. Buffer lengths are constrained by the need to meet delay guarantees.

- UBR cells can be dropped or delayed.

- Rate control signals can be used to vary the rates of ABR connections.

- Connection acceptance control (CAC) is used to limit the acceptance of new connections having throughput guarantees (essentially DBR and SBR connections, and ABR connections with non-zero MCR) so as to keep the total bandwidth demand within the resource available.

- Usage parameter control (UPC), or policing, is used to monitor connections to ensure that they stay within their traffic contract. Cells exceeding this contract may be tagged, and could be discarded.

Quality of service classes

The ATM Layer Transfer Capabilities have associated network performance parameters - these are cell loss ratio, cell transfer delay, and cell delay variation. In addition the traffic descriptor defines the cell delay variation tolerance where appropriate.

To complement the connection profiles described by the ATCs, and to describe the Quality of Service parameters of the connections offered by a network, ITU-T Recommendation I.356 [12] describes classes of Quality of Service. There are at present four QoS classes. Their main characteristics are outlined below. Values for the limits on cell delay and cell loss are given in I.356.

QoS classes

Class 1, the 'stringent' class, offers stringent limitations on both cell loss and cell delay, regardless of the CLP (cell loss priority) indication. The stringent limitations for delay apply both to the average cell delay on the connection and to the cell delay variation (CDV).

Class 2, the 'tolerant' class, likewise offers guarantees regardless of the CLP indication of each cell. This QoS class specifies limited cell loss, with limits that are slightly more tolerant than in QoS class 1. QoS class 2 offers no limitations on cell delay.

Class 3, the 'bi-level' class makes a distinction between cells with CLP indication CLP = 0, and cells with CLP indication CLP = 1. Guarantees apply only to cells with CLP = 0. The guarantees are limitations on cell loss, and they follow the values of QoS class 2.

Class U is the 'unspecified' class. Neither delay nor loss have specified limitations for connections of this class.

I.356 defines appropriate combinations of ATC and QoS class (marked o) as follows:

	DBR	SBR	ABT	ABR
1: stringent	o	o	o	
2: tolerant	o	o	o	
3: bi-level		o		
U: unspecified	o	o	o	o

Quality of service, resource usage, and charging

In practice there are no fixed rules to determine which services and applications will use each ATC. For the user there is a trade-off between cost and quality of service. Consider voice traffic as an example. Voice has traditionally been carried at constant bit rate in narrowband telephony networks, and would naturally use DBR in an ATM network. However with variable rate encoding it could use SBR with equally acceptable quality of service, or ABR with less reliable quality. The choice should depend on the pricing structure and on the quality of service achievable (the quality of service provided by an ABR connection would depend on network conditions, varying with time of day).

In a competitive environment one would expect that the usage-based component of charges for different ATCs should reflect the relative costs of resource usage in the network. This cost is not determined simply by the average bandwidth requirement of a connection - it depends also on the bandwidth variability, the peak rate, and the QoS requirement. For example, for an SBR connection with a highly variable cell rate and a low delay requirement the network might need to reserve bandwidth considerably greater than the mean rate of the connection (the average rate at which the connection generates cells) in order to meet the QoS guarantee. In contrast the network might need to provide very little capacity for elastic traffic (ABR and UBR) since these connections are rate-adaptable and can use the spare capacity left over by guaranteed services. Hence it has been suggested [116] that charges for different ATCs might differ by several orders of magnitude.

The problem for the network operator then is to devise a pricing structure for the ATCs offered. Competition should ensure that prices reflect relative network resource usage costs. The charging algorithms should convey appropriate incentives to users and should not be too complex. If these aims are achieved successfully then users will be able to make efficient choices of traffic contract, with a good correspondence between the utility to the user and the cost imposed on the network. It remains an open question as to whether a realistic pricing structure can support the full range of ATCs defined for ATM.

1.4   Requirements for charging schemes

Charging for telecommunications services has two main aims. The first is to generate revenue which enables network and service providers to operate profitably. The second aim, met by usage-sensitive charging, is to generate incentives for users to constrain their traffic demands appropriately, resulting in efficient network operation. This second aim is particularly important in broadband multiservice networks where user applications have the ability to generate high data rates - often much higher than the user needs to assure an acceptable quality of service. However it is likely to be difficult to characterise and predict resource usage in a multiservice environment, and the requirements for charging schemes should therefore be evaluated carefully.

The requirements for a charging scheme are imposed mainly by the two key roles - provider and customer. In the context of ATM networks we will focus on charging for ATM-level services provided by a network operator. Other roles can be distinguished (service providers, application developers, regulator) - their impact on requirements is considered later in this section.

We consider here high-level requirements that apply to the charging scheme as a whole. Network operators also have more detailed requirements for the charging system implementation - these will be discussed in chapter 3.

Customer requirements

Predictability

Charges should be broadly predictable, therefore the major part of usage charges should be based on measures that customers can understand and control.

Ease of use

Customers need to be given simple information through a clear interface to enable them to make correct choices of tariff and traffic contract.

Traceability

Bills should be clear and understandable to customers, so connection charges should have supporting information that indicates choice of service and tariff and measured usage parameters.

Network operator requirements

Revenue generation

Charging should generate the required revenue for the network operator. Telecommunications charging has traditionally been based on a combination of subscription and usage charges. Subscription charges provide a steady and predictable revenue. Usage charges provide a more variable revenue but one that is linked to variable network costs.

Cost-effective implementation

Usage-sensitive charging imposes several overheads on the charging system, in particular the collection and processing of usage measurements and the presentation of detailed data in customer bills. These overheads can add significantly to the cost of implementing and operating the charging scheme. The requirements for usage-sensitive charging, and the design of the charging system, must be carefully assessed to ensure that the cost is not too great.

Flexibility

The charging scheme should be adaptable to meet the requirements of all types of customer, to work effectively with user applications, and to serve as a basis for charges that are defined at the service level.

Usage incentives

Charges should generate incentives to users to constrain appropriately the traffic that they generate, so ensuring efficient network operation.

Interconnect

Different network operators may use different charging schemes, but the usage parameters on which charging is based should be standardised to facilitate interconnect charging. Chapter 6 includes a discussion of interconnect charging.

Requirements of other parties

Service provider

A service provider can offer to customers high-level services that operate over ATM connections provided by a separate network provider. The service provider is therefore a customer of the network provider in addition to being a supplier of services to the end-customer, and therefore has many of the requirements listed above. A more specific requirement of the service provider is to be able to charge at the service level in a way that relates logically to the ATM-level charges imposed by the network provider. Service-level charging is discussed more fully in chapter 6.

Some service providers might also provide and charge for content. Usually the service provider would like to offer an integrated charge to the end-customer, who would not then be able to distinguish between connection charge and content charge.

Application developer

The characteristics of ATM traffic will to a large extent be determined by software applications under the control of end-users (for example, applications such as videoconferencing, Web browsing, file transfer). The developers of these applications may be able to maximise their efficiency (in terms of bandwidth usage, for example by using sophisticated video coding methods), and to include controls which allow the user to trade data rate against perceived quality. Whether, and how, application developers will provide these facilities depends to a large extent on the charging schemes that users are faced with.

Regulator

Many countries now have regulatory bodies specifically responsible for overseeing the telecommunications industry and regulating the transition to a fully competitive environment. Charging, and in particular the level of charges, is naturally a key area for regulation. Within this area there are two requirements which might influence the charging schemes adopted by network operators:

- Charges should be cost-orientated. This should occur naturally in a fully competitive environment, and it is therefore a reasonable aim for regulation in markets where one operator is dominant [19]. This is a key issue for determining interconnection charges.

- Tariffs should be clear and understandable to users, and should enable comparison between different providers.

Discussion

It should by now be apparent that the desires of different parties are sometimes in conflict and it will be difficult, perhaps impossible, to design charging schemes that fully satisfy all of these requirements. Perhaps the most important difference is between the desire for simplicity and predictability and the need to generate appropriate usage-related incentives. Charging schemes that are closely usage-related are less likely to be simple, understandable and predictable. In the end it is a commercial decision for network providers to choose charging schemes weighing usage-sensitivity against customer acceptability.

One way to resolve or lessen this conflict is to ensure a good user interface - one that can help the user to make good choices of tariff and traffic contract and to understand the resulting charges. This issue came to the fore in the CA$hMAN project, which directed some of its work to the design of the user/network interface and of intelligent agent software to help users.

Another important issue concerns charging for elastic traffic (such as TCP/IP, and the ABR service in ATM). Incentive-compatible charging schemes for elastic traffic are congestion-sensitive - the busier the network the more the user must pay to achieve a desired throughput. The schemes investigated in CA$hMAN and described in Appendix B are certainly of this kind. This property conflicts with many of the requirements listed above (including simplicity, predictability, revenue generation), and customer acceptability must be a major concern. In fact this form of charging is not designed for predictable revenue generation but rather as a means of providing control signals leading to efficient network operation. The charges are an incentive to users to cooperate in this control, and may well be acceptable to users provided they are substantially lower than charges for guaranteed services.

1.5   The CA$hMAN Project

The ACTS Programme (Advanced Communication Technologies and Services) was established under the Fourth Framework Programme of European activities in the field of research and technological development and demonstration (1994-1998). The Programme aimed to support research and development in advanced communications in order to facilitate economic development and social cohesion in Europe. Under the Programme, individual companies, public sector organisations, research institutes, schools and universities agreed to work together as individual project consortia, pooling their knowledge and resources in pursuit of specific research objectives covered by the ACTS workplan. All ACTS research was conducted in the context of usage trials to ensure relevance of the results and to encourage a broadening of awareness of the benefits that advanced communications may bring. Twenty two National Host organisations supported project experiments and acted as a window to the many trials conducted.

ACTS Project AC-039 was named CA$hMAN - "Charging and Accounting Schemes in

Multiservice ATM Networks". CA\$hMAN ran for three years, from September 1995 to August 1998. Its objectives were to study and develop, implement, verify and compare charging and accounting schemes for ATM networks. It was a multidisciplinary project involving participants from university departments, telecommunications hardware and software manufacturers, and network operators:

Intrasoft SA, Greece
Ascom Monetel, France
ATecoM GMBH, Germany
Ericsson AS, Norway
ICS-FORTH, Greece
ISS University of Aachen, Germany
Lucent Technologies, USA
Lyndewode Research, UK
Royal KPN, Netherlands
Telenor Research, Norway
Telscom AG, Switzerland
University of California Berkeley, USA
University of Cambridge, UK

Appendix C provides a full list of the individuals from these organisations who participated actively in CA\$hMAN.

CA\$hMAN's main achievements were to develop a range of simple but effective pricing models for both guaranteed and elastic services, to design and implement a platform for charging and accounting management based on TINA principles and advanced technology, and to use this platform for trials that were able to demonstrate CA\$hMAN charging schemes in operation and to explore user-network interface issues and the use of intelligent agent software. The multidisciplinary approach was very successful, combining economic and mathematical models, hardware and software development, and operational network issues.

This book does not set out to describe all of the work done in CA\$hMAN. Instead we aim to present an approach to multiservice network charging that reflects the CA\$hMAN experience.

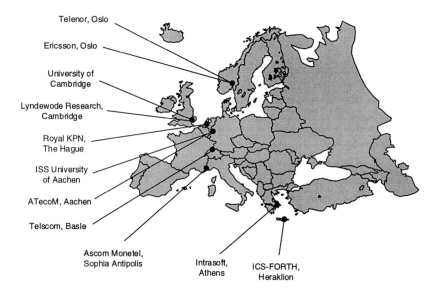

Figure 1.1: CA$hMAN partners

Chapter 2

The *abc* scheme

2.1 Introduction

Usage-sensitive charging schemes for multiservice networks must be carefully designed to meet a range of requirements - they should be sufficiently robust and effective to generate appropriate incentives for all classes of service, while being sufficiently simple to allow cost-effective implementation and interfacing with user applications. Mathematical models of network behaviour can be used as the basis for charging schemes that reflect resource usage. This also requires that connection acceptance control (CAC) schemes be designed appropriately. However this alone is not sufficient - in order to generate appropriate incentives for users, tariffs should be understandable and, in particular, should relate to connection traffic characteristics that the user (or the user's application software) can understand. These principles underpin the development of charging schemes, and their mathematical analysis, described in Appendices A and B.

The work described in the Appendices develops charging methodologies based on measurement of duration and volume of each connection, applicable to both delay-sensitive and delay-tolerant traffic contracts. This work is outlined in the next section. In the remainder of this chapter we describe how these methods can be brought together in a unified charging mechanism. This charging mechanism has been implemented within the CA$hMAN project for user trials in the context of ATM-level traffic contracts between user and network. After presenting the underlying charging mechanism we describe how this mechanism can be used to implement a range of charging policies and then discuss some of the issues relevant to the choice of charging policy. Chapter 6 describes how this charging mechanism might be extended to service-level charging and interconnect charging.

2.2   Models for charging schemes

Charging models for guaranteed services

When a network offers strong service guarantees it must apply connection acceptance controls in order to reserve the necessary resources to ensure that these guarantees can be met. Charging connections on the basis of their resource usage is a natural way to generate appropriate incentives. With correctly designed charges the system comprising users and network should move towards an efficient operating point. How can charges be defined so as to reflect resource usage adequately and convey appropriate incentives without being too expensive to implement or too complex to manage? The approach described in Appendix A uses charges based on effective bandwidth models for resource usage.

Consider a resource in a multiservice network, such as a link, which is shared by a mix of connections of different types. Effective bandwidth is a measure of the relative resource usage of each connection. The value of the effective bandwidth must lie between the mean rate and peak rate of the connection, depending on quality-of-service requirements and network conditions:

- For a large resource carrying many connections, or where QoS constraints are weak, the effective bandwidth will be close to the mean rate.

- For a small resource carrying few connections, or where QoS constraints are strong, the effective bandwidth will be close to the peak rate.

The influence of network conditions can be represented by two parameters, one representing space (such as buffer and link capacities) and one representing timescales. These two parameters can be expected to vary rather slowly and can be readily estimated by network operators.

The usage-sensitive component of connection charges should be determined in some way by measures of effective bandwidth. However the most obvious ways to do this have disadvantages:

- An estimate of effective bandwidth might be constructed solely from the traffic contract parameters agreed between user and network at the start of the connection. A charge is then applied at a fixed rate (per time unit) on the basis of this estimate. This gives the user no incentive to constrain traffic demands to anything less than the maximum achievable within the traffic contract.

- An estimate of effective bandwidth might be constructed solely from measurements of the actual cell rate of the connection. A problem with using this estimate as the basis for charging is that the network may have to reserve resources (on the basis of the traffic contract parameters) in order to ensure the guaranteed QoS. A connection with a low mean rate might not pay for the reserved resources.

The proposed solution is to construct tariffs that depend both on static parameters that are policed and on dynamic parameters that are measured. The tariffs offered to users are obtained from bounding approximations to the effective bandwidth function. Appendix A describes a simple charging mechanism where charges are linear combinations of the duration and volume of the connection. Users can minimise their charge by choosing tariffs corresponding to their expected mean rates. This charging mechanism forms the basis of the unified charging scheme that is discussed in this chapter, and which has been implemented and studied in CA$hMAN trials.

Appendix A also describes models based on more general linear functions of measurements, considers issues of accuracy and fairness in charging, and describes a connection acceptance control (CAC) mechanism that is closely related to the simple time and volume charging scheme.

Charging models for elastic services

In future communication networks there are expected to be applications that are able to modify their data transfer rates according to the available bandwidth within the network. Traffic from such applications is termed *elastic* [106]; a typical current example is TCP traffic over the Internet [76], and future examples may include the controlled-load service of the Internet Engineering Task Force [120] and the Available Bit Rate transfer capability of ATM (asynchronous transfer mode) networks [13].

The key issue addressed in Appendix B concerns how the available bandwidth within the network should be shared between competing streams of elastic traffic. Traditionally stability has been considered an engineering issue, requiring an analysis of randomness and feedback operating on fast time-scales, while fairness has been considered an economic issue, involving static comparisons of utility. In future networks the intelligence embedded in end-systems, acting on behalf of human users, is likely to lessen the distinction between engineering and economic issues and increase the importance of an interdisciplinary view.

Appendix B presents an approach based on a *proportional fairness* criterion, whereby a system optimum is achieved when users' choices of charges and the network's choice of allocated rates are in equilibrium. Simple rate control algorithms, using additive increase/multiplicative decrease rules or explicit rates based on resource shadow prices, can provide stable convergence to proportional fairness per unit charge, even in the presence of random effects and delays.

Appendix B also presents two possible ABR implementations of proportionally fair pricing, and a pricing scheme based on the sharing of effective usage rather than the sharing of simple rates. A simple implementation of ABR pricing is described in the next section, as part of the CA$hMAN unified charging scheme.

2.3   A general mechanism for usage-sensitive charging

The charging mechanism comprises a subscription charge and a per-connection charge.

The subscription charge can be related to many different aspects of the service being purchased, including:

- access rate

- the range of services available

- quality of service.

The per-connection charge takes the form

$$aT + bV + c$$

where T and V are the measured duration and volume of the connection, and a, b, c are tariff parameters applying to the connection. The tariff parameters a, b, c are agreed between user and network at the start of the connection, dependent on the traffic and service contract. They are static parameters (they are changed by the network only infrequently, typically at intervals measured in months).

These tariff parameters have a simple interpretation for the user. a is a charge for duration (for example in euros per second). b is a charge for volume (for example in euros per Mbit). c is a minimum charge for a connection.

As defined the abc scheme is deceptively straightforward. But we shall see that the dependence of a, b and c on static parameters, known to the user and the network at the start of a connection, allows the scheme to deal with both guaranteed and elastic services; indeed it even permits the network to offer subtle choices of tariff that might appeal to sophisticated users able to assess the statistical characteristics of their traffic.

Charging for guaranteed services

For guaranteed services the charging parameters a and b can be defined by tangents to the bounding effective bandwidth function, as discussed in section A.3 of Appendix A. For a given peak cell rate the user may be offered a fixed tariff whose parameters a and b are given by the intercept and slope of a fixed tangent; or the user may be offered several choices of tariff, corresponding to distinct tangents, as illustrated in Figure 2.1. Each tangent is a distinct linear bound to the bounding effective bandwidth function, touching at a specific value of the mean rate of the connection. The choice of tangents allows the user to lower the "per unit time" rate a at the cost of raising the "per unit volume" rate b.

The user can thus minimise the expected charge by choosing a tariff corresponding to the user's estimate of the mean rate of the connection. A user with a low expected mean rate should choose a tariff with small duration charge a (tariff 1), whereas a user with a high expected mean rate should choose a tariff with small volume charge b (tariff 2). The user's choice of tariff thus conveys information to the network which could be used in connection acceptance control (as discussed in section A.6 of Appendix A).

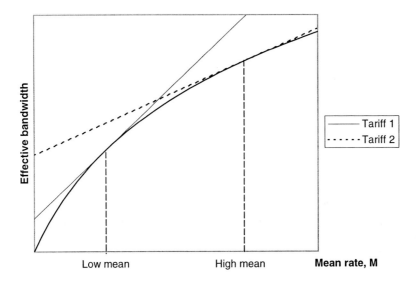

Figure 2.1: Tariffs for connections with low and high mean rates

The connection set-up charge (the parameter c in the tariff) represents the cost to the network, in switching and signalling resources, of establishing a new connection. Some services, such as intelligent network services, may use additional signalling resources which might justify a higher set-up charge. If an operator were to offer a facility to renegotiate connections then a similar renegotiation charge would be required. This might be the same as, or less than, the set-up charge. The user then has a decision problem - whether or not to renegotiate a tariff during a connection. This is a problem readily handled by user application software. Chapter 5 describes some of the CA$hMAN experiments with renegotiation and the use of such software to help the user in choosing a and b tariff parameters.

Charging for ABR

The *abc* scheme can also be applied to ABR charging. The essence of the scheme is that traffic up to the minimum cell rate (MCR) is charged at one rate, while traffic above the MCR is charged at a lower rate. If a resource within the network has spare capacity beyond that required for high-priority and MCR traffic, then it may be shared amongst ABR connections in proportion to their MCRs. Thus the choice of MCR by a user buys a share of spare capacity, as well as providing a minimum cell rate.

More precisely, we suppose that there is a charge of a times the chosen MCR per unit time, and additionally a charge of b per unit volume, where b may be zero. This is precisely equivalent to differential charges for volume above and below the MCR under the assumption that the cell rate does not fall below the MCR - in other words, the contracted MCR defines a minimum level for volume charging. Thus traffic above the chosen MCR is charged at a lower rate, possibly a substantially lower rate. To illustrate the properties of this scheme, consider a typical ABR application, such as a file transfer of a given size. By choice of MCR a user can obtain an upper bound on the time taken to transfer the file, although the user would expect a much faster transfer if the network were lightly loaded. Note the important feature that both the time taken to transfer the file *and* the total charge to transfer the file will be larger when the network is congested, since the higher charge a applies to a larger volume of the transfer. Users may of course complain that they are charged more for a slower service, but this is the key characteristic of any incentive-compatible scheme designed to ease congestion. At times of congestion the user can speed up file transfers by increasing the chosen MCR for connections: each user is able to act according to its own trade-off between delay and cost.

Note that users and network can achieve a co-ordinated response to congestion without the need for the charges a and b to depend upon the level of congestion or even upon factors such as the time of day. The key point is that for traffic that is not highly delay-sensitive, both price and delay are available as co-ordination signals (cf. [107]). The scheme described here allows delay to carry feedback on network congestion to users; the charges a and b turn the delay signal into a price signal with many of the attractive properties of the "smart market" of [91]. In particular, the price signal encourages the revelation of user preferences.

There are several ways to describe the above scheme, both practically and theoretically. The scheme closely resembles some of the existing tariffs for frame relay, where the committed information rate plays a similar role to the minimum cell rate. It can be described in terms of the effective bandwidths, where the charges a and b play the role of the respective shadow prices for the two constraints (equations (A.4) and (A.5) in Appendix A). It would be interesting to explore further relationships with the expected capacity service of [44], where packets tagged *out* might correspond naturally with traffic charged at the rate $b = 0$.

The simple pricing approach for guaranteed services could be readily integrated with the above scheme to price traffic below the MCR, and this may be worthwhile if the statistical properties of users' traffic are such that MCRs are frequently not filled. Similarly the approach will have relevance for the statistical multiplexing over short time-scales of delay-tolerant traffic that is bursty within its rate control envelope. A fuller discussion of rate control for delay-tolerant traffic would depend upon implementation details, and particularly upon the allocation of buffering across the network, but it seems unlikely that this level of network detail could usefully influence the structure of tariffs.

Early discussions of the above *abc* charging scheme were presented in [83] and [113].

2.4   A numerical example

We now present a numerical example to illustrate the charging scheme. The connection types in this example are all delay-sensitive, and the tariff parameters are calculated from expression (A.15). We will disregard here the per-connection charge c and only consider charges arising from the duration and volume tariff parameters a and b. Note that these tariff parameters generate charges that are in units of bandwidth. In other words, the total charge per second (arising from both duration and volume charges) is the linearly bounding effective bandwidth (in Mbit/s). In practice some constant factor would be applied to all of these tariff parameters in order to produce monetary values, but the important issue in this example is the relativity between different sets of tariff parameters.

Suppose that the predominant traffic offered to a link of capacity 100 Mbit/s falls into three categories, with peak and mean rates as described in Table 2.1. Then the choice $s = 0.333$ in expression (A.14) is reasonable [79]. Table 2.1 gives the tariff parameters $a(h, m)$, $b(h, m)$ for these connection types. Here we make explicit the dependence of a and b upon the peak rate, h, of the traffic contract and upon the user's choice of tangent, labelled by m. Note that almost all of the charge for these three connection types arises from the variable charge $b(h, m)$.

While the predominant traffic may be of types 1, 2 and 3, connections are not constrained to just these types. For example, a connection with a known peak rate of 2 Mbit/s could select any pair $(a(2, m), b(2, m))$ from Figure 2.2, or a connection with a known peak rate of 10 Mbit/s could select any pair $(a(10, m), b(10, m))$ from Figure 2.3.

Similarly tariffs may be calculated for sources with other peak rates. For a peak rate of 0.1 Mbit/s the bandwidth $B(h, M)$ is almost linear in M, producing a variable charge $b(h, m)$ per unit of traffic that is almost constant in m. Since statistical multiplexing is efficient for sources with such low peak rates, very little incentive need be given to determine mean rates accurately. Peak rates above 2 Mbit/s produce more concave effective bandwidths and hence more incentive to accurately estimate the mean.

Table 2.2 shows tariffs for other service types which have higher mean rates. The various charges shown in Tables 2.1 and 2.2 are expressed in the same units (of resource usage per

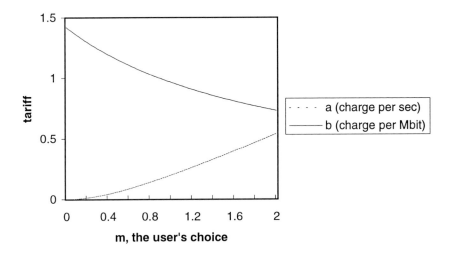

Figure 2.2: Tariff choices for a peak rate of 2 Mbit/s

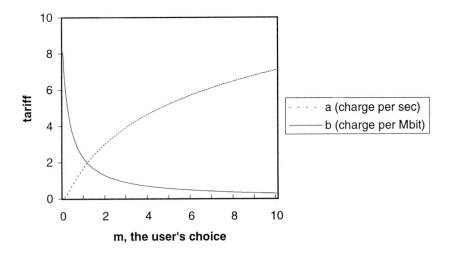

Figure 2.3: Tariff choices for a peak rate of 10 Mbit/s

Connection type	Rate (Mb/s)		Charge	
	Peak (h)	Mean (m)	$a(h, m)$ (per second)	$b(h, m)$ (per Mbit)
1	0.1	0.04	2.7×10^{-4}	1.0
2	2.0	0.02	1.3×10^{-4}	1.4
3	10.0	0.01	1.1×10^{-4}	7.9

Table 2.1: Typical charges for traffic with low mean rate

Connection type	Rate (Mb/s)		Charge	
	Peak (h)	Mean (m)	$a(h, m)$ (per second)	$b(h, m)$ (per Mbit)
4	2.0	1.0	0.2	1.0
5	10.0	1.0	1.7	2.2
6	10.0	2.0	3.0	1.3

Table 2.2: Charges for traffic with higher mean rates

second or per Mbit) and are directly comparable with each other.

Table 2.3 shows the total charge for a connection of 100 seconds duration, for each of the six connection types listed in Tables 2.1 and 2.2. We assume here that the mean rate of each 100 second connection is actually equal to the specified mean. Observe that the total charge for connection type 1 is higher than that for connection type 2: for these connection types at this resource statistical sharing is relatively easy, and the advantage of a lower mean rate outweighs the disadvantage of a higher peak rate. The total charge for connection type 3 is, however, much higher than for connection types 1 and 2: statistical sharing becomes more difficult with a peak rate as high as 10% of the capacity of the resource. Observe that for connection types 1 to 3 almost all of the total cost to the user arises from the variable charge. For connection types 4 to 6 much more of the total cost arises from the fixed charge, more than half in the case of connection type 6.

Comparison of the total charges for connection types 4 and 5 shows the saving to be made by reducing peak rate while maintaining the same mean rate. This indicates the incentive to the user to use shaping to limit peak rates without reducing the volume of data sent. This incentive is substantial when, as for connection types 4 to 6, peak and mean rates are high in relation to link capacity.

The above charges can be compared with those that might be appropriate if the link were entirely loaded by delay-insensitive traffic (that is, traffic whose effective bandwidth approaches its mean rate, and for which the average utilisation could reasonably exceed 90%). A variable charge of about 0.5 per Mbit would recover from such traffic about the same total revenue as can be recovered from a link loaded with high-priority traffic from the categories shown in Table 2.1. Note that delay-insensitive traffic does not directly substitute for high-priority traffic until its volume exceeds a certain level, about 50 Mbit/s for the numerical example of this sub-section. Distinct constraints of the form (A.4) and

Connection type	Rate (Mb/s)		Total charge (100s)
	Peak (h)	Mean (m)	
1	0.1	0.04	4.0
2	2.0	0.02	2.8
3	10.0	0.01	8.0
4	2.0	1.0	116
5	10.0	1.0	392
6	10.0	2.0	557

Table 2.3: Total charges for connections of 100 seconds duration

(A.5) apply to high-priority traffic and delay-insensitive traffic: if the first constraint is tight and the second is not, then the link is unable to accept any more high priority traffic and yet is capable of accepting more delay-insensitive traffic.

2.5   Charging policies

A practical charging scheme should enable network operators to implement a wide range of commercial charging policies. Some operators may well wish, for marketing reasons, to offer tariffs that are simple and easily understood. Others may put higher priority on using tariffs that closely reflect network resource usage. The choice of charging policy affects the attractiveness to users of the services offered by the network, and also has a strong influence on the traffic generated by users. In this section we list the distinct types of tariff that are possible with the *abc* scheme, and for each type of tariff we describe the corresponding charging policy and its applicability and advantages. See [111] for a study of the relative competitive advantages of choice of charging policy.

Flat-rate charging

A service is charged for on a flat-rate basis (subscription only) when the per-connection usage tariff is zero. Flat-rate tariffs are popular with users because they generate completely predictable charges and provide no disincentive to generate traffic. An operator might offer flat-rate tariffs for services which impose relatively low usage costs on the network even when demand is high. A flat-rate tariff may often depend on the user's access rate, which constrains the maximum demand.

Charging by duration

The per-connection charge is $aT + c$. From the user's viewpoint this charging would be seen as suitable for real-time services with delay guarantees, for example interactive speech or video. From the network operator's viewpoint it is clearly applicable to ATM DBR traffic contracts. An operator might also choose to apply duration charging to SBR traffic contracts - for simplicity, and to meet user expectations. However this does have some disadvantages. It may be difficult to differentiate between various SBR traffic contract choices, and between SBR and DBR contracts, via a single duration-related charge. There is also no incentive for the user to limit traffic volume below that allowed in the traffic contract, thus reducing the scope for network efficiency improvement.

Charging by volume

The per-connection charge is $bV + c$. From the user's viewpoint this charging would be suitable for non-real-time services with only weak guarantees (or none) on delay, for example for email and file transfer. From the network operator's viewpoint it is applicable to UBR, and also to ABR with zero minimum cell rate (MCR). An operator might also choose to apply volume charging to some traffic contracts which have guarantees on delay or throughput. However this is likely to present problems with user incentives. The user has no incentive to terminate a connection that is not sending data, even though the network has to have resources assigned to maintain the throughput guarantee. In addition, if parameters such as PCR and MCR are reflected in the volume charge b then the user may have an incentive to split the connection into several smaller ones with lower tariffs.

Charging by duration and volume

The per-connection charge is $aT + bV + c$. This charging scheme is suitable for variable bit-rate services with guarantees on delay or throughput. For SBR the network can offer, for each set of traffic contract parameters, one or more sets of tariff parameters. In this model, developed in Appendix A, each tariff represents a bounding tangent to the effective bandwidth function. The user's best choice of tariff depends on the estimated mean rate of the connection.

In the case of ABR the duration-related charge is proportional to the requested MCR and the volume-related charge is typically very much smaller, as presented in section 2.3. This scheme is able to implement the desirable feature of proportional fairness, applicable to elastic traffic (including ABR and TCP/IP).

2.6   Implementation and user issues

The *abc* charging scheme is designed to be as simple as possible while still providing appropriate incentives. Implementation in real networks, however, raises many practical issues. A major part of the CA$hMAN project was devoted to examining implementation and user issues of charging schemes, through experimental implementation and user trials in an ATM environment. In this section we outline some of the issues of network implementation, user/network interface, and user understanding that motivated CA$hMAN work. The following chapter discusses architecture and design issues in much more detail, while the results from CA$hMAN work form the substance of the remaining chapters of this book.

Network implementation

Implementation of usage-sensitive charging in a real network environment involves a number of architectural and design decisions. The most basic requirement is the need to measure usage. For the *abc* scheme, usage is characterised by the measured duration and volume of each connection. Hence there is a need to count cells and accumulate cell counts for every connection. This imposes certain hardware and software requirements, but in principle this is not more onerous than the policing function for ATM connections, which also requires cell counts.

Raw measurements require processing to generate charging information. This may include some statistical treatment of the measurement data, followed by combination of this data with tariff information to produce charges. It is necessary to consider at what level in the network such processing is carried out, and how the data is stored and transmitted to appropriate points in the network. It is conceivable that some charging schemes might be based on complex statistical functions of connection cell rates, for example to reflect burstiness over short timescales. For such schemes it might be necessary to carry out a significant amount of processing on a real-time basis. The *abc* scheme does not pose such requirements.

Real networks must collect and process charging information for large numbers of simultaneous connections. The design solutions adopted for these functions must be scalable to ensure efficient operation with acceptable performance across entire networks.

User/network interface

The user/network interface must be able to show tariff information to users in association with traffic contract information, and enable the user to make sensible choices of tariff and traffic contract. It should also have provision for charging information to be displayed to users during connections and on their completion, and might also enable users to renegotiate tariff or traffic contract parameters during connections.

The *abc* scheme uses linear functions of time and volume and thus enables the adoption of a standard form of tariff comprising the three charging parameters a, b, c. This in turn allows the design of a simple user/network interface for ATM-level charging that is common to all ATCs. This interface would, in general terms, be between a Tariffing Agent in the network domain and a Purchasing Agent in the user domain. The Tariffing Agent passes traffic contract and tariff options to the user domain, and receives back the user's choice of tariff and traffic contract. The Purchasing Agent mediates between the human user, the user's application, and the network. In the simplest case the Purchasing Agent might be just a Java applet that is downloaded from the Tariffing Agent and displays to the user the available choices of traffic contract parameters and tariff parameters. More sophisticated Purchasing Agents might provide a higher-level display to the user (for example, showing estimated costs of connections for different tariff choices), and might be linked to the user's ATM application in order to provide intelligent assistance with choice of contract.

A user/network interface of this form was developed in the CA\$hMAN project and used in user trials of charging schemes. This interface is described in chapter 4.

It is essential for any charging scheme that the charges as presented in customer bills should be clear and understandable and auditable. This requires the storage of all of the data that determines each connection charge. For the general charging scheme discussed here this comprises the following information:

- The identity of the tariff selected, which fixes the tariff parameters a, b, c.

- The measured duration (T) and volume (V) of the connection.

- Any further information which may underlie the tariff choice, for example the time of day, call destination, ATM traffic contract.

User understanding, acceptance, and incentives

The user viewpoint is critical for the acceptance of new kinds of charging schemes. Users should feel that they are able to understand their charges, and that they should be fair and predictable. In a multiservice environment it is inevitable that usage-based charging must present some difficulties for non-expert users, in particular in selecting appropriate tariff and traffic contracts and in understanding the resulting charges. From the network provider's viewpoint, a charging scheme is designed to convey certain incentives to users, and efficient network operation depends on users reacting appropriately to these incentives. This in turn requires a certain level of understanding on the user's part. Software agents can help users in this process. Such agents could be closely linked to (or part of) the user's ATM applications. In CA\$hMAN some experiments were made with user agents, primarily in order to demonstrate that such agents could use simple algorithms to make good tariff choices on the user's behalf. This work is presented in chapter 5.

Predictability of usage charges is an important issue for customers. A subscription-only scheme (no usage charges) is completely predictable. Usage charges based on duration only (for real-time voice and video) or on volume only (for non-real-time data transfer) are likely to be understandable and thus moderately predictable. Charging based on both time and volume would seem to present the most difficulty for users. However for many services time and volume charging will be necessary to provide the right incentives and enable the full benefits of ATM to be achieved. Economic considerations should favour the adoption of time and volume charging, but this will require that operators present a suitably clear charging interface and that users are helped by application software that can deal intelligently with tariff and traffic contract decisions.

It is not easy to determine how to set relative prices for services with different QoS characteristics - and in particular relative prices for guaranteed and elastic services. Such relativities depend upon relative resource usage (which may not be readily quantifiable), customer utilities (i.e. the valuations that customers place upon different levels of service), and the actions of competitors. An approach to this problem is outlined in chapter 6.

Chapter 3

Design and Implementation Concepts

3.1 Overview

Flat-rate and capacity-based pricing policies have been widely adopted by telecommunications operators and service providers. These policies can be easily supported by charging mechanisms that do not closely involve the service logic and the control of the resources used. However the deployment of charging mechanisms over broadband networks, combined with usage-based algorithms, has a very tight relationship with the service provision mechanisms at all levels of the hierarchy, which imposes the use of sophisticated accounting management mechanisms. From the network level, where the resource usage and utilisation are monitored, up to the service level where integrated per-user pricing information is produced (service-level charging), the charging functions should be designed in an efficient manner, in order to minimise the cost of the management infrastructure and also to avoid performance bottlenecks.

The various architectures used for service provision refer to the modelling of the functions and the building blocks that constitute the service management and control. This modelling includes the identification of the business roles and their relationship, the definition of the different views of the service, as exposed for each role, the definition of the functional and computational entities of the service and the way they are deployed on the computational and the switching resources of the physical network.

Existing service architectures present a high degree of differentiation in terms of capturing the relationship between the service logic and the required network resources. Each architecture focuses on some specific applications and services that best match the network characteristics and exploit the provided resources most efficiently. For example the Internet architecture places the service logic at the access points of the network and at the user terminal equipment, while the network is used only for its transport capabilities. By contrast, in the Intelligent Network (IN) architecture the service control and call processing functions are placed within the network.

A charging and accounting architecture can be considered as the part of the service architecture that is related to the collection and processing of usage and charging data according to a specific pricing policy. The design of a charging architecture usually depends on the nature of the supported applications in terms of requirements and service control functions. "Interactive", "Messaging", "Distribution", or "Retrieval" classes of applications may exhibit quite different behaviour when referring to video, audio, text/data, or image information transfer. In the same way, "Interconnection" applications - such as aggregated LAN, remote terminals, distributed file systems, and general distributed processing communication - may require a different approach to defining the relationship between resource usage and charge. This variety in the behaviour and the requirements of the services should be captured by the corresponding charging algorithms and more generally by charging systems having the ability to monitor and process efficiently the resource usage, service control, and pricing information.

The functionality of an accounting and charging architecture extends beyond the domain of a single service provider or network operator. Usually many business parties are involved in this process such as end-users, customers, service providers, content providers, brokers, and network operators. The individual nature of these roles, their interests, the various contractual agreements between them, and the technical grounds upon which these agreements are realised, should be taken into account when designing an accounting architecture.

In this chapter we try to identify the generic requirements of the accounting system and to describe the corresponding functionality and information exchange between the independent building blocks, providing a simplified and representative view of charging and accounting in general. For example the lower level functions for monitoring, storage, and reporting of resource usage can be identified independently of the service architecture or the network technology. This can be done by defining the interactions and the transferred generic information elements through specific reference points. At the higher layers, where charging and billing is performed according to specific user and service profiles, there is an additional requirement to define reference points for the communication between the service provision and charging functions. These reference points between end-users, service providers and network operators should be independent of the service architecture and the adopted network technology, and should be based on a generic business model within which the roles and responsibilities of each stakeholder are specified.

The flexibility and efficiency of an accounting system can be guaranteed only by a decentralised distributed model, where the computational entities are able to communicate and act in an independent way. Among the reasons that justify this requirement are the following:

- The volume of the processed information in usage-based charging systems can be very high, and consequently there could be a need for distribution of functionality amongst the network and the processing resources.

- The control and management of the system can be a relatively complicated task, so there is a need for components that are able to "absorb" the complexity of specific tasks, and expose a simplified view of them to the other components of the system.

- The rapid development of new services should be followed by update and modification of the corresponding systems. The responsibilities of the computational entities should be very clearly defined, so that each one of them can be easily updated or modified without affecting the operation of the whole system.

These computational entities with incorporated intelligence and ability to act on behalf of users, business roles or even functional entities are known as "intelligent agents". In terms of implementation, the distribution of the charging and accounting functionality amongst independent building blocks can be supported by the corresponding "middleware" technologies, which are responsible for providing an environment that facilitates the deployment and interworking of the components.

The chapter concludes with an indicative, rather than exhaustive, list of problems and considerations about the performance and scalability of accounting systems. The deployment of the system over large-scale networks and the potential impact on the overall performance may introduce a significant communication and processing cost for the management system, and thus for the delivery of services to the users. The minimisation of this cost is a prerequisite for the acceptance of usage-based charging mechanisms and sophisticated accounting systems by service providers and network operators.

3.2 Business model

The business model describes the different roles involved in service provisioning and the relationship between them in a generic and commonly accepted way. The term "role" is assigned to a set of actions and responsibilities of a business, which acts autonomously and for its own interest, providing specific functionality or resources. The delivery of services to the end-user usually requires the collaboration of more than one business role, depending on the service and network architecture of the system, and on the specific requirements of the service.

A generic classification of the business roles involved in telecommunication services includes the following parts:

End-User: The end-user role refers to the party to which the service is delivered in its final form. The end-user gains directly from using the service, and in most cases is responsible for the payment of the bill.

Customer: The customer is a role usually assigned to corporate users of telecommunication services. Since the relationship between customers and end-users that are included in this corporate environment is internally defined and usually not exposed to the general business model, the customer and the end-user roles are equivalent for many service architectures. Consequently the customer is responsible for the payment of the bill on behalf of the end-users.

Service Provider (Retailer): The service provider provides to customers the only access point to the telecommunication services, and exposes the overall view of the service logic and functionality. Even if other roles are also involved in the service provisioning, their contribution is not directly exposed to the customers, and it is the retailer's responsibility to coordinate the required resources and functions. The retailer is also responsible for charging for the services provided, including the delivery of bills to customers.

Third Party Provider: This business role is assigned to the providers of services or resources on a wholesale basis. A retailer may utilise more than one third-party provider for providing services, on the basis of contractual agreements between them. These contractual agreements describe, among others, the provided control and management functionality, and potentially the exchange of usage or charging information.

Content Provider: This role is assigned to the stakeholders responsible for providing the information that is sent to customers through a telecommunication service. This information may be text, images, video, audio, or other data, and its content strongly affects the utility of the whole service and thus the corresponding charge. The content-based part of the service charge is normally related to compensation of the content provider, while the usage-based charge refers to the utilisation of resources for distribution of the information and control and management of the service.

Network Provider: The network provider controls the telecommunication resources and provides the network connections upon which the service data and management and control information are transferred. This role is usually assigned to telecommunication operators that own the network infrastructure. Service providers and third party providers make use of network connections through the corresponding control interfaces offered by network providers. The extent of the functionality that is supported through these interfaces, as well as pricing and billing issues, are part of the corresponding contractual agreements.

Broker: The role of the broker is mainly market-oriented and it is not directly related to service provision. The broker maintains information about service, third party or network providers and their characteristics, such as supported services and the corresponding tariffs, and makes this information available to potential customers. This gives the customers the opportunity to select the best offer that fulfils their requirements. A representative example of the proliferation of the broker role is the existence of several Internet-based exchanges (such as www.band-x.com, www.interxion.com, and www.ratexchange.com) that constitute virtual markets for buyers and sellers of bandwidth.

All the above roles may be assigned a specific part of the service provision mechanisms according to technical, business or regulatory grounds. However, more than one business role may be assigned to a stakeholder, and in fact it is a common practice for network providers also to be service providers. The model of "consumer-supplier" is representative of the relationship between the different stakeholders. The service provider for example is a consumer of the network provider's services, and a supplier for the customers. Similarly, a network provider may be a consumer of the resources of another network provider. The Consumer, the Broker, the Retailer, the third party Service Provider and the Connectivity Provider are the business roles upon which the Business Model of the Telecommunications Information Network Architecture (TINA) is based [23]. In this model, the consumer refers to the end-user or customer, while the connectivity provider is equivalent to the network provider (see Figure 3.1). Similarly, the Network Management Forum (NMF) [1] has defined a Business Model where all roles involved in the service provision process are classified as follows: the end-customer, the service provider, the other provider, and the supplier (Figure 3.1). The broker, the retailer and the third party provider are embodied into the service provider role in the NMF model. An example of a third party service provider is a content provider.

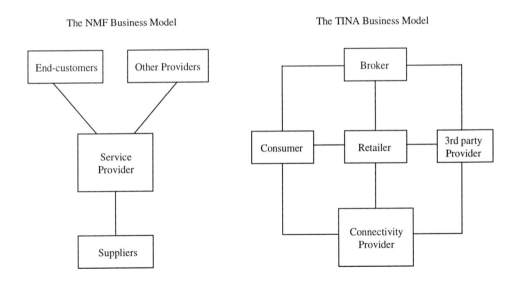

Figure 3.1: NMF and TINA Business Models

---

[1]NMF is an international consortium of communication service providers and their suppliers, dedicated to promoting industry-wide agreement for the exchange of management information between business roles

The corresponding standardisation effort of EURESCOM, which is a consortium of European operators, is based on a business model that includes the user of the service, the customer that subscribes to a service provided by a Public Network Operator (PNO), the Customer Premises Network Manager (CPN-manager) responsible for operating the service on behalf of a customer network, and the PNOs (see Figure 3.2). The role of the service provider is assigned to the PNO, since it is mainly communication services that are taken into account by the architecture.

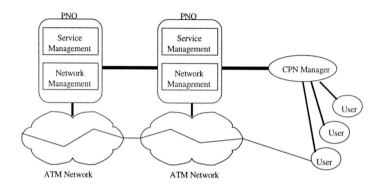

Figure 3.2: Business Model for Communication Services

The various standardisation bodies and consortia are also working on the modelling and specification of the interactions and of the information exchanged between the different business roles. This work is realised by defining interfaces (or reference points) that each business role should support in order to co-exist in a service provision environment, and be compatible in terms of service control and management. This modelling may either be of a conceptual nature, such as the TINA reference points and the NMF Business Agreements, or in the form of extensions to already implemented interfaces that facilitate the information exchange between different management domains.

3.3   Accounting management service

Accounting management deals with the collection of usage data for the resources involved in service provision and also the generation of a bill according to the pricing policy associated with the service. Three sub-processes of accounting management have been identified by ITU-T [9]. The *usage metering process* is responsible for the creation and logging of usage metering records upon the occurrence of accountable events. This process includes the sub-process called usage data collection process, which is in charge of the reliable and timely collection of usage data from the physical network equipment. The *rating and discounting process*, also called charging process, is responsible for the charge calculation according to a specific pricing policy and using the collected usage data. The charging information is structured as "Service Transaction Records" in order to be easily transferred and maintained. The *billing process* is responsible for collecting the Service Transaction Records, associating them with a specific customer, and distributing the bill. Figure 3.3 presents the Accounting Process as defined by ITU-T.

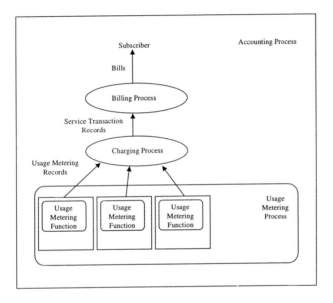

Figure 3.3: The Accounting Process

Usage metering process

Usage metering is defined as the set of activities that monitor the usage of resources for the purpose of accounting and controlling the recording of usage data. The usage metering process defines the generation and logging of specific usage information structures, called Usage Metering Records (UMR). Many vendors of switching systems use specific structures for reporting usage information, called Call Detail Records (CDRs). However the format of CDRs is not yet defined in a standard way between different vendors or standardisation organisations. Among usage metering responsibilities are the collection of usage data, their storage in persistent storage structures, and their processing and conversion to information structures that are sent to the computational entities where the charge calculation is performed. These information structures should have a predefined standard format, since they are part of the service-to-network-provider interface.

Network element usage metering functions (UMF)

Usage metering includes a critical set of functions upon which the whole process of charging and accounting is based. Within this set of functions three main tasks are identified for usage metering:

1. Usage Metering Control (UMC) is responsible for the generation and reporting of UMRs. In addition UMC identifies the accountable resources from where usage data are retrieved, and the events and the conditions under which the generation and reporting should be triggered.

2. The Usage Metering Data Function (UMDF) is responsible for the emission of the UMR notification defined by the usage metering control function. Usually this occurs when the service is terminated or changed, when a threshold is reached, or at regular intervals during the service transaction.

3. The UMR Reporting Function controls the transmission of notifications, and includes real-time (e.g. hot-billing service) and non-real-time mechanisms. For purposes of efficiency a block transfer of UMRs may also be supported.

Usage metering is usually performed close to the switching systems or other equivalent network elements including software and hardware modules involved in the provision of services. Specifically for switching equipment the nature of the delivered accounting data depends on the underlying network technology, and thus their format varies, for example between ATM, SDH-SONET, Frame-Relay, Internet or X.400 networks.

Usage data collection function

The collection and processing of usage information includes mechanisms for the aggregation, correlation, filtering, distribution, validation, surveillance and conversion of the received data, for monitoring or accounting purposes.

- The aggregation function is used for reducing the volume of the transferred information. According to the granularity required by the consumers of the usage information, this function combines many usage records into a single one with aggregated information.

- The correlation function is defined as the association of usage records, typically generated from different locations (e.g. origination network element, intermediate/terminating network element) into a single one that represents resource usage in an unambiguous way.

- The filtering function is generally used to discard faulty, redundant or undesirable usage records.

- The distribution function is the filtering and forwarding of usage records to different applications or outgoing files.

- The validation function checks the data integrity for missing, duplicate or out-of-sequence usage records.

- The surveillance function is the monitoring of usage records to detect deviations from the established norms.

- The conversion/formatting function consists of transforming the raw usage data into a common format (e.g. Bellcore AMA Format) or of transforming a usage record from one format into another required by a specific function within the rating and discounting process.

Charging and discounting

The charging mechanisms are responsible for service-usage correlation and charge calculation, using as input the usage data received from the usage metering functions and the subscription information existing for each customer. Typical charging mechanisms include one or a combination of the following:

- Flat-rate charging

- Duration charging

- Distance charging

- Time-of-day charging

- Day of the week/year charging

- Volume charging

- Call set-up charging

- QoS charging

- Content-based charging

In general the charge calculation is based on specific tariffs within which the relationship between service usage and charge is identified. All of the above charging mechanisms, with the exception of flat-rate charging, will generally be usage-related, i.e. charges will depend on the characteristics of individual connections. The administration of the tariffs refers to the creation/deletion and maintenance of tariff classes that may correspond to specific classes of subscription contracts and services [7]. Using these tariffing functions the service provider can apply a pricing strategy that usually varies with the target market and the positioning of the service within the general business and technical environment.

Special discounts may be applied according to the customer's profile, the time of day, day of year, or other parameters related to the pricing policy adopted by the service provider. The system may use input from Performance Monitoring and Service Quality Management (as well as from other Network/Systems Management and Maintenance functions) in order to verify that the delivered service quality complies with the contractual agreements between consumers and suppliers of the service. If it does not comply, discounts or a zero charge may be applied.

Billing

The Billing functions are related to the process of selecting the service transaction/cost records and distributing these costs to the customers. The billing mechanisms may vary according to the billing options that are offered by the service provider, including the form of the bill (aggregate, itemised) and also the delivery time/date:

1. Periodic billing: A bill is sent to the customer regularly (e.g. weekly or monthly).

2. On-demand billing: A bill is sent to the customer upon request.

3. Per-call billing: A bill is transmitted upon completion of the call or service. Per-call billing has real-time characteristics since the data should be delivered to their destination as soon as possible.

4. Advice of charge or real-time/hot billing: This is the most constraining case in terms of performance and consumption of processing and communication resources. The records are generated and transmitted during the lifetime of the service instance, mainly to provide a real-time indication of the charge.

5. Pre-paid billing: This mechanism limits the usage of services according to a specific predefined amount of charging units. Although the billing records are not required to be sent to the user in real-time, the calculation of charge should be performed in this way in order to check if the usage/charge limit is reached. In addition, this mechanism should be combined with service control functions in order to restrict further access to the services.

The configuration of the billing functions depends on the specific pricing policy adopted by the service provider, on the supported billing modes, on the nature of the charged service, and optionally, on the profile of the customer.

The on-line delivery of billing information to the customers through the service provision system can be very useful for users and service providers, especially if used in conjunction with on-line digital payment systems. Representative examples of work towards this direction of "Micropayments" [17] are the payment system introduced by Digital Equipment (Millicent), and also the "CyberCash" and "DigiCash" systems. The "Micropayments" paradigm provides an environment where electronic financial transactions can be accomplished, even for low-priced services where the value of the sale cannot cover the cost of conventional methods of payment such as credit card transactions.

Generic requirements for charging and accounting systems

The introduction of a charging and accounting system in a service and network management architecture must always take into account basic business and technical requirements imposed by the different business roles involved. Since service, network and content providers and customers have a different perspective of the mechanisms involved in the calculation and distribution of charging information, a generic set of requirements must be defined in order to provide a common view of this issue. These requirements are independent of the pricing policies adopted by the providers of the service.

Accuracy: The accuracy of the information that represents resource usage and charge is a basic requirement for all interconnection agreements between business roles. It should be preserved both at the points where it is collected or calculated and at the communication interfaces between the components of the system. Loss, duplication or corruption of usage and charging records should be avoided by using fault management mechanisms.

Timely delivery: The delivery of usage and charging information can take place after predefined time intervals or upon the occurrence of specific events (e.g. the invocation or termination of a service session). In both cases it is very important for the system that the records do not experience unnecessary transmission or forwarding delays, and that they can be delivered to users at the time periods specified in the subscription contracts.

Flexibility in supporting various pricing policies: The system should be designed in a way that allows the introduction of new policies, parameters or mechanisms for processing the usage and charging information. The usage information should be structured in a generic and standardised way in order to be easily transported, maintained, and utilised by various pricing schemes.

Adaptability to Services and Users: The system should be able to discriminate among users (according to subscription contracts and predefined user profiles) and classes of services and applications. Thus it should be able to cope with specific operation requirements and characteristics posed either by the nature of the requested services or by the user's contracts and preferences.

Security: As for all management services a very important requirement in a charging and accounting architecture is the secure delivery of the information to authorised parties. Authentication, data integrity and confidentiality functions should be associated with the accounting and charging mechanisms.

Performance and Scalability: The performance of the system should be maintained at an acceptable level regardless of the number of users, their physical locations, the amount of information transferred, and the service being charged.

Auditability: The system should provide auditing functionality for two reasons. First, to allow the network manager to monitor and audit the accounting records generated, received, and processed by the various components. Second, to provide the customer with the ability to verify the results of the charging process through a detailed audit trail.

3.4 Service provision and charging - the common framework

The deployment and operation of charging and accounting mechanisms within a service provision system depend heavily on the basic characteristics of the service architecture, the classes of applications supported, and the underlying network technology. In this section we provide an overview of the most important architectures for service provision and their relationship with charging.

Services and network technologies

The wide range of existing applications that make use of telecommunication networks is made possible by a corresponding variety of terminal equipment for end-users, and by the network technologies used for the transfer of data and control information. A telecommunication service can be classified as one of the following categories:

- Communication (e.g. videoconference, telephony)

- Messaging (e.g. e-mail and the "push" model for the Internet)

- Distribution (e.g. cable TV services)

- Retrieval (Web browsing, data retrieval services)

- Interconnection (aggregated LAN, remote terminals, distributed file systems, distributed processing applications)

The service logic and communication requirements for the above services vary according to the nature of the transferred information (video, audio, text/data, or image), and to the specific characteristics of the underlying network technology. The network technologies used for the transport of data and control information can be summarised as follows:

- Public Switched Telephone Networks (PSTN)

- Integrated Services Digital Networks (ISDN)

- Data networks (X.25, Frame Relay)

- Broadband ISDN networks with ATM technology

- The Internet and Local Area Networks (LAN)

- Cable TV networks

- Multi-megabit services via Low and Medium Earth Orbit satellite (LEO) systems.

Some of these network technologies have been designed for specific applications, while others can handle more general classes of services. In some cases these services are designed and deployed in a manner that exploits the specific characteristics of the network technology, something that may be positive in terms of performance and implementation but which limits the choices for integrated solutions for service provision. Consequently the introduction of additional management services, especially accounting, may be constrained by the service and network characteristics.

The need to support a wide range of service categories is reflected in the recently introduced network technologies, such as the LEO systems, where in addition to data, telephony, fax, paging, and messaging, the services targeted include Internet access, videoconferencing, and tele-medicine. However, for older and well-established technologies, the transition to a multi-service provision environment requires the deployment of sophisticated mechanisms for the management and control of the existing system.

Service provision architectures

Service provision architecture refers to the modelling of the functions and the building blocks that constitute the service management and control. This modelling includes:

- Identification of business roles and their relationships.

- Definition of the horizontal layering that exposes different views of the service for consumers and suppliers.

- Identification of generic functional entities that constitute the core of the service logic.

- Distribution scenarios for the deployment of the building blocks on the physical network computational and switching resources.

Among the best known (and some of them widely adopted) architectures are the following:

The Intelligent Networks (IN) architecture

The introduction of the IN architecture as an extension of the classic telephony service aimed to move the service control from the local node (the exchange) to a centralised service control point (SCP). Although the main task of the SCP in the early intelligent networks was to set up simple telephony services in the network, this separation of the service control from the call processing facilitated the enhancement of more complicated services on the existing network infrastructure.

The "conceptual model" of the IN architecture makes a clear distinction between the different views that a service may exhibit to the different stakeholders involved in the provision of services. The user's view of the service is called "service plane", while the modelling of the service independent building blocks (SIB) is described within the "global functional plane". The "distributed functional plane" provides a decomposition of the service building blocks to functional entities, and the "physical plane" refers to the deployment of the computational entities to the physical system. It is worthwhile noting that IN provides a particular SIB that processes the calls (basic call process) and also a charge SIB which allows specific charging for IN services. This latter can log a usage record, apply a specific charging policy to a call, or monitor accounting events.

The Telecommunications Management Network (TMN) architecture

The TMN architecture is orientated to the management of network resources through predefined interfaces. The TMN - Logical Layered Architecture (TMN-LLA) uses a hierarchical approach for the modelling of the deployment of resources and management entities within the system. The document "Principles for a Telecommunications Management Network" [4] identifies the decomposition of the TMN functions to the following management layers:

- Element management layer deals with the lower level network resources (e.g. the switching systems), and it depends on the technical characteristics of the managed equipment. Performance monitoring, control, and collection of accounting metrics are among the responsibilities that correspond to this management layer.

- Network management layer provides a wider view of the network within which the connections are deployed and managed. The hierarchical grouping of switching systems can be used for the definition of layer-networks, where groups of nodes at one layer appear as a single node for the upper layer.

- Service management layer is the environment where the service logic is implemented and the network resources are utilised for providing services. The service control and management mechanisms are deployed through interfaces that facilitate communication with adjacent administrative domains and management systems.

- Business management layer deals with the business-oriented relationships between stakeholders and owners of different portions of the infrastructure. This layer is not strictly defined since it is supposed to accommodate functions that correspond to the business aspects of service deployment.

The Internet

The Internet applications and services are based on a widely adopted network infrastructure, the development of which was driven more by the technical and commercial requirements of its users and suppliers than by the guidelines of a service reference model. Internet services assume that the intelligence or the service logic is implemented on the edges of the network, or on the terminal equipment of the consumers and suppliers. The network itself is used only for its transport capabilities, without any involvement in the service provision. However, the best-effort nature of the Internet services, where resources are not guaranteed but given to users according to their availability status, may be changed with the introduction of quality-of-service guarantees. These assume the use of signalling (e.g. the Resource Reservation Setup Protocol - RSVP) and/or service differentiation mechanisms, which transfer part of the service logic from the user to the network side.

Simple end-user pricing schemes have been adopted for Internet services, namely flat-rate, capacity-based, and time-based charging. However the introduction of new services, competition between providers, and the need for QoS guarantees, may require more complicated usage-based charging schemes, with corresponding accounting architectures.

The Telecommunications Information Network Architecture (TINA)

The TINA architecture identifies the characteristics of a universal distributed processing environment for integrated service control and management. TINA extends the frameworks of TMN and IN, aiming at supporting a wide range of services and applications, independently of the underlying transport network.

TINA has extensively adopted the main principles of object-oriented design, modelling the service functional, computational and information entities to independent building blocks. Communication between the objects is established through the Distributed Processing Model, according to the definitions of the Object Management Group [10].

The service control part of the TINA paradigm, and the corresponding distinctions between the user and provider view that TINA provides through the session model, can facilitate the integrated design and implementation of charging and accounting mechanisms. The TINA approach to the latter is described in the TINA Accounting Management Architecture [1].

The Digital Audio Visual Council (DAVIC) architecture

This architecture [2] is orientated to the applications and services in which digital audio and video components are involved. Its target is to provide the design and implementation framework for interactive multimedia services, the deployment of which would be independent of the network technology, including cable TV, ATM, and Internet networks.

The "delivery systems" defined in the architecture are responsible for information transfer, and specifically for service and network-related control functions. The service-related control includes broker mechanisms, address resolution, security and session control services, while the network-related functions include call and connection control, resource allocation, routing and identification of the terminal equipment.

Each one of the above architectures aims at satisfying the requirements of specific applications and services by defining the relationships between the roles involved in the service provision process, and identifying the corresponding functional and computational entities and building blocks. The convergence of these architectures to an integrated solution able to support all classes of existing and future applications is considered as very beneficial for all the business roles. However this target does not seem to be feasible at least for the near future, since service provision systems are driven by different network architectures and use different views of the service provision mechanisms. The fact that most of these systems are already deployed and operational with a large number of users and suppliers makes the transition to an integrated architecture, which has not been tested in real-usage environments, even more difficult. Collaboration and inter-working between the heterogeneous systems appears to be the only viable solution.

In a similar way, the existing charging and accounting systems correspond to the service provision system, and inevitably depend on the class of service and application and on the underlying network technology. However, although these dependencies might need to be reflected in a pricing scheme it is desirable that they do not affect the deployment and operation of the charging mechanisms in general.

Generic view of the service

The design of charging mechanisms applicable to a wide range of services has to bypass the specifics of service architectures and focus on the core functions of service provision. The identification of these core functions can provide a representative view of the generic service characteristics upon which pricing can be properly introduced.

Service logic and service requirements

The common characteristic of all telecommunication services is the need for network connections, and consequently many architectures, services and applications consider the control of network connections as the main part of their functionality. Other services, such as cable TV, are orientated to the content of the provided information and not to the transport characteristics. However, the new interactive multimedia services have additional requirements related to more sophisticated service control, both in terms of information content and transfer capabilities. In that sense, the value of the service depends not only on the nature of the transferred information, but also on the flexibility provided to users in terms of service customisation, management and control. For example in a videoconference application, invitations to other users to join a session, parallel views of image or video data, and collaborative document editing are service features that require complicated service control functionality.

According to the above, the more demanding the services become, the greater becomes the need to separate the service logic from the management of the utilised information, network, or computational resources. This is the direction of the TINA, IN, and TMN architectures, although they start from different viewpoints.

This separation is clearer in the TINA architecture, where the service control and management [22] are confronted independently of the network connection management [18]. Specifically, TINA is based on the notion of the "session", which is an instance of the abstract modelling of the functions that constitute the service logic. The mechanisms that establish and control the network connections (communication and connectivity sessions) are modelled in a similar way. The basis of this modelling is the service session, with which are associated the users that participate in the session (and have a customised view of it), and the corresponding connections (see Figure 3.4).

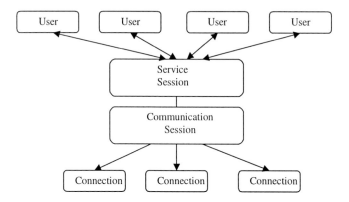

Figure 3.4: The Session Model

Conceptually this separation significantly facilitates charging of services, since it associates users, service sessions and communication resources in an integrated way. Thus in the lower level, where the establishment and control of network connections takes place, the system maintains a connection-oriented view, while at the higher service level the view becomes service-oriented. In a similar way the users maintain a separate view of the service that corresponds to the part of the session that is user-dependent, both in terms of service control and charging.

Service phases

The interactions between users and service providers for the access and usage of services can be divided into the set-up phase, service execution phase, and wrap-up phase [1]. In the first phase the user presents to the provider the relationship between his needs and his "willingness to pay". The provider uses the above information in order to define the tariff that corresponds to the user's profile. Within the second phase the service is delivered to the user, with the corresponding pricing information. The third phase refers to the appropriate service delivery verification process. This process should verify that the service was delivered according to the agreement between user and provider, and that the cost corresponds to the actual service usage.

Set-up phase

Within the set-up phase the user and the provider come to an agreement upon the way the second will charge the first. The user's view on the quality-to-cost relationship represents the subjective value of the service for the user. The latter also indicates parameters related to the customisation of the charging process and delivery of the charging information. The provider presents its own pricing policy in terms of tariffs, and the corresponding service quality offers, and only if the two views are identical are the service provision and charging mechanisms instantiated. However, since the two business roles are trying to protect their own interests, they usually see the service provision and the corresponding charge from a different perspective.

Thus, the existence of a mechanism responsible for resolving the disputes between consumer and supplier is necessary. This mechanism may support a renegotiation sequence, by trying to adjust the two different views to a common one that satisfies both parties. This policy is the most effective, since it can avoid deadlock situations, while at the same time it satisfies all the parties involved in the negotiation. However, the drawback is that this policy imposes the deployment of intelligent mechanisms both at the user and the provider domain (with a correspondingly advanced communication protocol) in order to support the renegotiation interactions between the two parties.

Another potential solution to this problem is to weight the provider's opinion more and force the user to accept it. In this way, the user's proposal is taken into account only as a "hint" for the provider to determine its policy. Although this solution is easy to implement, it is not flexible since the user is limited to a specific range of choices that may not correspond to his requirements.

Service execution phase

During this phase the service is activated and offered to the user. The latter controls the service by using the service control and management mechanisms, while at the same time charging information may be obtained in specific time intervals or upon the occurrence of specific events.

The renegotiation of the service quality or billing configuration parameters provides significant flexibility to the user for dynamically controlling the quality-to-cost relationship. This feature is even more important for usage-based charging schemes, where the charge is dynamically changing with time, or other usage metrics.

Wrap-up phase

After the end of the service session the components of the individual sessions are terminated after reporting their final status to the corresponding persistent storage systems. Particularly for the charging building blocks, the reliability, the consistency and the accuracy of the charging data are verified, before the final charge is sent to the users and the session charging processes are terminated. The users receive the total charge for the service usage, and depending on the provider's policy, they may receive performance metrics or usage information that can be used to verify that the service was received according to the agreement with the provider, and that the charge for the service corresponds to the actual usage.

In the case of service failure the provider's contractual agreement with the customer may include compensation actions, the nature of which depend on the subscription contract with the consumer, on the nature of the delivered service, and on the value of the portion of the "non-compliant" service already delivered.

3.5 Interfaces and information flow

The control of the accounting and charging process and the exchange of usage and charging information are realised through the corresponding interfaces between the customers, providers, and network operators. The design model for the interactions between the various business roles and the exchanged information determines the performance of the system and its ability to adapt to various pricing policies.

In this section we present an outline of those interfaces, along with the corresponding information structures. Specifically, as shown in Figure 3.5 we focus on the interfaces between the end-users and the service providers, and between service and network providers.

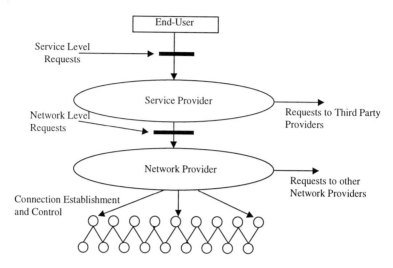

Figure 3.5: Interfaces between service and network providers

Customer to service provider interface

The relationship between customers and service providers is basically defined on a long-term basis through subscription contracts, within which the terms and the guarantees of the cooperation are described. In a similar way, this relationship can be defined on a short-term basis, since the contractual agreements cannot usually cover the service customisation in every detail. Thus, the negotiation of some service parameters at the service set-up, or during the service usage, may be allowed by the contractual agreement.

The billing functionality is usually realised through invoices and other commercial documents sent to the customer periodically. However in some classes of services and pricing schemes it is important that billing information is transferred upon the occurrence of specific events, on a real time basis. In all cases it is important that this information transfer takes place through predefined interfaces. The user may utilise this information and actively influence the charging and accounting process on a per-call basis (or even within a call) by tuning some service or pricing-specific parameters, and by redefining the quality requirements of the service.

The customer to service provider interface is usually service and not resource-oriented. The user/customer requests a service, providing information about the preferred quality (according to subjective criteria), and tuning other service delivery customisation parameters. The service provider is then responsible for identifying the communication requirements of the requested service, in terms of network connections that the network provider will be asked to establish. However there are cases where the customer explicitly requests transport connections or is provided with the ability to customise the number and the nature of the underlying network connections.

The customer to service provider interface includes two distinct information flows: the upstream information flow that is related to the control information, and the downstream information flow related to the charging feedback from the network to the customer.

Upstream information flow

The control and service customisation interactions can be considered more as part of the service transaction than part of the charging and accounting process. However the service customisation capabilities inherently have a strong impact on the ability of the customer to control the amount of payment that corresponds to the service usage. The efficient selection of service quality, with implicit or explicit declaration of QoS and traffic contract parameters for the underlying connections, are very important functions for the customer in terms of determining a convenient quality-to-cost relationship that best suits his requirements.

In addition it is possible that the pricing policy adopted by a service provider gives incentives to the customers to declare an estimation of their behaviour in the future (e.g. on a per-call basis, or for a specific time period, etc.). Thus the interface should be open enough to accommodate additional charging configuration information that is specific to the adopted pricing strategy.

Billing configuration capabilities should also be supported by the interface, since it is possible that various users or applications may have specific requirements in terms of the content, generation and transmission of billing records.

Downstream information flow

The billing (or advice of charge) information is encapsulated in the billing records sent by the service provider to the customer/user, upon the occurrence of a specific event or periodically within specified time intervals. The information contained in these records should be detailed enough to provide to the customer a clear illustration of the payment that corresponds to the usage of a specific service for a given time period.

The billing records are service-oriented; thus the chargeable entity is the service instance. The record should indicate the service instance identifier and the identifier of the customer who uses the service. A summary of the more basic information fields that can be part of the billing record is the following:

- User identity: The user to whom the billing record is delivered.

- Service instance: An indication of the service entity upon which the record is referred.

- Time information: The generation time of the record and the chargeable time period to which the charging information refers.

- The charge that corresponds to the specified time interval for the usage of the indicated service instance.

- Service-level requested quality.

- Aggregated usage information.

- Indication of potential rebates from inability to meet the requested quality requirements.

All the above information fields are service-oriented. However the customer requirements or the nature of the service may imply the need to receive also charging or usage information for the individual connections established through a service instance, and the billing record could also accommodate this information. For example the billing record may contain additional separate parts - one per connection used - where charge and usage information would be inserted. The basic parts of this sub-section could be the following:

- Connection identifier.

- Time information.

- Charge related to the connection in question.

- Requested network-level quality parameters (e.g. QoS parameters for ATM transport service).

- Measured quality parameters during usage of service.

- Usage information. This part is specific to the nature of the underlying network, but its content is equivalent to the information included in the Usage Metering Records.

- Tariffing information. This part refers to the tariff parameters used for the charge calculation.

- Indication of rebates. This part is related to potential inability of the provider to meet the quality requirements of the specific connection.

The pricing policy adopted by the service provider determines how the network-level usage information is correlated and aggregated in order to provide the service-level integrated usage and charging information. This aggregation policy should also be included in the main part of the billing record; otherwise the additional information for the individual connections could not be used for the verification of the total charge for the service.

A more detailed example of billing records and the interactions between customer and service provider can be found in the next chapter, where the charging and accounting platform of CA$hMAN is presented.

Service provider to network provider interface

The "consumer-supplier" relationship that exists between customers and service providers is also applicable between service and network providers. In this section we present the main parts of the interface to a provider who is responsible for the control and management of the network connections required by the telecommunication services. Network (or connectivity) suppliers are usually the telecommunication operators that own the network infrastructure.

The relationship of network providers with consumers of the transport services is connection-oriented, since the connections are the commodity that is actually traded between them. The connection control capabilities, to the extent that they are provided to consumers, are determined by the corresponding contractual agreements and realised by on-line negotiation mechanisms. On the other hand, the exchange of connection usage or charging information is a basic requirement for the consumer to confirm that the provided transport services comply with the terms described within the agreements. At the same time, this information may be used by the service providers when applying usage-based pricing schemes.

Control interface

Contractual agreements between service providers and the underlying network providers identify the level of control that the former may have on the established connections. For example if the network provider offers SVC connections, then the service provider may have direct on-line control over the establishment of connections and the network resources used. In this case the customer's service quality preferences are directly mapped to the corresponding connection control calls to the network provider. By contrast, if only permanent trunks (with fixed reservation of resources) are offered, the service provider has no control over the network resources, so a more simplified interface between them can be used.

The customer's billing requirements (content of information records or generation conditions) may also need to be announced to the network provider, particularly if they affect the transmission conditions of the usage metering records.

Usage metering report interface

The generation and transmission of usage metering records is the cornerstone of the billing process. Independently of the record generation conditions, or of the peculiarities of the underlying network technologies, the records should be detailed enough to give a clear view of the resource usage to the service provider, and open enough to accommodate the specifics of different transmission technologies. Usage metering records are connection-oriented, since the chargeable entities are the established connections.

According to the information structures defined for the needs of the CA$hMAN project, and related recommendations from the Network Management Forum [15] (definition of the Universal Accounting Record) and ITU-T [9], a basic set of information entities that can be included in the usage metering records is identified as follows:

- A connection identifier which defines the connection to which the usage data refer.

- A technology-dependent part of connection identifier like the VPI/VCI pair of the UNI interface for ATM networks.

- Addressing information for the initiator of the service and all the parties involved in it, such as the E.164 address.

- Time information. The generation time of the record and the time period to which the usage information refers.

- Class of service indication (technology-dependent).

- Traffic contract parameters for the connection (technology-dependent). A technology-independent part for this information entity could be the definition of the maximum allowed transmission rate, the average bandwidth, and generally transmission parameters applicable to all kinds of transport networks.

- Requested quality of service parameters (technology-dependent).

- Measured usage. This information may include both technology-independent and dependent parts.

- Measured quality of service (technology-dependent).

In Figure 3.6 the information flow between customers, providers and network operators is presented. Additional information that is related to the format of the usage metering records and the technology-dependent metrics of usage can be found in [14], [9], and in the TINA Network Resource Architecture document [18]. The usage metrics and the accounting information collected from the inter-carrier interfaces can be found in [6], where emphasis is given to the metering capabilities of originating, intermediate and terminating carrier networks. An indicating implementation example is the realisation of the CA$hMAN charging and accounting system presented in the next chapter.

3.6   User and network intelligent agents

The introduction of charging and usage metering mechanisms in service provision systems should exhibit significant flexibility in the way the functional entities are distributed among the available computational resources. Moreover, especially from the supplier's

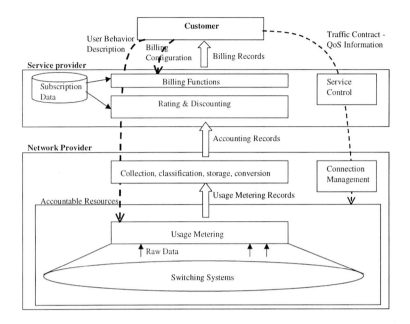

Figure 3.6: Accounting Information Flow

perspective, this flexibility should be combined with high performance and reliability of the system. On the other hand, for end-users and customers, in addition to reliability and the accuracy of charging information, simplicity and predictability of the charge are of major importance. The latter depends heavily on the adopted pricing policy, but also on the way the charging information is presented to the user and correlated with "real-life" qualitative and quantitative parameters. The maintenance of a clear view of the pricing aspects included in a contractual agreement between consumers and suppliers is the basis of a trusted relationship.

For all these technical and business-oriented considerations there is a need to develop service provision and charging mechanisms in terms of self contained independent building blocks called "agents", that can be easily transferred and adapted to the whole system. The modelling of complicated functions by means of agents is a technology that is very widely adopted in many applications and frameworks, from adaptive user interfaces to distributed network management and service control. The inherent cooperation capabilities of the "client-server" architectures and many distributed processing technologies make the "agent" modelling even more popular and widely spread.

Characteristics of intelligent agents

The term "agent" is assigned to an independent computational entity, which is responsible for the implementation of a specific process [92]. The responsibility of an agent is usually to "absorb" the complexity of a task (or a decision process), exposing a simplified view of it. Thus it is commonly used to act on behalf of humans, business parties, or even functional entities that are not capable of handling very complicated processes. The intelligence included within an agent may vary from the simple processing of data to be presented through a user interface, or the simplification of user interactions, to the complicated data correlation of network management information collected from various points of the network.

In addition to the intelligence incorporated in the agents, their communication capabilities are very characteristic of their role in the service and management architectures. Agents able to search for and collect distributed information, to send notifications for specific events or errors to other agents, or to control remotely the resources of large systems, are very common in the network and service management areas.

The latest direction in the development of intelligent agents is to facilitate their transfer and execution in various environments. This functionality would provide the opportunity, for example, for network management systems to distribute the agents to network nodes where a distributed set of management functions can be performed. The Java technology used for the transfer of executable code for the servers to the client terminal equipment is another example of the wide range of applications that intelligent agents may have.

While "agent mobility" refers to the act of transferring the code of the agent to remote machines, "agent migration" includes the transfer of the execution state along with the code of the agent. The agent may suspend its execution (saving its state and data), and resume on another machine exactly from the same execution point.

Service provision, management and charging with agents

The utility of agents in the service provision, management, and charging architectures is steadily increasing, as the complexity of the provided services and the customer needs increase. This utility may be identified in the following fields:

Service provision and customisation

The design and deployment of services in distributed environments can take place through independent and reusable building blocks, which perform portions of the service logic in a collaborative fashion. Agents with remote execution capabilities can be used by providers for on-line customisation of services according to specific requirements imposed by the nature of the applications or the network technology.

With the use of intelligent agents the service logic can be provided in terms of independent sub-services and functions, the collaboration and correlation of which is among the responsibilities of intelligent agents that belong to the consumers of the services.

System upgrades

Rapid changes in the requirements of users and applications should drive the upgrade of systems and services, and thus this is a process that requires considerable effort and resources from the supplier's point of view. The use of intelligent agents can facilitate the process of distributing service provision building blocks to the corresponding system resources and points of service logic execution. At the same time, software upgrade on the user's terminals can be performed with automatic transfer of new software modules to the user side.

The automatic distribution of agents to the consumers of services can be used in conjunction with the "broker" concept, for advertising services and applications. The delivery of software components to the customers may be part of the access session to the service provider.

Service usage

The deployment on user sites of an agent that represents the provider, and of an agent on the provider's sites that represents the user, is an interesting approach in terms of modelling the relationship between the two roles. When the user accesses a provider or requests a service, the corresponding agent is transferred to the user's terminal, and upon its execution it helps the user to customise the service according to his needs. This functionality is particularly important especially when the service control functions are complicated for the user to handle. On the other hand, when a user subscribes to a provider, an agent of the user is created on the provider's site. This agent is aware of all the user's preferences as they were described in the subscription contract with the provider. Additionally the agent may obtain information about the terminal equipment of the user, about historical data that reveal the user behaviour, and generally about everything that the service provider would need to know when providing a service (see Figure 3.7). The TINA architecture has adopted this model by using the "User Agent" and "Provider Agent" as parts of the computational modelling.

Generally, intelligent agents can negotiate on-line "open" contracts between consumer and supplier, and resolve or clarify conflicts and problems that cannot be described in every detail in a subscription contract.

In addition to service control, intelligent agents may be used for evaluation of the service provided and of the relationship between cost and service quality. Agents with functionality customised according to the user's subjective criteria and to the specific application requirements can be executed on the terminal equipment, monitoring parameters of the

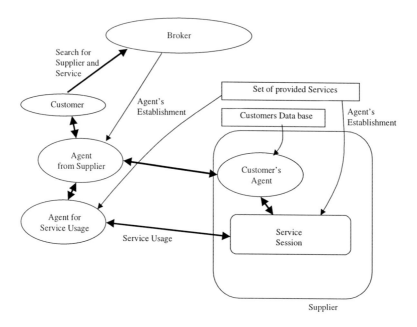

Figure 3.7: Use of intelligent agents for service provision

service delivery. The cost of the service may be calculated by the agent in order to provide a verification of the payment requested by the provider.

Feedback-based service control mechanisms

Intelligent agents can handle network feedback information related to the quality of the service, the congestion of the network, or the price that corresponds to the service usage. When this information is retrieved in real time, and the consumer has to react to this feedback as soon as possible, intelligent agents can provide this functionality without waiting for user involvement in the process. Of course the user can personally customise the criteria used by the agent to correlate the received information and derive the corresponding decisions, in such a way that his interests are sufficiently protected. The definition of the service quality / cost relationship by intelligent agents is a representative example of this functionality.

Distributed management and load balancing of computational resources

Distribution of functionality to different administrative domains and computational resources of the network, in order to improve the performance and the scalability of the system, is a very important part of the design of network management systems. To minimise the information transfer between the computational entities there is a tendency to establish the management mechanisms as close as possible to the managed resources. Thus the deployment of intelligent agents by the network equipment facilitates the collection and processing of management data "on the spot", while only the significant and filtered part of this information is delivered to the higher layers of the system (see Figure 3.8).

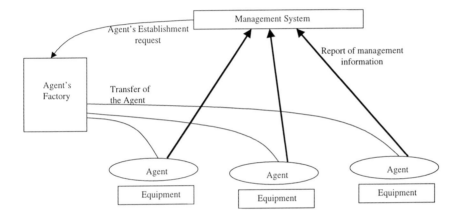

Figure 3.8: Use of agents for network management

The introduction of usage metering for pricing purposes, and specifically for usage-based charging schemes, may induce significant performance and scalability deterioration to the system. The use of distributed agents for control of the accountable resources, in conjunction with the corresponding asynchronous notification mechanisms, can guarantee the effectiveness of the usage data collection process.

3.7 Performance considerations

The flexibility of an accounting architecture to accommodate a wide range of services, applications and pricing policies, and the ability to adapt to various network and service provision technologies, are very important qualifications for the acceptance of the accounting system by service and network providers. Equally important is low installation and maintenance cost. However a fundamental prerequisite of any management system is to limit the communication and computational overhead to acceptable levels, so that the cost of accounting is relatively low in comparison with the cost of providing the service.

The performance of an accounting system that is deployed on large-scale multiservice networks is affected by many factors related to the design, implementation and deployment aspects of the system. Among the key factors that can drastically affect the overall performance of the accounting system are the efficient collection of usage information, selection of middle-ware platforms and communication protocols, distribution of functionality among the communication and computational resources, and configuration of the accounting functionality according to the requirements of users, services and applications.

Usage data collection

Usage information for network resources may be obtained either by means of network probes that monitor the traffic on the corresponding links, or directly by the switching systems that handle the traffic. The usage data collection equipment should individually handle each data flow in terms of counters, statistics and temporary storage. Therefore, in order to avoid performance bottlenecks, the usage metering functionality should be attached to edge devices of the network, where the number of flows and the processed volumes of traffic are low. The edge devices may need to handle traffic originated from (or terminated at) end-users and transferred over the link that connects them with the network, or may handle aggregate traffic from other corporate or public networks. In the last case the term "flow" refers to the aggregate traffic from one network to the other, and consequently the pricing scheme and the corresponding charge are applicable for the aggregate usage information. In this way usage data collection can be feasible even for very large networks.

In addition to the performance limitations of the equipment in terms of collection and processing of usage data, another important issue is its temporary storage capability. The maximum length of usage data reporting intervals from the collection equipment to the management system is proportional to the temporary storage capabilities of the first. Low storage capability means that usage data must be reported very frequently, even when not required by the management system, resulting in waste of computational (and probably communication) resources.

Communication protocols / middle-ware and management platforms

The communication cost of transferring control and management information in a distributed system is a very important performance consideration. This cost is related to the modelling of functionality and information in terms of independent building blocks, to the way these components are distributed among communication and computational resources, and to the mechanisms that support the communication between them (communication protocols, marshalling of data, etc.), and coordinate their operation.

The communication and the coordination of the different parts of the accounting system can be based either on standard or on more proprietary solutions, according to the generic requirements of the accounting system. The ITU-T recommendations on network management are based on the Common Management Information Protocol (CMIP - [21]). This protocol is usually adopted by telecommunication operators since it provides robust control of network devices and ensures the reliability and scalability of the management system. However due to the multi-layer OSI structure of the protocol stack, this protocol is expensive to develop and introduces a high communication overhead. A lighter and more widely adopted solution for the management of IP networks is the Simple Network Management Protocol (SNMP - [40]). This protocol, although it does not provide the robustness of CMIP, is easy to develop and is supported by most of the vendors of telecommunication and switching equipment.

Although the main consideration for the standardisation of management protocols is the interoperability between management domains (administrative areas managed by the same management system), there are cases where proprietary protocols are used, especially at the lower management layers. This happens mainly to cope with equipment specialties, and also for performance reasons. For example when usage data are collected on a network element (e.g. switching system) and must be rapidly transferred to the management system for on-line processing, a fast proprietary solution can be used in order to ensure the timely delivery of the information.

Another possibility for the implementation of management systems in general is the adoption of the distributed computing paradigm, where the management functions are distributed among independent computational entities (objects). These objects are instantiated in an environment that supports their communication through pre-defined interfaces, providing implementation and location transparency. This environment is implemented according to a distribution architecture such as the Common Object Request Broker Architecture (CORBA) [11] described by the Object Management Group (OMG), and the Distributed Component Object Model (DCOM) defined by Microsoft [105].

The transfer syntax and a standard set of message formats for the communication of the objects in the CORBA architecture is specified by the General Inter-ORB Protocol (GIOP). GIOP is intended to be a light and flexible protocol that is able to support specific implementation for each different transport network. For example a specific description of GIOP over TCP/IP transport network is specified by Internet Inter-ORB Protocol (IIOP) [11].

Although the robustness and flexibility of these distribution architectures are indubitable, it seems that there are performance and scalability problems, especially when used for real-time transactions. The required marshalling and de-marshalling of the data structures and the conversions between layers of the protocol stack inevitably produce a computational overhead. However this overhead depends on the specific implementation of the distribution architecture. For example, as described in [67], the latency overhead for two commercial CORBA implementations is due to non-optimised buffering techniques, and unnecessary function calls, layer conversions, and data copying. In addition, the lack of integration with the underlying operating systems and network technologies produces performance and scalability bottlenecks for the system. There is continuous research activity into improving the performance of the distribution architectures, and the products are expected to be widely adopted by the network management community.

Issues related to the design of the accounting management system can also greatly affect its performance and scalability. A representative example is the use of the asynchronous delivery of information mechanisms, which can be used for avoiding undesirable blocking situations between the components of the system. These mechanisms are supported by most of the management and distributed computing architectures. For example ITU-T Recommendations on the Event Reporting Management Function [5] define the Event Forwarding Discriminator (EFD) as a class of managed objects responsible for filtering and forwarding events to other components of the management architecture. The hierarchical event management system of the TMN architecture is based on the notion of EFD, since the notifications are either handled by the components of a specific level of hierarchy, or forwarded to the above layers. Another example is the asynchronous delivery of "Events" as defined by CORBA, and called "Event Service". This service is part of a coordination technology, called "CORBA-Services" [16], that handles the details of the coordination between objects, instantiated in a distributed computing environment.

Deployment of components

The control and management of services is generally based on components located on the user or the network side. The components that are distributed on network nodes or other computational resources can either be specific to users/providers, or be related to the core service functionality. In the first case they are usually deployed close to the access nodes of the network, so as to handle efficiently issues related to service customisation according to customer profiles. A very important feature of this deployment is that it can scale easily to very large networks, since only a small group of users/customers is handled by each access point of the network. However for the core part of the service there is not a straightforward way to decide where these components should be located. This deployment usually depends on the service provision architecture, on the distribution capabilities provided, and on specific load-balancing techniques.

The components of the accounting management system can be co-located with the corresponding service provision components. In this way the interaction between service control and accounting is facilitated (in terms of communication cost), something that is particularly important for usage-based charging for services exhibiting high interactivity. However if free distribution of components is allowed by the service and accounting architectures, then the distribution criteria depend on the network topology, the available processing and communication resources, the adopted pricing policies, and many other factors.

For usage-based charging the objective is to minimise the communication cost induced by the transfer of the usage information to the components where charge calculation is performed. By keeping these components close to the usage metering equipment we can ensure the fast calculation of charge according to usage of network resources in a real time fashion. The charging information may be transferred offline to a centralised persistent storage unit for post-processing (e.g. billing). Inevitably there would be a communication cost for the control and customisation of the charging components from a more centralised system that provides the tariffs according to which the calculation of charge takes place. However this cost is relatively low compared to the cost of continuously transferring usage information between components.

The problem becomes more complicated if we assume that (near) real-time advice of charge is provided to users/customers. In this case there is an additional data flow from the charge calculation components to the user side, with significant communication cost. Considering also that the point where usage information is collected and processed may be different to the access point of the user that uses the service - in fact it could be at the opposite end of a network connection - this communication cost may be relatively high. Therefore a load balancing mechanism is required, in conjunction with the dynamic instantiation and distribution of the accounting components according to the service requirements and the physical distance between the usage metering points, the charge calculation points, and the receivers of AoC information.

Configuration of accounting mechanisms

The configuration of the accounting mechanisms should be based on various considerations, such as the available computational and network resources, the provided services and the adopted pricing schemes. Among others, the granularity of the usage information in terms of data flows, and the usage data and AoC reporting intervals, need to be very carefully selected in order to provide the required functionality without introducing excessive overhead to the system.

The granularity for usage metering varies between per-flow or aggregated counters, and depends on the collection point, the pricing scheme and the service contract between the supplier and the consumer of the communication resources. For example a pricing scheme may require traffic volume information at the egress point of a network, on a per flow basis, in order to charge the traffic flows that are inserted in a neighboring network. When usage metering and charging are applied on a per-flow basis, more resources are required, and therefore a different contractual agreement should exist between customer and provider.

The usage and AoC reporting intervals should also be configured according to the requirements of services and pricing schemes. For example for services with high interactivity and variations in the consumption of system resources, short intervals may be required in order to provide a more representative view of the service usage. The pricing structure should accordingly provide compensation for the overhead introduced on the accounting management system.

Another important issue is the potential for the customer to renegotiate service and traffic contracts during the service provision. In some cases it is in the interest of a provider to support this functionality - for example when providing charging feedback to the user as an advice for a wiser selection of the service parameters. However the communication and computational cost of the renegotiation should be taken into account. The provider should discourage users from performing frequent renegotiations (e.g. by using the appropriate pricing scheme) when elements like the nature of the service or the profile of the customer do not justify this overhead.

Chapter 4

The CA$hMAN charging and accounting system

4.1 Overview

The implementation of usage-based pricing in telecommunication services is very different from flat-rate and capacity-based charging schemes, mainly because it is tightly related to service control and management mechanisms. This relationship is imposed by the fact that the user may influence the charge by controlling specific parameters of the service, such as quality parameters, and thus affect the utilisation of system resources. Additionally, usage-based pricing introduces an overhead to the service provision and management system, since usage data must be retrieved from various points, transferred to the corresponding charging modules, and processed for the calculation of the charge that corresponds to the service usage. The adoption of usage-based charging schemes by a service provider imposes additional complexity also for end-users and customers of the services since they are not able to predict and verify charges in such a straightforward way as with flat-rate pricing policies.

This chapter presents the design and implementation of the CA$hMAN charging and accounting management system that provided specific solutions to these issues by realising an integrated and realistic environment for the deployment and evaluation of usage-based charging schemes. The design of the system was based on the principle of combining the service-oriented view of charging with resource-oriented charge calculation at the lower management levels. Although the pricing schemes of CA$hMAN take into account the utilisation of network resources, the system is able to associate the charge for each individual connection used by a service to a total charge that corresponds to the service usage as a whole. The implementation of the system was based on current network management and distributed processing technologies, preserving the reliability, scalability, performance and flexibility of the charging and accounting functions. The TINA service architecture

71

and connection management is the adopted framework upon which the CA$hMAN system was built.

Additionally, strong emphasis was given to the way the charging information is transferred and presented to the user, and to providing the user with the ability to efficiently control the service quality and cost relationship. Intelligent agents and advanced user interfaces have been implemented for this purpose.

The presentation of the design and implementation of the CA$hMAN system in this chapter aims at revealing the specific choices made by the Project in terms of:

- Collecting usage data (time and volume) for each network connection.

- Real-time transfer of usage and charging data to the system components located in the domains of the service provider or the user.

- Defining interfaces for the exchange of usage and charging information between different business roles, namely customers, service providers and network providers.

- Defining data structures for the maintenance and transport of the information.

- Adopting and extending the existing recommendations on accounting management and service control.

- Distributing the functionality among independent building blocks, increasing the scalability and the flexibility of the system.

- Designing advanced user interfaces and agents that handle the complexity of the system on behalf of the user, presenting a simplified view of the service control and charging functions, without restricting the user choices and customisation capabilities.

Specifically, section 2 gives a general description of new challenges for accounting management and a presentation of the requirements for the CA$hMAN accounting system. The requirements are based on the general accounting and billing objectives presented in the previous chapter, and on the experimental characteristics of the system, as posed by the aims of the CA$hMAN project and its associated trials.

The mapping of the requirements to the corresponding operations and functional entities is described in section 3, both in terms of service provision and accounting management. In section 4 there is a presentation of the architectural framework upon which the CA$hMAN management system was based. In this section are presented the main principles of the TINA recommendations as they were introduced in the accounting system. Thus, the corresponding charging information structures and computational entities are described, in conjunction with the service provision entities of the TINA architecture.

The hardware equipment for the real-time usage data retrieval of the CA$hMAN project is presented in section 5, where the critical hardware design and implementation issues of usage metering are discussed. In section 6 integration and deployment issues are briefly discussed, including the inter-working of the system's components with external applications and devices used for the experiments. Additionally, some performance and scalability considerations for the usage data collection mechanisms are presented.

The principles upon which the Graphical User Interface (GUI) design of the system was based are described in section 7. The objectives of the GUI design and implementation process are described in conjunction with specific evaluation experiments. Within these experiments, evaluation feedback from real users and specialists was used as input for the progressive improvement of the way usage and charging information are presented.

A general operation scenario is provided in section 8, where the information exchange between the components and the action sequence are presented. The action sequence is described in conjunction with the corresponding user interface entities giving a view of the system from the user's perspective. The conclusions in section 9 present the experience gained from designing and implementing the CA$hMAN charging system.

4.2 Motivation and objectives of the system

The new challenges for accounting management

According to the Network Management Forum [15], among the problems of today's accounting and billing process are the following:

- The existing accounting and billing applications for services based on new network technology cannot accommodate usage data collection and billing.

- Introduction of a new service is either slow (because new software has to be developed) or is prohibitive in terms of cost.

- Inflexible rating and discounting schemes prohibit innovative rebates, multiple-currency, and satisfaction of additional needs of global customers.

- Collection from distributed collection sites in the network or from heterogeneous networks is difficult.

- Few standards have been implemented in the area of usage data collection and billing.

Accounting management in multiservice networks involves the coordination of various complex activities at different levels. The monitored and collected usage information spans from the network connections and their associated resources, to the service-level resources and the content utilised by customers. This complexity is increased by the distributed nature of the metering points, the diversity and volume of the monitored and collected information, and the variety of the applications that use this information. For example, accounting components should be deployed in cooperation with other management mechanisms such as performance reporting and service quality management, in order to be aware of potential service level agreement violations.

In today's highly competitive business environment, rapid availability and quality of billing information is of prime importance. A major success factor for the telecommunications service provider depends on how services are priced and also on how they are billed and invoiced. Additionally, the emerging multimedia services pose additional complexity related to the use of multicasting and multi-party features, that impose the sharing of resources in some portions of the communication tree for the participants of the session, and also additional service control and management functionality. These new services pose key design challenges and stringent flexibility constraints to the accounting management infrastructure, which require new design and implementation approaches. These approaches should also take into account the increasingly changing market environment that requires the fast deployment, modification or withdrawal of services and pricing policies.

The choice of pricing policies by a service provider can be dramatically restricted by the design of the service and accounting management architecture. For example, the pricing policies in Internet are limited by the structure of IP addresses, which hide the distance information between the physical locations of the interconnected parties. Additionally, the Internet's connectionless and unreliable information transfer, and its receiver-driven nature, restrict service providers to adopt mainly flat-rate and capacity-based pricing policies. Paradoxically, due to positioning requirements, some telephony services offered over the Internet make use of traditional telephony time-based pricing policies.

Objectives and requirements for the charging and accounting system

The design and implementation of the CA$hMAN accounting management system aims at providing a flexible and customisable environment, where various usage-based charging schemes can be tested and evaluated. The accounting system should be an efficient tool that can be used for producing useful experimental results. In addition the scalability of the proposed solution, the performance of the system, and the ability to adapt to the existing commercial hardware equipment were important factors that influenced the design and implementation choices. The CA$hMAN system can be seen as a generic service provision and accounting management framework that applies to most multimedia applications. Information to support charging and billing must be collected from many locations and transferred to different external support systems (such as marketing components, network planning components, finance components). This accounting management system should offer services to both users and service providers. The general functions needed by users include the ability to:

- be informed of the cost of services prior to use, perhaps based on historical data from previous similar sessions

- be informed of the costs (e.g. accumulated, current period) of the services during the session

- receive the billing information in different forms (e.g. itemised, accumulated)

- negotiate the charge for the service via the QoS choice or the pricing options.

The general functions needed by service providers include the ability to:

- inform users of the costs of services and possibly influence their behaviour

- customise tariffs according to specific strategies (e.g. market segments, packages, special discounts)

- offer to customers several tariff options

- automate the interactions with customers, and control the corresponding service level agreements.

Briefly, the specific objectives of the CA$hMAN accounting and charging system are identified as follows:

- The system should comply with the generic requirements of accounting management, as defined by the standardisation bodies (such as NMF, ITU-T and TINA) and the corresponding service control and management frameworks. Among these requirements are the accuracy and reliability of the exchanged pricing information, and the timely delivery of the data either in predefined time intervals or upon the occurrence of specific events. The pricing information exchange between the components of the system and between different administrative domains should take place through predefined interfaces in terms of self-contained data structures.

- It should be flexible in accepting various usage-based pricing schemes, by supporting the collection of a wide range of usage metrics, and by having the ability to calculate the charge correlating the corresponding usage and pricing information from various management levels and administrative domains. This information should be structured and processed by mechanisms that can be easily adapted to various pricing schemes. The system should be able to provide on-line delivery of the charging and accounting information (advice of charge).

- The system should be built according to a service architecture that is sufficiently flexible to accommodate a wide variety of applications and services. Specifically, for interactive multimedia services where sophisticated service control mechanisms and real-time event handling are required, the charging functions should be introduced smoothly and tied to the service provision and network management frameworks.

- The customer domain components of the architecture should export the service customisation and control functions in a user-friendly way. The billing customisation and the correlation between service control and charging should also be presented in a simple way, hiding the potential complexity of the pricing schemes, while exporting their most important aspects. This is a particularly important feature for usage-based charging, where a close connection between the transport and the service usage data is sometimes too complicated for users to understand. It is important that the customer is provided with intelligent agents that automate the processes of tariff negotiation and billing data exploitation. In this way the customer can better predict and verify the impact of his actions on the consumption of network resources and on the corresponding charge.

- The system should provide extensive customisation capabilities to service/network providers, for configuration of charging algorithms, billing parameters, and the processing and presentation of billing data to users.

- The system should be open enough to integrate new components and modules that facilitate the exploitation of the collected data. A very critical part of the system's functionality is the processing of network feedback in terms of monitoring and even redefining the quality-to-cost relationship for the service. For this purpose the system provides Application Programming Interfaces (APIs) in order to facilitate the integration of independent components. Part of the functionality of these external components may be the selection of optimal traffic contracts taking into account the quality of service requirements.

4.3 Service provision and accounting management

The charging system provides an integrated infrastructure where usage-based charging algorithms are implemented and evaluated. Part of this evaluation focuses on the impact of the integration of the algorithms with the service management system, and on the user's behaviour in response to pricing signals. The generic service provision systems implemented in the CA\$hMAN charging system, and the use of interactive, broadband, multimedia services and applications, aim at providing these realistic conditions where charging can be integrated with service management and control.

In an open service provision environment the user initially contacts a service provider, authenticating himself, and receives a list of supported services. This list usually depends on the contractual agreement between the customer and the provider. Upon selection of a service, the user is requested to specify the required quality for the service and the corresponding pricing choices. Although this is an initial definition of the quality-to-cost relationship, this relationship may be renegotiated and refined on-line even during the service session. The service provider may send charge information to the user at regular time intervals, upon request, or upon the occurrence of specific events. The main parts of this process are related to both service provision and accounting management (see Figure 4.1), and are based on the generic requirements of an accounting system (see the previous chapter) and on the specific experimental needs of the CA$hMAN research activities.

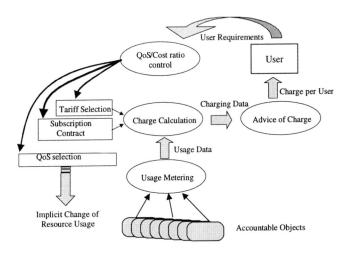

Figure 4.1: The reference model of the charging system

Service provision functions

The generic functionality of the services and applications that can be supported by the system can be represented by a set of operations. Briefly, these are the following [30]:

Service provider selection, user authentication and authorisation

After the selection of a service provider by the user, the latter is prompted to identify himself. According to the subscription contract the user is allowed to access a specific list of supported services, and possibly to claim special treatment from the provider in terms of pricing and service quality.

Selection of service

Within the list of services provided, the customer selects the one that satisfies his requirements. For the supplier, the service selection requires the instantiation of specific components that provide the requested functionality. Additionally, the communication requirements of the service are identified, such as the class of service (e.g. ABR or SBR class for ATM networks).

Selection of traffic contract and service quality parameters

According to the selected application and service category, the user selects the traffic contract and service quality parameters from a predefined value range specific to the application and to the subscription contract with the provider. The user's choices represent the value that the user assigns to the service in terms of quality.

Indication of user behaviour

An early estimation of the user's behaviour (in terms of connection traffic characteristics) may be requested by the supplier. This estimation can be used for more efficient handling of the traffic and better resource utilisation of the provider's network. Through a corresponding charging scheme, a provider can give pricing incentives to users to declare this information.

Upon request for a service, all the service and network components are instantiated and utilised for the service provision according to the adopted service architecture principles.

Core accounting and charging functions

The charging system accommodates the following functional entities, in terms of charging and accounting [30]:

Usage metering

Usage metering is defined as the usage data collection process, from the accountable objects of the system. An accountable object can be associated with a switching device or any other device that provides usage data. The usage metering function is heavily related to the connection and resource configuration management mechanisms adopted by the connectivity provider.

Charge calculation

The *calculation of charge* for a service takes place through dynamically created components that are instantiated concurrently with the rest of the service components. The calculation uses the accounting data collected by the usage metering function, and a tariff structure that provides the relation between service/network usage and prices. The contents of the tariff structure depend on the specific characteristics and customisation parameters of each service, and on the user profile as described in the subscription contracts with the provider.

Advice of charge

The charge that corresponds to a specific user can be transferred to the user domain by using the *advice of charge* (AoC) function. The way this information is presented to the user depends on the capabilities of the terminal equipment, and on the potential intelligence located on the user side, responsible for filtering and evaluating the charging data received. The CA$hMAN platform has focused more on the AoC than the general billing functions because the key feature of the system's charging mechanisms is to provide real-time feedback to users and not to deal with all the problems of invoicing, payment collection, and service level agreement.

QoS-cost ratio control

The user has basically two ways of influencing the way he is charged for the service usage. The first one is by tuning the QoS parameters for the received service. The second is by selecting the correct tariff, subscription contracts and charging parameters when exchanging information with the network provider (implicitly giving a prediction of the service usage in the future). The customer domain components can provide to users the ability to efficiently control the QoS-cost relationship according to their requirements.

In some cases, an important feature that should be provided to users is the ability to continuously tune the QoS-cost relationship during the course of a connection. This is especially important for congestion pricing models, where there is a continuous update of prices in a short time scale. The architecture should utilise intelligent agents in the user and provider domains, responsible for on-line monitoring and renegotiation of contract parameters.

4.4 Architectural framework

The CA$hMAN charging system has been designed using TINA recommendations. The fundamental concept of the TINA business model [23] that distinguishes between service provider, customer and connectivity provider is particularly representative also for describing the business roles involved in the charging and billing processes. We describe briefly the basic principles of the TINA framework which have influenced the deployment of the charging functional and computational entities.

Adoption of the TINA framework

TINA has adopted TMN functional layering except in that the network management and the network element management layers have been grouped into one layer called the resource management layer. For each of these layers (service management, resource management) is defined a corresponding set of concepts, principles, rules and guidelines to be applied during design and deployment phases.

TINA Service Architecture [22] defines a set of reusable and interoperable components with the corresponding interfaces between the roles involved in service provision. TINA aims at offering the same management functionality provided by the TMN functional areas (namely fault, configuration, accounting, performance, and security) integrated with the service management and control mechanisms. It makes use of a distributed processing environment (DPE) that offers a distributed execution and communication environment for the independent building blocks of the architecture.

The network architecture [18] defines concepts related to the control and management of transport networks. This architecture is described in a generic way using abstractions of real network components (such as switches and routers). The network resources and switching systems are represented in a hierarchical way since they are grouped in sub-networks. Each sub-network is part of a higher level sub-network, and at the top hierarchy level there is the layer network which includes all the sub-networks of a specific domain. Switching systems, sub-networks, and layer networks are controlled by the corresponding components defined in the resource architecture of TINA. Resource configuration management is responsible for the way that the switching systems and the sub-networks are distributed and grouped, and the allocation of the corresponding components for controlling them. The process of utilising all these components in order to provide network connections is described in the TINA "Connection Management" specifications [18].

In addition to resource-oriented components used to support the service connectivity requirements, there are connection-oriented components, dynamically created and associated with specific sessions. These components are used to represent the network connections to the higher service levels, providing control and transport interfaces.

TINA has adopted four of the Open Distributed Processing (ODP) viewpoints, complementary to each other, that focus on a different sub-set of the system's characteristics. The four viewpoints are:

- Enterprise viewpoint, which presents the purpose, scope and policies for the system.

- Information viewpoint, which defines the semantics of information and information processing activities in the system.

- Computational viewpoint, which decomposes the system into a set of interacting objects which are candidates for distribution.

- Engineering viewpoint, which focuses on the infrastructure required for supporting distribution.

Hereafter are presented the most important modelling concepts that have been used to design the accounting management architecture. Information modelling is concerned with the objects, their relationships, and the constraints and rules that govern their behaviour (e.g. creation and deletion). Computational modelling specifies the functional decomposition of the system into components (computational objects) suitable for distribution.

The session concept is a key element in the modelling of the TINA architecture, since it allows activities and information elements to be grouped, associating them with the corresponding roles involved in the service. The different types of sessions are defined as follows [22]:

- The Access Session allows a user to access a service provider and request a service. Authorisation and authentication of the user's request is performed within this session. Access session components decide whether a requested service should be provided, according to the usage context of the user who requested the service (e.g. the terminal equipment capabilities). It is service-independent and its primary purpose is to instantiate the service session components that correspond to the requested service. The initial configuration of the access session is performed through the subscription process.

- The User Session deals with a single user's interaction with a service session. It is a representation of the local view of users as participants of a service session. It keeps track of all the user's activities and the specific resources allocated to them. The CA$hMAN architecture defines in this session all the accounting, tariffing and billing information related to a single user.

- The Service/Provider Session performs the core functionality of a specific service and maintains a global view of the service usage, for example the resources used by all participants. The charging system defines in this session all accounting, tariffing and billing information shared by all participants. The participants of a service session communicate by means of stream flow connections (SFC) which represent a point-to-point or point-to-multi-point connection between application-level end points. The distinction between the user and the provider service session aims at decoupling the user-specific aspect of the service from the common parts.

- The Communication Session provides a view of communication resources, as seen by the service level components and the user applications. It is common to all services and independent of network technology. It is responsible for the management (e.g. establishment/release, customisation) of stream flow connections.

- The Connectivity Session is responsible for providing to the communication session the required interfaces for controlling the network connections utilised by a particular service session. Hence the connectivity session defines components that utilise the underlying network architecture components providing the corresponding network connections [18].

Information model for charging and accounting

The network-technology independent view of the communication resources utilised within a service session provides a suitable framework for modelling the charging and accounting information structures. In addition, integration with the service control functions is facilitated, which is particularly important for the association of pricing and service quality notions. Through the communication session the establishment, negotiation of traffic contract and QoS, and release of multiple connections are realised. The service session controls the SFCs through the communication session, while the mapping of them to network flow connections (NFC) is performed through the connectivity session. NFCs are defined as uni/bi-directional point-to-point or point-to-multi-point flow connections between network flow end points (NFEPs). For the sake of simplicity the end-user's terminal ATM adapters can be seen as NFEPs.

The usage information is collected from the low-level communication session components, and transferred to the components responsible for the charge calculation. The information generated by the metering functions contains simple usage data for a specific network connection. Using specific tariff structures, the charging modules process the usage data for each NFC and produce the corresponding charge. Although the system aims at providing an open charging and accounting environment, able to cope with all different kinds of pricing policies and provided services, the work of the CA\$hMAN project was mainly focused on usage-based pricing of network connections, namely the network flow connections (NFCs). This connection-oriented pricing is realised by the CA\$hMAN charging schemes, and it is represented in the corresponding tariff data structures. In our case, a tariff structure consists of $a(x), b(x)$ and $c(x)$ parameters used for the charge calculation as:

$$\text{Charge} = a(x) * T + b(x) * V + c(x)$$

where T is the time and V the volume of ATM cells transferred in the corresponding time interval. The x parameter describes tariff choices offered to the user by the network during call set-up, including the service class (for example variable bit rate or available bit rate), and the user-network interface choices (such as the peak cell rate and cell delay variation tolerance). These choices allow a user to lower the "per unit time" rate $a(x)$ at the cost of raising the "per unit volume" rate $b(x)$. The charge for the connection establishment is represented by $c(x)$. The natural choice of units for T and V by the provider will depend upon whether connections are permanent, semi-permanent or switched. The $a(x), b(x)$ and $c(x)$ depend on various parameters (reflected in the tariff choice x) such as the user's policed peak rate, estimated mean rate, and the desired quality of service, through the effective bandwidth concept. The effective bandwidth of a source depends sensitively upon the statistical properties of the source, and is used as a measure of resource usage, which adequately represents the trade-off between sources of different types, taking proper account of their varying characteristics and requirements.

The usage-based charge calculation for each network connection produces the corresponding charging information structures. Among the elements defined in this structure are:

- VPI and VCI identifiers of the access (UNI) virtual channel connection

- ATM traffic class

- Traffic contract parameters

- QoS parameters

- Total time since the establishment of the connection

- Ingress/egress direction total charge measured since the establishment of the connection

- Tariff structure used for the calculation of the charge

- Usage information records.

At the higher levels, where the charging information from more than one connection is aggregated and associated with a service-level cost, additional information structures are used for describing the pricing policy adopted by the provider. This association depends on the weight that is assigned to the connectivity cost, compared to other service-oriented usage metrics, or the value-based charge for the service.

The aggregation of network-connection specific charging data produces the corresponding application-level connectivity charge, in terms of stream flow connection advice of charge records. These records contain not only the aggregate charge but also the charge for the individual network connections and the tariff description used for the aggregation (see Figure 4.2).

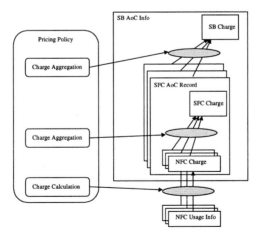

Figure 4.2: Accounting information structures

The charge produced for each SFC must be aggregated according to a specific pricing policy in order to produce the charge for the whole stream binding, which denotes the complete set of connectivity requirements used by a service. The records produced contain the total connectivity charge and additionally the charge for each included SFC and the tariff structure used for the association. The record is structured as follows:

- Service session identifier denoting the individual service

- Requested service quality

- Total time since the beginning of the service

- Total charge measured from the beginning of the service

- SFC information records for the individual stream flow connections

- SFC usage records

- NFC usage records

- SFC charge records

- NFC charge records

- Tariff structure for SFC charge

- Tariff structure used for the calculation of the total charge.

Although the service-oriented modelling of the charging information provides a detailed view of the cost of the service, the information that is important for the user should be user-oriented. The generation process of these records is a very important part of the charging and billing functions, and depends on the policy adopted for distributing the service charge among the participating users.

It should be noted that the reason for including in the AoC records the detailed accounting data from the network connections to the service level charge, is to provide the maximum flexibility for a service provider to support any kind of pricing scheme. This principle is useful not only for calculation of network connection charges, but also for aggregation of the charge at the higher management levels. However in a real operational network, where the performance and efficiency are of major importance, this information can be omitted if not required by the pricing scheme.

Computational modelling of the system

Computational objects (CO) are defined as units of programming and encapsulation, and the communication between them takes place through the corresponding interfaces. Generally there are two kinds of interfaces: the stream interfaces that are used for transporting information such as voice and video bit streams, and the operational interfaces that represent a set of defined operations.

The provider agent (PA) is a TINA CO that is located on the user domain. It is used for establishing a trusted relationship between the user and the service provider. A corresponding access-related part of the user application uses the PA in order to connect to a provider and request a service. On the side of the provider domain there are the user agent (UA) that represents the user, and the initial agent (IA) that is responsible for user authentication and authorisation.

The access session end point (ASEP) and the service session end point (SSEP) are also located on the user-side, and belong to the user access and service sessions respectively. These two components are normally parts of a TINA-compliant application, since they support all mechanisms for controlling the service.

The service components are instantiated by the service factory (SF). These components are the user session manager (USM) that maintains a user-oriented view of the service, and the service session manager (SSM) that provides a service-oriented view. The session objects are instantiated according to the user profile, as defined by the subscription contract with the provider and the specific customisation parameters defined within the access session.

The user billing manager (UBM) and the user tariffing manager (UTM) are responsible for the billing functions and the charge calculation according to the selected tariff (see Figure 4.3).

The communication requirements of a service are handled by the communication session manager (CSM) that receives requests for the manipulation of SFCs. These SFCs are mapped to the corresponding sets of NFCs. The manipulation of the latter is the responsibility of the connectivity session components, such as the connection coordinator (CC). The layer network and the sub-network components defined by the TINA architecture were only partially used, since the connection establishment process was beyond the scope of the implementation. However for design purposes the notion of the element management layer connection performer (EML-CP) was maintained, associated with the low-level usage metering components.

Communication and connectivity sessions are handled on the user-side by the terminal communication session manager (TCSM) and the terminal layer adapter (TLA) respectively.

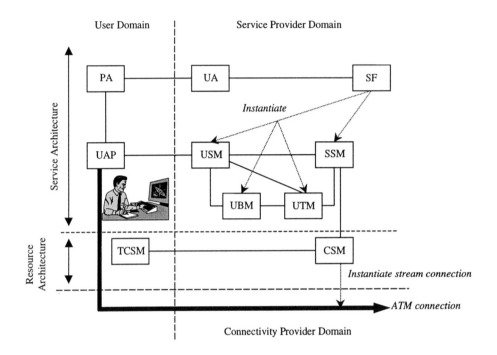

Figure 4.3: The computational model

Purchasing agent

The *purchasing agent* (PuA) is part of the service session end point (SSEP) in the TINA service architecture, and it has generic and service-dependent parts. The generic part is responsible for the lifecycle control of the session, while the service-dependent part provides service customisation and control capabilities. The PuA and SSEP may be part of, or closely linked with, the user application (UAP).

The PuA provides to the user the means to define or negotiate the traffic contract with the retailer. Since it is part of the SSEP, it is related to the generic functionality of the latter as defined by TINA service architecture, which is to enable the user to make use of the capabilities of a service session through an appropriate user interface. These capabilities are enhanced with charging-related functions, such as the selection of available tariffs or the customisation of the AoC process.

The PuA should be able to incorporate intelligence mechanisms for on-line processing of the network feedback. These mechanisms are assigned not only "advisory" responsibilities, but also actively participate in manipulating the generated traffic according to the user's subjective criteria for optimisation. It was also very important to provide open interfaces to the PuA for easy integration of different algorithms for processing those data on behalf of the user. For that reason the functionality of the PuA includes the following:

- The PuA can give advice to the user or propose the best traffic contract or tariff for a specific application. This advice can be based on the billing data sent by the network during the connection duration, or on historical data from previous calls and applications.

- The PuA can use AoC data in order to decide whether the selected tariff or traffic contract is the most appropriate, and if not, it can initiate a renegotiation process with the UBM without interaction with the user.

- When the user selects the preferred traffic contract and QoS parameters, the PuA can automatically adjust the behaviour of the application according to these selections.

A specific renegotiation function was built into the PuA to renegotiate the service contract during the connection. This is applicable in particular to congestion pricing schemes in ABR-like services, where dynamic adaptation of the demand to the network conditions is supported. The input to the renegotiation function is the pricing feedback from the network.

User tariffing manager

The *User Tariffing Manager* maintains all the available pricing options for the specific service session, for an individual user or customer. All the available tariffs for the selected traffic contract are included in this component, and a specific interface is provided so that the user can negotiate and select the best tariff. Briefly the User Tariffing Manager is responsible for:

- Managing the traffic contract and the subscription contract parameters from the USM

- Managing the available tariffs

- Negotiating, via the USM, the tariff selected by the user

- Collecting usage data from the metering manager

- Calculating the charge for the consumed resources that is associated with the specific user service session.

User billing manager

The *user billing manager* is responsible for managing the persistent storage of billing information and for supporting the advice of charge functionality. The UBM customisation information is obtained from the subscription contract between user and service provider, and from the preferences declared by the user before or during the session. The user billing manager collects the charging information from the user tariffing manager, filters it according to the billing options, logs it in a database and forwards it to the user or any other component that is interested in this information (e.g. a marketing component used by the service provider).

Metering manager

The *metering manager* is a component that is used for collecting usage information from the lower connectivity-session accounting components (usage information per NFC and SFC). This information is then transferred to the service session accounting components. The MM is informed by the CSM about the established SFCs and NFCs, so it can interpret the received notifications and aggregate them in terms of SFCs before sending them to the service-level components. It should be noted that the MM receives notifications containing usage information in terms of NFCs and correlates them with the corresponding SFCs.

CA$hMAN charging unit agent (CCUA)

The collection of usage data in the implemented charging system is performed by the corresponding hardware equipment, called CA$hMAN charging units (CCUs). Having a complementary role to switching systems, the CCUs provide real-time, per-VC, accurate cell counts for customisable time intervals. The collection of the raw usage data, and its forwarding to the charging system in terms of notifications, is the responsibility of the CCU agents (CCUA).

CCUAs correspond to element management layer components of the architecture. Their role is to hide the equipment's technology dependencies on the usage metering hardware, facilitating the usage of alternative devices or switching elements with integrated usage metering mechanisms.

4.5   The CA$hMAN charging unit

The collection of volume data for different connections is a time-critical issue that might in principle be carried out using any of the following:

- FPGA (field programmable gate array) chips, i.e. pure hardware (HW),

- DSP (digital signalling processor), i.e. HW and assembler software,

- pure software (SW).

For CA$hMAN, collecting charging data in software was not feasible owing to the heavy requirement in processing power. Hence at the start of the CA$hMAN project it was planned to develop and use two different hardware units for charging. These CA$hMAN charging units (CCU) have the function of collecting the data necessary for charging each ATM connection and passing this data in an appropriate form to network management via a CCU interface. The CCUs also have a policing capability.

The two available units were the SAPU (Stand-Alone-Policing-Unit) developed by ATecoM and previously used in the ACTS EXPLOIT project, and the EPCU (Ericsson Policing and Charging Unit) developed by Ericsson. The SAPU is a specialised measurement unit for usage parameter control (UPC) using FPGA chips to ensure that time critical tasks do not have to run in assembler software. The SAPU was developed for policing functionality within EXPLOIT, and charging functionality was added subsequently for CA$hMAN. The EPCU is based on general purpose processors with integrated DSPs, and was developed specifically for charging. Policing functionality was added subsequently.

When CA$hMAN was planned, the range of charging schemes to be studied was not known. While some schemes might be quite simple, other schemes might require very fast real-time processing of ATM cell-level data. The two CCU designs embodied two different approaches to the collection of usage data. However, if the charging schemes need only measurements of connection duration and cell counts, the fast hardware-based solution, especially the UPC in the SAPU, is not essential. In general, it is more convenient with respect to development time and cost to deploy functionality in software rather than hardware. ATecoM withdrew from CA$hMAN after the first year and the SAPU units were not used for the later experiments.

SAPU implementation

The SAPU architecture comprises a charging function, a policing function, line termination units, and a 68030 CPU board. It is based on a VME bus. The operating system for SAPU is pSOS+, which is a commonly used real time operating system offering TCP/IP and SNMP support. The EPCU also offers TCP/IP, but lacks the SNMP support.

Line termination

At most two line termination modules can be plugged into the carrier board at the same time. These modules translate SDH/PDH layer to ATM layer and vice versa. Each physical medium is assigned one line termination module. Different kinds of line termination can be used simultaneously. SDH multimode STM-1 (155.52 Mb/s) and PDH electrical G.703 terminations were used.

Policing

The enhanced SAPU also uses a modular approach to traffic management. It is possible to extract any 16 bits out of the header of 32 bits. Any combination of these 16 bits has its own leaky bucket parameter set. Thus up to 64k of connections could be policed by one module.

The policing used by SAPU is compliant to ITU-T Recommendation I.371. The module supports the use of dual or single leaky bucket algorithms. Thus the user can set up connections compliant to PCR, CDVT, SCR, and MBS policing parameters.

The module supports cell discarding as well as cell tagging options. It provides cell-counting information such as passed cells, discarded cells, and all cells for any policed connection.

Charging

A programmable board is used for the SAPU charging functionality. Xilinx boards are programmable in terms of logical programmable field gate arrays (FPGA). This means that it can be programmed to hold a range of different charging algorithms.

EPCU implementation

This section describes the architecture and functionality of the individual Exchange Terminal (ET) and the integrated EPCU.

Exchange Terminal architecture and functionality

The EPCU is based on Exchange Terminal (ET) units. The reason for adding the charging and policing functionality to an ET was that DSPs able to run time-critical charging and policing tasks were already present on the ETs. In the EPCU two 34 Mbit/s ET units are used, but the EPCU could be based on any other type of ET unit. An ET unit includes both hardware (comprising assembler software) and software. The hardware deals with traffic and time critical computations, and the software handles (among other things) the TCP/IP and CCU interfaces. The ET terminates the physical layer, performs the ATM transmission convergence, and carries the ATM traffic part to the specific functions on the ET board. The ATM functions are policing, fault management and performance management.

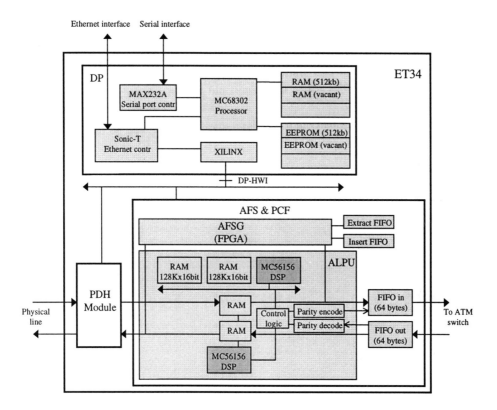

Figure 4.4: ET-34 architecture

The architecture of the ET-34 is outlined in Figure 4.4. As can be seen from the figure, the ET-34 consists of three main modules:

- A PDH module (plesiochronous digital hierarchy).

- An AFS & PCF module (ATM fault supervision and parameter control function). In this module a sub-module - ALPU (ATM layer processing unit) comprising the DSPs - is also shown.

- A DP module (device processor). The DP module is a general purpose processor exercising the general control of the ET-34 board. The AFS & PCF and PDH modules are more specialised hardware modules performing the most critical real-time tasks.

General purpose computing and specialised hardware

The ET-34 contains

- Specialised hardware for handling real-time critical operations that must be executed as the traffic passes by (the AFS & PCF and PDH modules).

- A general purpose processor (the DP) handling less time critical tasks, including various kinds of post-processing of data supplied by the specialised hardware, supporting control interfaces, and general control of the board.

Device processor - HW interface

An interface - DP-HWI (Device Processor - HW Interface) - is defined between the general-purpose processor and the specialised hardware. This interface has two parts:

- PDH-HWI. The interface between the DP and the PDH module.

- AFS & PCF-HWI. The interface between the DP and the AFS & PCF module.

The PDH module implements a traditional PDH interface for carriage of ATM cells. The functionality used in CA$hMAN is located at the ATM layer or above, and thus does not affect the PDH functionality.

The ATM layer functionality, however, is highly relevant to the CA$hMAN functions. Necessary changes and additions to the functionality are accomplished by programming of the DP and even the DSPs, accompanied by necessary adaptations to the interface.

Traffic functions of the ET

The ET-34 offers a wide area of functions. However, in this description only some of the most relevant traffic functions are presented.

The functions in this category process the traffic on the line connected to a 34 Mb/s port of an ATM switch. The processing occurs at two distinct protocol layers: the physical layer and the ATM layer.

The *physical medium functions* handle traffic processing of the G.703/G.804-based, 34 Mb/s PDH electrical interface used at the physical layer of the protocol suite.

The *ATM transmission convergence functions* act on the PDH payload.

The *ATM layer functions* perform the traffic processing of the ATM layer of the interface. The most important functions are:

- VPI/VCI identification and discard of cells with unrecognised VPI/VCI

- Usage parameter control (UPC) UNI, NNI policing

- Fault management

- Insertion and extraction of other types of OAM cells

- Counting

    - Total number of cells in ingress direction
    - Total number of cells in egress direction
    - Number of cells with unknown VPI/VCI in ingress direction
    - Number of cells in excess of the allocated bandwidth for a connection in ingress direction (UNI and NNI)

The integrated EPCU

Due to the relatively limited available DSP RAM, the charging and policing functionality is deployed on two different ET boards. The EPCU unit consists of two ET boards placed back to back. One ET board implements the policing functionality and one the charging functionality. What differs regarding the policing and charging functionality is the ALPU part of the AFS & PCF module. The back ends of the ETs are connected to an interconnect board. This board performs the relay of ATM traffic between the ETs, handles physical layer synchronisation, and provides power to the two ET boards.

The EPCU module is equipped with an Ethernet connector for facilitating LAN traffic, typically IP traffic. This is used by a management application to control the module. On the EPCU, a command agent receives the commands carried by the IP traffic and calls upon the correct traffic functions implemented on the EPCU.

The positioning of the EPCU module will typically be on the UNI at an access switch, located in front of the switch.

Architecture

Figure 4.5 presents an architectural model of the EPCU. The traffic is fed over a trunk and received by the module handling the physical layer. The physical layers (F1, F2, F3 and ATM Transmission Convergence Layer) are terminated and the ATM traffic is fed to the ATM module. The physical module is controlled by a control module, which is also in charge of the rest of the EPCU.

The ATM module receives the ATM cells and performs the necessary ATM functions, primarily the traffic control function (policing) and the charging functions (measurement,

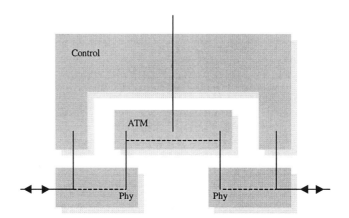

Figure 4.5: EPCU architecture (logical modules)

counting, reporting, and optionally calculation). As mentioned, the ATM layer is controlled by the same control module as the physical layer. This control module communicates with the CCU agent over the CCU interface.

The traffic is then fed back to the physical layer, through the ATM transmission convergence layer, and sent out on the trunk. With bi-directional connections, traffic also flows in the opposite direction.

The implementation of EPCU according to the general model described in this section is presented in Figure 4.6.

A number of software and hardware enhancements have been implemented in order to provide the necessary charging functionality in EPCU. The most time critical charging functionality, such as the real-time estimation of ATM traffic characteristics, is implemented on the DSP functional block. The ET DP software supports the following charging and policing functionality:

- Connection table that holds the charging and policing parameters.

- Storage and transformation of these parameters to a format used by the DSP software.

- Request of charging and policing data from the DSP.

- Management interface for providing access to the charging and policing functions.

- Manager communication support. An agent on the ET receives messages, interprets them and invokes the corresponding function. Results are then packed into a reply message and sent back to the manager.

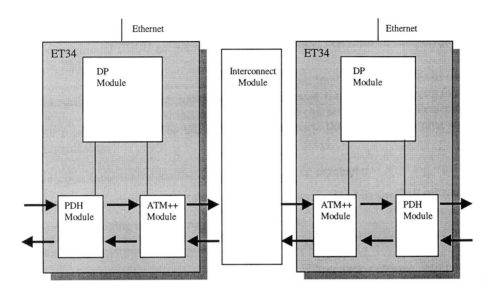

Figure 4.6: Implementation of EPCU

4.6 Integration and deployment of the system

The processing environment

The implementation of the system was based on the OMG-CORBA [10] middle-ware (IONA-Orbix), while the user domain components were implemented using the Java and CORBA technologies (IONA-OrbixWeb). The latter treats all the software components of the architecture as distributed objects whose interfaces are defined in Interface Definition Language (IDL) and implemented in various programming languages. In this way the details of their implementation and location are completely hidden (location transparency).

The introduction of CORBA in the extended management architecture significantly facilitates the implementation and the deployment of the components:

- All the management software components of the architecture are accessible via a common reference point, which is the Object Request Broker (ORB). In this way, all the current and future requirements that involve information exchange between components can be satisfied without extensive additional effort.

- CORBA Services can be used for extending the functionality of the components, and for supporting their generic requirements, in terms of their smooth integration to a distributed processing environment. For example, the trading and naming services provide an efficient way to locate objects by name or type and properties. Using traders, the components of the system may dynamically bind to each other without having to be "hardwired" to dedicated servers running on specific network nodes.

The use of TINA principles and concepts for the implementation of the CA$hMAN system facilitates in an integrated way the fast and flexible specification, design and implementation of accounting management services in an architecture based on an open and distributed computing environment.

While the distribution of functionality is reflected in the design of the information and computational entities, the distribution of components to different threads, processes and machines provides additional flexibility to the deployment of the architecture, while maintaining the performance of the system at acceptable levels.

However, for the customer domain components there were additional requirements related to portability and the ability to easily adapt to different terminal operating systems and environments. Additionally, the ability to download these components on-line to the user terminal upon request by a service can be supported by the use of Java technology. This would enable service providers and third-party providers to update those components frequently with additional functionality and intelligence.

Although the data and control information transfer between the system components takes place through predefined interfaces, considerable effort was spent on providing maximum flexibility in terms of the adaptation of the system to various communication and service equipment.

Interfaces to external components

The deployment and operation of the system presupposed its interworking with external software and hardware modules. Although this interworking was not identified within the objectives of the CA$hMAN project, the need for a "real" environment, where the user behaviour experiments would take place, made it necessary to confront this issue. The adaptation of the system in heterogeneous environments is based on the following interfaces as presented in Figure 4.7.

1. Interface to the accountable objects. These can be network elements (e.g. switching devices) from which the usage information (such as ATM cell counts) is retrieved in predefined time intervals, or network probes responsible for traffic measurements at the lowest level. In the presented system, the usage data are collected by the CCUs, using the corresponding interface. Within this interface the main control operations for the CCU are exported, including the retrieval of detailed usage data per connection.

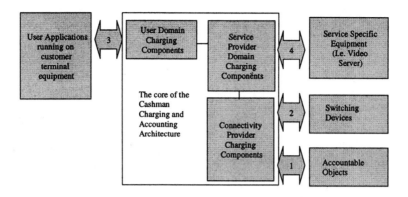

Figure 4.7: Adaptation to existing devices and components

2. Interface to the switching devices and the terminal adapters for the control of connection establishment and the traffic characteristics of the network connections. The information structures used for this interface are sufficiently generic to provide an integrated view of the equipment, and sufficiently detailed to accept various equipment-specific parameters.

3. Interface to the user applications, to enable their communication with the user domain components of the system. Usually the exchanged information includes service control messages between the application and the system's components.

4. An interface to other service-specific equipment that is required for supporting the service (e.g. video servers).

The user-domain components of the system contain service access and control functions compliant with the adopted service architecture (TINA). However, these functions are normally part of the user application, and even if implemented as separate modules they should be tightly adjusted to the application. Due to lack of TINA-compliant applications that could utilise the features provided by the system, the application service control functions are separated from the corresponding functions implemented within the TINA user-domain components. The interworking between TINA and non-TINA-compliant applications is generally a very important issue for the viability of the architecture. The solution to this problem is the definition of intermediate gateways (interworking units) that would translate the control functions between the different frameworks (this translation should incorporate some intelligence since the control operations of various applications may not be mapped to the TINA control operations in a straightforward manner). In the presented service provision and accounting system, interoperability with user applications is restricted to a minimal set of functions that fulfil the objectives of the project.

Performance and scalability considerations

The operation of the charging and accounting system in conjunction with usage-based pricing schemes and real-time advice of charge provision to customers is based on low-level usage data collection mechanisms implemented in hardware, and on the corresponding functions that transfer this information to the service management level components. There are some interesting considerations about the performance and the scalability of the system, when the usage monitoring mechanisms are handling data from thousands (or more) concurrent users.

Specifically for the EPCU each traffic flow is monitored by dedicated hardware in real time. This implies that the EPCU can handle a strictly limited number of concurrent connections, which is equal to 1021 [1] for the version of EPCU that was used for CA$hMAN. Since dedicated hardware was used to monitor the traffic, analytic considerations can be used to see how this mechanism operates at full speed. Due to the chosen implementation, the worst case for the EPCU is when all 1021 connections are active, and all the bandwidth (34 Mbit/s) is in use. Computation done in the project showed that even under these conditions the monitoring does not introduce significant delay to the traffic. In theory, this means that the number of concurrent monitored connections can be doubled if the clock speed of the processor and memory is doubled.

Another important consideration is the amount of collected usage data that has to be transferred from the CCU to the accounting system. If all 1021 connections are active, and a time window size of 50 msec is used for the usage data retrieval, a dedicated link of about 2.5 Mbit/s is needed to transfer the raw data (greater when protocol header information is taken into account). However, although a 50msec update window was the fastest considered in CA$hMAN, this is very unlikely to be required in practice - a 10 second update interval should be sufficient.

In general, a service provider should customise the offered choices of usage and charging data reporting time intervals, according to the specific requirements of the services, and to the ability of the service level components to handle the corresponding processing and communication load. From the network provider's point of view, the usage data retrieval and notification intervals should be customised according to the requirements of the service providers that utilise the network resources, and the performance constraints of the usage monitoring and reporting system.

4.7   User interface design

The Graphical User Interface (GUI) design for the CA$hMAN charging and accounting system was a particularly challenging task since it should handle the complexity of usage-based pricing schemes and convey the information that is essential for end-users to under-

---

[1]$1021 = 2^{10} - 3$ (used for internal communication)

stand and use these schemes effectively. In the CA$hMAN case the charging information is composed of various parts associated with different management levels. For example, in addition to the charging information that refers to the service, there is also charging information specific to the network connections used. A similar situation exists for the customisation parameters of the service, which also have service and connection-level parts. Consequently the presented information and control actions should be able to switch between the different levels, maintaining a clear view of the relationship between usage and charging.

The GUI design was based on general design principles, and also on a sequence of progressive improvements according to feedback from GUI specialists and users who were actually using the system. A well-designed GUI should combine simplicity and flexibility, without restricting the user choices and customisation capabilities. The information and the control functions should be presented in a friendly and consistent way, helping the user to understand the main concepts of the system and to control it according to his requirements.

GUI experiments and feedback from users

Although the CA$hMAN charging schemes contain the right incentives and offer the required flexibility, there is no guarantee that users understand them or respond appropriately to the built-in incentives. Even when they understand the scheme they might not have sufficient information to choose the right tariffs. While these issues play a role before a call starts, during the call the user may need feedback of charge to check whether the chosen tariff was the most appropriate one. Finally, after having finished the call, the user may want to evaluate the corresponding charge in relation to service quality in order to make better tariff choices in future. Some of the problems investigated in the experiments of CA$hMAN were therefore:

1. What information should be presented to the user before, during, and after a session?

2. How should information best be presented to assist user understanding?

3. What functions can be embedded in software to assist this process of information exchange?

By means of these questions the project team aimed to gain a better understanding of whether and how users can understand and use the CA$hMAN usage-based charging schemes. One experiment involved specialists in user interface design. Their task was to make progressively improving tariff choices during several Web sessions of duration five minutes each, and to assess the quality of the user-network interface. The aim of the experiment was to identify desired functionality of the user interface. After this experiment the GUI was improved and additional experiments were made in order to evaluate whether the improvements to the GUI helped non-technical users to interpret the information shown and to respond to the incentives of the tariff.

A typical experiment configuration (Figure 4.8) comprised two interconnected workstations, one of which was used as a Web browser and the other as a Web server. The server contained a database with text and pictures. The point-to-point connection between browser and server was an ATM PVC opened for the entire session. A CA$hMAN charging unit (CCU) measured traffic volume and duration of connection. Traffic information from the CCU was presented to the user in the CA$hMAN charging window. The CA$hMAN charging window is a graphical user interface (GUI) which is placed on the screen next to the Web browser.

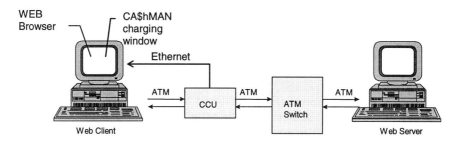

Figure 4.8: GUI experiment configuration

Users taking part in the experiments were asked to retrieve certain information (text and images) during a Web session. They were offered several tariffs, one providing a time-only charge and the others having time and volume components. The users were asked to try to choose the best tariff, which would depend on the volume of data retrieved during the session.

During the Web session the CA$hMAN charging window showed a graphical real-time display of the charges corresponding to the different tariffs (Figure 4.12). These graphs were regularly updated with a period of 10 seconds. After each session the user was able to compare the total cost of the Web session for the selected tariff with the charge for the other tariffs.

Conclusions from the GUI experiments

Although introducing a charging mechanism based on time and volume could be confusing to users, usage-based charging was considered to be understandable by users given sufficient guidance. The main conclusion from evaluating the interface was that the interface should be clean and simple.

During the Web sessions the feedback of charge was highly valued. Even though the tariff is more complex, users feel more secure when they are informed about the status of their charge.

Users have difficulty with providing a prediction of their traffic, therefore it is not easy to make an accurate choice for the optimal tariff. A helper application or software agent should be used. Processes like choosing the cheapest tariff should be fully automated by a software agent in the user's equipment. The experiment showed that the user is not really interested in monitoring alternative tariff choices. A software agent may track alternative tariffs internally for optimisation reasons, but it should not convey this knowledge to users. The software agent can signal the user when the current tariff is wrong and help to renegotiate with the network for a better tariff.

The experiments demonstrated that the CA\$hMAN platform provides an interface which enables users with varying levels of expertise to understand the concepts of tariffs that use volume charges, and to respond appropriately to the relevant incentives. These results justify further research into general acceptance by a broad public of usage-based charging for Web services with different QoS classes.

Users valued the possibility of choosing between two QoS classes, one offering good but expensive quality, the other standard but cheap (here QoS classes differ in the peak cell rate of the ATM traffic contract and thus affect transfer times of files). However, when users get a very good QoS so that transfer times are short, even for large files, this transfer time can be less than the reaction time to interrupt the transfer of the file. In this case users have less ability to control the charge that they have to pay. Clearly the applications that initiate these transfers need to be adapted to inform users about expensive file transfers.

Although it is sub-optimal to offer only one tariff per QoS-class, the participants considered the task of choosing the right tariff (by estimating their mean rate) complex and unfair: complex because of the large number of different tariffs (at least two per QoS class); unfair because they expect the operator to give them the best tariff from the start (this is however in principle impossible for tariffing schemes based on a priori expectations of usage of network resources, as discussed in Appendix A). Commercial customers such as Internet service providers might nevertheless value the additional control of tariffs that this option provides.

4.8 Operational scenario

An important contribution to the functionality of the system is the provision of advice of charge (AoC) information by the service provider (SP) to users. AoCs are used to inform users in real time about the progress of the service charge. It is normally only an indication of charge but can also be used for hot billing. The scenario focuses mainly on passing charging information to users in real time, and not on implementing the complete infrastructure to generate and deliver the bill. Charging and billing between SPs is also outside the scope of the scenario. Therefore we consider only the case of calls completely performed within one SP administrative domain. The AoC notification does not include installation fee, general subscription fee, subscription fees for different services, and service profile management charges, but it is focused on the usage-based charge that represents the utilisation of network resources.

Among the services charged in the scenario are data retrieval services, video on demand, Web browsing, and multimedia multiparty conferencing services. The network infrastructure on which the experiments were conducted consisted of three ATM test-beds that were interconnected over the European ATM pilot. The connections (permanent virtual channel) were pre-established via management interfaces.

The managed network elements (NEs), namely the CCUs, consist of stand-alone units with ATM interfaces at 155 Mbits/s SDH or 34 Mbits/s PDH. In addition to the policing functionality, the NEs support accounting functionality in terms of counting the transmitted cells over the connection in 50msec time slots. Connection management functions are also provided on the NEs to control the lifecycle of the managed objects that represent the monitored connections. The NEs generate usage records, which contain detailed low-level information about the service transaction. These usage records are processed in the network management and service management layers to deliver accounting reports that are used to generate the AoC notifications sent to users.

The interaction sequence between the user and the service provider starts with the presentation to the user of a login dialog within which the access session can be initiated (Figure 4.9). The user specifies the name of the provider he wants to contact (in the form of a host address) and is asked to submit username and password in order to be granted access. After the user is identified by the system he receives the list of supported classes of services. For each class a list of services may be requested, and upon service selection the service session is instantiated. All of these operations take place via the provider agent (PA) which resides in the user domain, and the user agent (UA) existing in the provider domain, which maintains the user profile and identity information.

The access session initiation on the provider domain is performed by the initial agent (IA), according to the user profile and the corresponding subscription contract. The PA requests from the IA a reference to the user agent (UA), with which it interacts directly to grant the user access and to get the list of services.

In order to start a service session the UA requests the service factory (SF) to instantiate the service session components that correspond to the service instance. This is realised by an instantiation of the user session manager (USM), the user tariffing manager (UTM), the user billing manager (UBM), and eventually the service session manager (SSM) if it has not already been instantiated by another participant of the same session. The references to all these components are returned to the user application (UAP) via the UA and PA.

When the service is started the service part of the UAP interacts with the service components via the USM to negotiate the service characteristics, the traffic contract parameters,

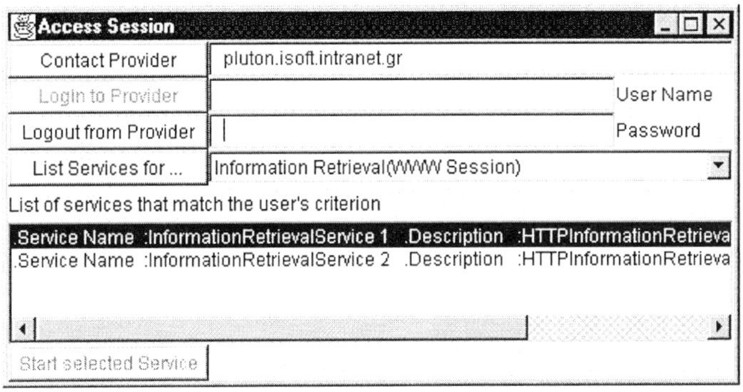

Figure 4.9: The login dialog

the tariff contract and the billing options. The corresponding user interface provides the means for the user to select these parameters from a list of supported choices (Figures 4.10 and 4.11).

When the user selects the traffic contract and QoS parameters for the requested service, the SSM decides the number of SFCs to be requested from the communication session manager (CSM) and at the same time performs the mapping from the service-oriented parameters to the connection-oriented ones. The CSM receives this information and is then responsible for establishing those SFCs between the applications involved in the service. In the same way the CSM requests the communication session components to establish the network flow connections (NFCs) between the terminal devices of the session participants. At the same time the identifiers of the SFCs and the NFCs are communicated to the corresponding accounting components of the system (metering manager), in order to be able to correlate the received usage metering information with the utilised connections.

When the session is active, the AoC information elements are received by the UAP, and an indication of the charge and the usage is presented to the user (Figure 4.12). The charge may be presented at a service level (where the total charge for the service is shown) or at a connection level, where the charge for individual connections is presented. The time interval upon which AoC information is transmitted is also configurable by the user (Figure 4.13).

The user may want to modify the tariff or traffic contract parameters on the basis of the AoC feedback received from the network and his evaluation of the received service quality. This can be done by using the on-line renegotiation functionality provided by the system. The tariff choice, traffic contract and QoS parameters can all be changed during the service. This process may be automated by enabling the corresponding renegotiation agents, which monitor the historical and real-time usage and charging data and decide when to request

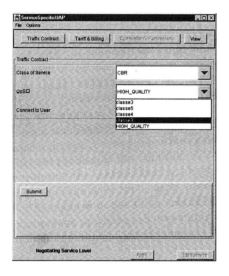

Figure 4.10: Traffic contract dialog

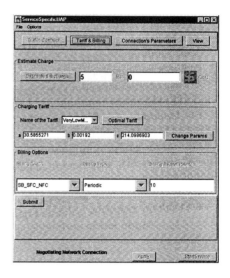

Figure 4.11: Tariff and billing dialog

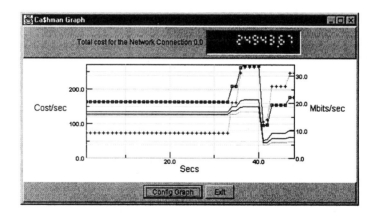

Figure 4.12: Presentation of advice of charge and usage information

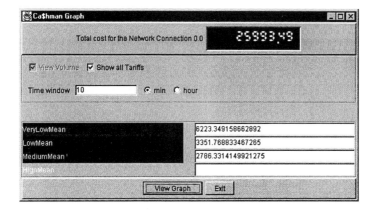

Figure 4.13: Customisation window for the presentation of charging information

a new traffic contract, QoS level, or tariff. In addition, these renegotiation changes may happen either on the "service" level, where the network is implicitly authorised to adjust accordingly the connection level parameters, or directly at the connection level, since the user is given direct control of the traffic contracts of these connections. The system allows the user to switch easily between service and connection views (Figure 4.14). We should note here that this functionality may be too complicated for the non-expert user, but it was very important for experimenters and expert users who needed a detailed per-connection view of the service configuration (Figure 4.15) and the charge and usage information.

4.9   Conclusion

A fundamental business concept in telecommunications, and more generally in economics, is the ability to offer differentiated services to customers. These services should come at different prices, and therefore they create a need for an appropriate accounting system to support the pricing policies. Cost/performance (or Cost/QoS) is one of the key metrics in telecommunications business since the provider with the best ratio should attract customers and achieve a high revenue. Then it is important to provide customers with functionality, implemented in the accounting management system, that allows them to modify this ratio according to the pricing policies implemented in the network.

Another important objective for the accounting management system is to provide a flexible and realistic environment where various usage-based pricing schemes can be deployed and evaluated at a reasonable cost. This evaluation focuses on the impact of deploying these schemes for the service providers and the users. From the provider's perspective, among the

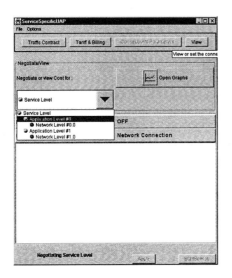

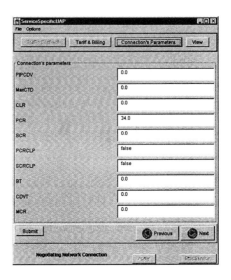

Figure 4.14: Switching views dialogue

Figure 4.15: Connection-level traffic contract and quality of service

main considerations are the performance, flexibility, and scalability of the system. Some accounting functions should be located close to the network elements, while others are much more related to the service-level management and control. Some functions are also likely to evolve over time with new services, new network infrastructures or new requests from customers. The globalisation and integration of telecommunications services make scalability one of the major issues for the design of services. An additional difficulty for the accounting management system is the ability to adapt to different pricing schemes since there is always a non-negligible level of uncertainty over their acceptance by customers. This flexibility is difficult to achieve because of the differentiation of network technologies and the inherent complexity of usage-based pricing methods. From the user's perspective, the system should export the charging and usage information and control operations in a friendly and understandable way, while at the same time maximum flexibility and customisation capabilities should be offered.

The reaction of users to the pricing schemes adopted is expressed through variation in the demand for services, or through preferences for specific values of the service customisation parameters. The need for retrieval of representative metrics for user behaviour requires a realistic service provision system, where the charging mechanisms are smoothly integrated and co-exist with the service control and management functions.

The accounting management system presented here lies across several management levels. At the service level it is mainly concerned with the application of tariffs to usage of the services, the computation of charges and the delivery of bills. At the network and network element levels it focuses on the collection, aggregation, correlation, filtering, and processing of resource usage information.

TINA recommendations that have been used to implement the CA$hMAN system provide an efficient tool to design the complex mechanisms required by an accounting management system in a distributed environment. The main objective of this accounting system is to provide charging both for network and service usage, taking into account the stringent requirements of the emerging multimedia services. These new services (Information, Telecommunication, Management) pose numerous challenges to accounting systems, such as the splitting of the service costs between customers and content providers (as in 800 service), and among the customers of multi-party services. The service characteristics and value also affect the association of usage and charge, as defined by the corresponding pricing schemes. Telephony over IP is an example of the emerging class of services on the Internet, where although pricing is based on the traditional flat-rate scheme, these services tend to be priced individually as a supplementary service. It is the demand for new services, requiring some QoS levels, that has convinced some Internet researchers to revoke the "best-effort" paradigm in favour of a differentiated services one. These differentiated services have to be supported by administrative policies such as authentication, authorisation and accounting.

The session concept, as a fundamental part of the TINA architecture, facilitated the introduction of the charging mechanisms within an integrated modelling of the management and control of the service. In this way, although the system is based on the TINA specifications for the service provision architecture, the selected charging and accounting functions and the corresponding information structures maintain a generic view of the accounting principles. TINA recommendations facilitate the adoption of the end-to-end service management approach, focusing on the service requirements instead of the resource-oriented approach that is found in TMN. One important and complex aspect that can be considered as an extension of CA$hMAN's work is the use of the service transaction concept which should be associated with the interaction and information exchange sequences in the system.

The processing of usage and charging information has different objectives for the user and the provider, and thus specific mechanisms such as intelligent agents were employed for the corresponding filtering, forwarding and presentation of the information. The experience gained from the implementation of the charging schemes and the continuous improvement of the user interfaces according to feedback given by the users and experimenters showed that the presentation of charging information to the user is an issue of major importance. Thus it should be taken into account when applying a charging scheme and designing the corresponding functions and mechanisms. The following chapter presents some of the CA$hMAN work on developing and evaluating some examples of charging agents.

The adoption of distributed processing technology for the implementation of the system proved to be very convenient for the integration of new specialised components during the design and implementation phases, and for distributing the functionality between components and network locations. Specifically for usage metering, where substantial implementation and maintenance costs exist for an operator, the usage data collection took place by using specific hardware equipment that provided accurate counts of ATM cells per connection.

Chapter 5

Agents

The CA$hMAN platform described in chapter 4 uses a simple interface that gives the user current information on charges but provides relatively little supporting information to help the user make tariff choices. The human user is expected to make these tariff choices on the basis of his or her expectation of the traffic characteristics and quality of service requirements of the connection. In user experiments employing this interface with the *abc* charging scheme it became clear that users were generally not able to make informed choices of tariff or to react quickly to changes in charge. Most users expected that the charging system should make such choices on their behalf. ABR charging schemes present a particular difficulty since users may need to react to varying rate allocation (and varying charge) during a connection.

A natural approach is to investigate the use of software agents to make tariff and traffic contract choices for users. Such agents could provide a simple and high-level interface to the user while incorporating useful intelligence, in particular through being customisable to the user's requirements and application software. Suitable agent functionality could be located in the network domain, where it would be linked to specific services that are offered. Alternatively it could be located in the user domain as part of user applications that use basic ATM transport connections. The functionality would be rather similar in either case, although agents in the user domain might more readily be customisable for user traffic characteristics.

The CA$hMAN charging schemes were designed to provide a simple and uniform user-network interface that enables the transfer of appropriate incentives. In contrast to this uniform charging approach, helper agent functionality needs to be closely related to specific user applications, or to specific high-level services offered by the network. It was not a key part of the CA$hMAN project to develop such agents. However it became clear during CA$hMAN user trials that it would be very useful to implement some examples of agents in order to demonstrate the full potential of this approach.

This chapter presents some of the work of CA$hMAN in developing examples of user agents to make charging decisions. Section 1 considers ABR connections and describes an agent that aims to maximise the user's utility by varying the user's 'willingness to pay' in response to the network's rate allocation and charging parameters. Section 2 describes the extensions to the CA$hMAN platform through which this agent was demonstrated in user experiments, and presents the results from a simulation model used for quantitative evaluation of the performance of the agent. In section 3 we describe an agent for on-line renegotiation of tariffs for connections with fixed peak rates, under the *abc* charging scheme for guaranteed services. Experimental results using this agent are also presented. Section 4 describes an agent for on-line renegotiation of peak rates, together with simulation and experimental results.

A general conclusion from this work is that user agents incorporating well-designed algorithms can be very successful in making rapid decisions on the user's behalf in order to maximise user utility. One may expect more work to be done in the design of charging decision agents as the concepts of dynamic pricing and renegotiated services gain ground.

5.1   A user agent for ABR connections

We consider two of the ABR charging schemes that were studied within CA$hMAN. In the first scheme, described in section 2.3, prices are based on the minimum cell rate (MCR) and involve measurements of the duration of a connection (time, T) and the total number of cells transferred (volume, V); the total charge of the connection is $a \cdot MCR \cdot T + b \cdot V$, where a is the charge per unit of time and unit of MCR, and b is the charge per unit of volume transferred. The second charging scheme (in its simplified version) deals with connections with zero MCR, and is justified by the theory of social welfare maximisation (see section 3 of Appendix B). Prices per unit of volume vary dynamically in response to varying conditions of network load in such a way that, in equilibrium, the demand for bandwidth will be equal to the supply. With appropriately defined user demand functions, in the state of equilibrium, social welfare (i.e. the aggregate utility of the users) is maximised. This scheme is referred to as the dynamic pricing scheme for ABR. According to this, each user i declares his willingness-to-pay w_i, and is allocated a corresponding portion x_i of the capacity available to ABR; this portion is proportional to w_i, i.e. $x_i = (w_i / \sum_j w_j) C_{ABR}$. This structure is also applicable to the MCR-based charging scheme, provided that each user expresses his willingness-to-pay in terms of the quantity of MCR he wishes to purchase; that is, $w_i = a \cdot MCR_i$, where $\sum_i MCR_i$ is guaranteed by CAC to be available to ABR connections. Demand for bandwidth, expressed through the willingness-to-pay, varies with time because users may enter or depart the system, or modify their willingness-to-pay during an ABR connection. Moreover, C_{ABR} varies with time, because so does the set of DBR and SBR connections, the residual capacity from which is used by ABR. Thus, for an ongoing ABR connection, offering the same amount of money will not (in general) lead to the optimal 'utility-for-money' under different conditions. Thus, it is necessary for the user to *vary* w_i if it does not constitute a satisfactory choice: either because the previously attained QoS is not 'worth the money' anymore (because it costs more due to increased demand or decreased supply), or because better QoS is achievable at little additional cost due to a decrease in demand/supply. One context to which this situation applies involves transport of video on demand over ABR, with variable-rate encoding of movies (eg. MPEG). There have been developed video servers that can *adapt* the quality of the video sent to the bandwidth x instantaneously available: this can be done by either selectively discarding frames, or by varying a quality factor; see [34] and references therein. When the transport of video is charged, this introduces an additional component to the feedback loop of video adaptation. As will be discussed at the end of the section, the approach to be presented also pertains to Web browsing over ABR, and to other cases where the QoS perceived by the user is mainly related to the mean bandwidth offered to his connection.

In large systems with many users, it is envisaged that small variations of w_i may be necessary rather frequently. In such a case, it will be difficult (and maybe annoying) for the user to perform these variations manually. On the other hand, this appears to be a suitable task for a *software agent*, residing at the user side; such an agent can prove a valuable tool, constantly maintaining a good level of the net benefit - that is, the difference between the utility acquired by the QoS and the willingness-to-pay. Of course the user should have the ability to bypass the agent in case he is not satisfied by its selections. In this section, we formulate an optimisation problem for a user sharing a single ATM link with other users; each user is served by an ABR connection. It is assumed that the user values the instantaneous peak rate x allocated by the network, so that his utility function $u(x)$ is an 'explicit' function of x. The user does not know this function explicitly, yet has knowledge of its derivatives, since he can figure out (by also observing the QoS) whether his net benefit increases or not when he perturbs his willingness-to-pay. On the other hand, the ABR agent can only observe the amount of bandwidth allocated by the network for differing selections of the willingness-to-pay. This is a reasonable assumption, because standard ABR flow control does offer this information. We show that the problem of the ABR agent learning the user behaviour reduces to a curve fitting problem, which under the assumption of *concave* utility function is solved by means of a special algorithm (namely, antitonic regression). The selection of willingness-to-pay by the ABR agent is performed on the basis of the curve fit. We also extend the ABR agent approach to more general cases of economic sharing of network resources. It should be noted that although we deal with ABR connections, the approach is applicable to other elastic services such as TCP/IP. In the following section we evaluate the approach by means of simulations, the main conclusion of which is that the ABR agent leads to *almost optimal* net benefit with very small computational overhead; we also show that such an accuracy cannot be attained with a certain simpler method. The ABR agent approach is rather general: users do not have to be identical, their number need neither be fixed nor known at any point.

The model - the optimisation problems

We consider a system where multiple users with ABR connections share network resources, which are also used by guaranteed QoS connections. For simplicity, we consider the case of a single ATM link; the approach to be presented extends to the case of a network, as explained later. The total capacity available to ABR is denoted as C_{ABR}. For each user i the *net benefit* function is assumed to be quasi-linear [115]. In particular, this equals

$$u_i(x_i) - w_i$$

where the function $u_i(x_i)$ gives the utility due to the QoS attained when bandwidth x_i is allocated to the user and w_i is the willingness-to-pay of the user, i.e. the amount of money to be paid for this bandwidth per unit time. (In fact, $u_i(x_i) - w_i$ equals the net benefit per time unit.) Note that the function $u_i(\cdot)$ need *not* be common to all users. However, it is assumed that each of the functions $u_i(x_i)$ is an *increasing concave* function of x_i. This is a standard assumption (see [97, 84]) indicating a diminishing marginal utility as x_i increases; representative such functions are $u(x) = (1 - e^{-x/B})\tilde{u}$, $u(x) = (x/(x+B))\tilde{u}$, where $\tilde{u}, B$ are constants, or $u(x) = -(-\log(x/C))^\alpha$, where C is the total capacity of the link and $\alpha \geq 1$. Henceforth we focus on a particular user i, and we drop the subscript i from the various quantities concerning this user, who will be denoted as U. We shall study the behaviour of this user throughout multiple ABR connections, and assume that his utility function $u(x)$ does *not* change from connection to connection. Otherwise, we could associate a different utility function for each *mode* of operation of user U, and study such modes separately; for example, the user may value differently some amount of bandwidth when served for professional purposes than when served for private purposes. It should be noted however that the number and the set of other users contending with U may *vary* during a connection of U, and the same applies to their willingness-to-pay and to the value of C_{ABR}.

From the theory of proportional fairness presented in section 2 of Appendix B we know that a network planner aiming to optimise social welfare should allocate to U a bandwidth

$$x = \frac{w}{w + W} C_{ABR} \tag{5.1}$$

where w is the willingness-to-pay of this user per time unit, and W is the total willingness-to-pay of the *other* users. This result can also be extended to networks. Bandwidth allocation according to (5.1) is referred to as proportional sharing of bandwidth, and can be interpreted as follows: Users buy bandwidth at a *price p* per unit, according to their willingness-to-pay; there exists a price p and values of users' willingness-to-pay such that if the network planner sets the price p to $(w + W)/C_{ABR}$ then all individual net benefit functions are maximised, and so is *social welfare*, i.e. the sum of the utilities of all users. Thus the price is determined by both the demand (through the total willingness-to-pay $w + W$) and the supply of capacity, i.e. C_{ABR}. The pair (W, C_{ABR}) will be henceforth referred to as the *link state*.

Since w, W and C_{ABR} may vary with time, it is reasonable to assume that the goal of user U is to always select such a willingness-to-pay so that the bandwidth x allocated according to (5.1) leads to a maximum of $u(x) - w$. Using (5.1), it follows that the user optimisation problem is:

User Problem:

$$\max_{w \geq 0} \left\{ u\left(\frac{w}{w + W} C_{ABR}\right) - w \right\} \tag{5.2}$$

It is easily seen that this problem has always a unique solution, to be denoted as $w^*[W, C_{ABR}]$; given the function $u(x)$, the value of this optimal solution depends only on the link state (W, C_{ABR}). Indeed, due to concavity of $u(x)$, the function under maximisation is concave in w; moreover, its first derivative (with respect to w) either is always negative (in which case its maximum is attained for $w = 0$) or vanishes at a single point w^* which is the maximising point in question.

For the optimisation problem (5.2), we can define a doubly parameterised set $\mathcal{O}$ of points

$$\left(w^*[W, C_{ABR}], x^*[W, C_{ABR}] \right) \tag{5.3}$$

each satisfying (5.1) and being optimal under a pair (W, C_{ABR}). In fact, for any fixed value of C_{ABR}, by treating W as a free variable we obtain a curve of optimal points (5.3). Therefore, in general the set $\mathcal{O}$ of optimal points is *not* just a single curve, but it is rather a family of curves defined as above, parameterised with C_{ABR}. Figure 5.1 depicts these curves for an analytically solvable case of the problem; in particular, we have taken $u(x) = 1 - e^{-x}$, where x is expressed in Mbit/s. The topmost part of each curve corresponds to $W \approx 0$, while the bottom part corresponds to $W \to \infty$.

It is easily seen for the case depicted in Figure 5.1, that for $W \to \infty$, w^* goes to 0, thus implying $w^* \ll W$. Moreover, in the bottom part of the curves, there are points that are optimal under distinct link states, while being very close to each other. This occurs because, due to the fact $w^* \ll W$, (5.1) reduces to

$$x \approx w \frac{C_{ABR}}{W} = \frac{w}{p} \tag{5.4}$$

where $p = W/C_{ABR}$. This parameter can be interpreted as the *price* per unit of bandwidth per unit of time. Thus, if the same value of the price p corresponds to two (or more) distinct link states, then the corresponding optimal points $(w^*[W, C_{ABR}], x^*[W, C_{ABR}])$ are very close to each other.

The above observations motivate us to consider henceforth only the special case where user U has *limited 'market power'*, so that when he enters the system, the extra bandwidth he receives has a negligible influence on the initial price $p = W/C_{ABR}$. In this case, the User Problem (5.2) now reduces to

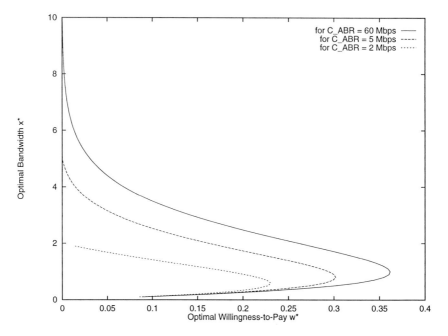

Figure 5.1: The curves of optimal points

Special Case of User Problem:

$$\max_{w \geq 0} \left\{ u\left(\frac{w}{p}\right) - w \right\} \tag{5.5}$$

Equations (5.4) and (5.5) pertain to the case of a large system, if the user U is small enough so as to buy bandwidth according to the price $p = W/C_{ABR}$ per unit of bandwidth per unit of time, without his demand further influencing the price.

The Special Case of User Problem is indeed applicable to the case of a system of many users, provided also that the function $u(x)$ is such that it discourages user U from desiring high values of bandwidth, so that $w^* \ll W$. This is not an unduly restrictive assumption, since users also have budget constraints which in a large system will in general enforce this condition.

Furthermore it is readily seen from (5.5) that the optimal point of the Special Case of User Problem only depends on the price $p = W/C_{ABR}$. Thus, for link states (W, C_{ABR}) where W/C_{ABR} is equal to some constant p, the corresponding optimal points of the User Problem collapse to a *single* point $(w^*(p), x^*(p))$ depending only on p.

So far we have not dealt with *how* user U would actually find the optimal selection of the willingness-to-pay. In practice, the user knows neither an analytical expression for the utility function $u(x)$, nor the values of C_{ABR} and W. Nevertheless, since by assumption the user can evaluate the derivatives of $u(x)$, he can assess whether or not a perturbation of his willingness-to-pay leads (under the same link state) to an increase of his net benefit. Thus, optimisation can be performed by the user by means of successive *trials*. Furthermore, in a varying system, upon a change in the link state, the allocated bandwidth x and hence the value of the user utility will also change. Thus user U has to modify his willingness-to-pay again until he reaches a point where $u(x) - w$ is maximised again. In the next subsection we illustrate how this can be done by means of a software agent.

The ABR agent

The main issues

The objective of the ABR agent (AA) to be developed is to tune the willingness-to-pay on behalf of the user, so that the user's net benefit is steadily maximised despite the variations in the link state. Before explaining how this can be done we clarify the assumptions regarding the *information set* of the AA, which in general should comprise both *prior* information on *user preferences* and *dynamic* information on the *link state*.

The *perfect* information set of the problem would be for the AA to have both:

1. complete prior information on user preferences, that is knowledge of the family of curves $\mathcal{O}$ *and* of the link state under which each point is optimal, and

2. complete dynamic information, i.e. know the link state at each time.

Such a case is easy to deal with: the AA would at each time accurately select the willingness-to-pay that is optimal under the present link state. However, such a case is unrealistic because the information on the link state requires additional probing of the system (see below); the information obtained through the ABR flow control is not sufficient.

A more realistic case with imperfect prior information would be one where the ABR agent only has recorded previous points of the curves $\mathcal{O}$. Each such point however has to be associated with the corresponding link state (W, C_{ABR}) for which it is optimal, for otherwise it conveys *no* information on the user preferences. Indeed recall that, due to (5.1), each point (w, x) is feasible for infinitely many pairs of (W, C_{ABR}), provided that $C_{ABR} \geq x$, yet for only one such pair is this point optimal. In fact, there are utility functions for which this always holds, and thus the set $\mathcal{O}$ comprises all points (w, x) with $w > 0$ and $x > 0$.

Of course, the link state (W, C_{ABR}) can possibly be determined by probing the system: that is, by the AA offering another amount of money w' (for test purposes), recording the corresponding amount of bandwidth x' allocated, and then solving a system of two equations with respect to the unknown link state (W, C_{ABR}), namely the equations $x = (w/(w + W))C_{ABR}$ and $x' = (w'/(w' + W))C_{ABR}$. However, such a procedure would introduce additional delay in the AA selection, since it would require probing the network in order to determine the current link state. This procedure increases the possibility of an outdated selection; moreover, it may result in QoS deterioration, because (w', x') may constitute a selection that does not please the user. It is important for our purposes that the algorithm makes a reasonably good choice *quickly* since the link state is assumed to vary frequently. In the case where the user U has limited market power, the aforementioned information (i.e. record of previous optimal points) is interesting and useful. Indeed, the system is now operating in the region where it suffices to parameterise the optimal points with the price p set by the network. Each recorded point (w, x) can be associated with a *price* (rather than the link state) which can be estimated as $p = w/x$, *without* requiring any additional probing. Therefore, the ABR agent, prior to being activated, can *learn* the user behaviour, by recording points previously achieved by U; the AA can subsequently select the willingness-to-pay based on the price.

Let us denote by $\mathcal{R}$ the set of points recorded by the AA. Ideally, $\mathcal{R} \subseteq \mathcal{O}$, that is all points recorded by the AA correspond to previous *optimal* selections of the user, without any inaccuracies in the observations (this issue will be dealt with in detail later). Since the points recorded would constitute a single *curve* (see Figure 5.2) the set of prior information is well-structured, thus attaining complete encoding of user preferences: for each price p, there exists a unique point $(w^*(p), x^*(p))$ on the curve; thus, when the current price is given, if the AA knows the curve then it can determine the optimal selection of willingness-to-pay.

It should be emphasised that the AA learns and subsequently *imitates* the behaviour of user U on the basis of *different information*. In particular, the user observes the QoS *without* knowing the exact value of the allocated bandwidth x, estimates his current derivative of the net benefit, and selects w in order to maximise (or at least improve) $u(x) - w$. On the other hand, the AA can only observe the bandwidth x allocated for the selections of w it (or the user) makes.

Finally, since the user actually performs trial-and-error successively, $\mathcal{R}$ also comprises near-optimal points, as well as points corresponding to highly unsatisfactory selections; this imposes an important task for the AA, namely to *filter out* the 'noise' from the set $\mathcal{R}$ of recorded points. Thus, the AA has to *fit a curve* $\mathcal{R}_{fit}$ to the set $\mathcal{R}$ of recorded points, since if only optimal points were recorded then these would constitute a single curve. One can apply standard curve-fitting techniques, in order to fit this curve directly on the (w, x) plane. This approach suffers from the fact that the above curve has no interesting properties that can be exploited to improve the accuracy of curve-fitting. The approach to be presented exploits the assumed *concavity* of the utility function $u(x)$ and leads to an easier curve-fitting problem. This is explained later; for the present, we assume that such a curve is already available.

The algorithm of the ABR agent

Let us assume that the system is initially in equilibrium, i.e. that for the particular link state (W^0, C^0_{ABR}), the values of which are not known, AA has reached the corresponding point (w^*_0, x^*_0) for user U that is optimal for this state. The initial estimate of the price is $p_0 = w^*_0/x^*_0$; the aforementioned point will be henceforth denoted as $(w^*(p_0), x^*(p_0))$. The link state then changes to (W^1, C^1_{ABR}), the values of which are not known either. The change will be detected by the agent, through a change in the value of the allocated bandwidth, from $x^*(p_0)$ to x_1. Thus, U is now at the point $(w^*_0(p_0), x_1)$. This in general is a *non-optimal* point under the current link state; that is, it does not belong to the curve $\mathcal{R}_{fit}$. The AA will then adjust the willingness-to-pay by guessing the *new* value of the price, which should be taken as

$$p_1 = \frac{w^*(p_0)}{x_1}.$$

Then, the AA will select the willingness-to-pay $w^*(p_1)$ that corresponds to the point of $\mathcal{R}_{fit}$ for price equal to p_1; see Figure 5.2. Following this choice, the AA will record a new point $(w^*(p_1), x'_1)$; ideally, there should hold $x'_1 \approx x^*_{fit}(p_1)$; that is, the bandwidth allocated to user U as a consequence of this choice of willingness-to-pay should approximately equal the bandwidth specified by the corresponding point of the fitted curve $\mathcal{R}_{fit}$. However, it is possible that this does not hold, due either to the various approximations involved, or to a change of the link state in the meantime. In any case, the AA should estimate the price again and suggest a new choice of the willingness-to-pay. As already mentioned, it is important in the cases of interest that the algorithm makes a reasonable choice *quickly*. Our algorithm has this property as will become apparent by the results presented in section 5.2.

Curve fitting algorithm – antitonic regression

Our objective is to find the optimal choice for the willingness-to-pay $w^*(p)$ under price p, on the basis of the available set $\mathcal{R}$ of measurements (w, x). This will be done by means of curve-fitting. The straightforward approach would be to fit a curve $\mathcal{R}_{fit}$ directly on the (w, x) plane. We follow a different approach, exploiting the assumed *concavity* of the utility function $u(x)$.

As a first observation, it is easily seen from (5.5) that, for a price p, there holds

$$p = w^*(p)/x^*(p) = u'(x^*(p)) = \left. \frac{du(x)}{dx} \right|_{x=x^*(p)} \tag{5.6}$$

Since $u(x)$ is concave, $u'(x^*(p))$ is a non-increasing function of $x^*(p)$. Since $x^*(p)$ is the inverse function of $u'(x^*(p))$ it is also a non-increasing function of p. Instead of fitting a curve to the points on the (w, x) plane where the original measurements reside, we opt

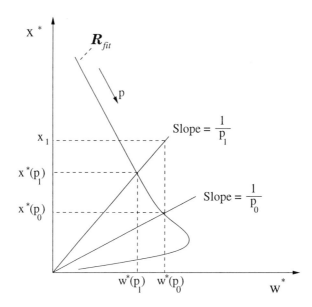

Figure 5.2: The algorithm of the ABR agent

to *transform* the measurements into points on the (p, x) plain and then fit a curve $g(p)$ to those points. Thus, we can derive the value $g(p) := x^*_{\text{fit}}(p)$ which will constitute an approximation of the optimal bandwidth $x^*(p)$ for price p. As will be explained below, this fitting is simpler, because it is restricted over the set of *non-increasing* functions and can thus be solved by means of a special algorithm. Hence, given the current value of p, the agent will use the curve $g(p)$ to compute the recommended willingness-to-pay as $g(p) \cdot p$.

For each price p, let $x(p)$ be the recorded allocated bandwidth. The function $g(p)$ is referred to as the *antitonic regression* of $\{x(p)\}$ with weights $h(p)$, if $g(p)$ minimises the sum

$$\sum_{p \in P}[x(p) - f(p)]^2 h(p)$$

in the class of functions f satisfying, over the set of points P,

$$f(p_i) \le f(p_j), \quad \text{if} \quad p_i > p_j, \quad \forall p_i, p_j \in P \,.$$

In our case, P is the set of prices for which there are available measurements of bandwidth x. $g(p)$ is a *step* function and can be derived by means of the *Pool Adjacent Violators* algorithm [31]. According to this algorithm, the antitonic regression function g partitions X into subsets on which it is constant, i.e. into level sets for $g(p)$, called solution blocks. On each of these solution blocks, the value of the function $g(p)$ is the weighted average of the value of $x(p)$ over the set of prices within the block, using weights $h(p)$. Note that the above function $g(p)$ is defined only on isolated points of the set P; yet $g(p)$ can be naturally extended to a piece-wise constant function, by associating the value corresponding to a solution block to all p within the extreme points of the block.

In order to find the solution blocks, the Pool Adjacent Violators algorithm proceeds broadly as follows:

Assume that $p_0 < p_1 < \cdots < p_k$. If

$$x(p_0) \geq x(p_1) \geq \cdots \geq x(p_k) \, ,$$

then this partition is also the final partition and $g(p) = x(p)$ for all $p \in P$. Otherwise, the algorithm should select any of the pairs of *violators* of the ordering; that is, select a j such that $x(p_j) < x(p_{j+1})$; a new block $\{p_j, p_{j+1}\}$ is formed by *replacing* the ordinates of the points $(p_j, x(p_j))$ and $(p_{j+1}, x(p_{j+1}))$ with their weighted average value

$$\frac{x(p_j)h(p_j) + x(p_{j+1})h(p_{j+1})}{h(p_j) + h(p_{j+1})}$$

which has the new associated weight $h(p_j) + h(p_{j+1})$; see Figure 5.3, where it is assumed that all points have initially unit weight. The algorithm then proceeds with finding another pair of violators, also taking into account the solution blocks already formed; the *order* of considering violators does *not* influence the final solution. If no other violators can be found, then this implies that the current set of blocks (with their associated values) do satisfy the required inequalities, and thus it yields the desired function. Since $g(p)$ is only defined for prices within solution blocks, the agent must use interpolation to provide selections for other prices. Figure 5.4 depicts the corresponding curve on the (p, w) plane.

It should be noted that the above algorithm is very *simple* to implement, and has small computational overhead, because it only makes comparisons and computes weighted averages.

Enhancing the antitonic regression algorithm

The above algorithm of [31] fits the non-increasing curve $g(p)$ to the set of measurements $x(p)$ so as to minimise the mean square error. In our case, it performs more efficiently if we introduce some additional steps which further reduce the processing overhead while improving the performance of the AA.

The modifications introduced are as follows:

1. *Group points* corresponding to identical or almost identical values for p. The reason for this is twofold: (a) such points may anyway have to be grouped by the algorithm, and (b) we are interested in finding quickly a good choice of $w^*(p)$ in order to adapt as rapidly as possible to the varying conditions in the network, rather than

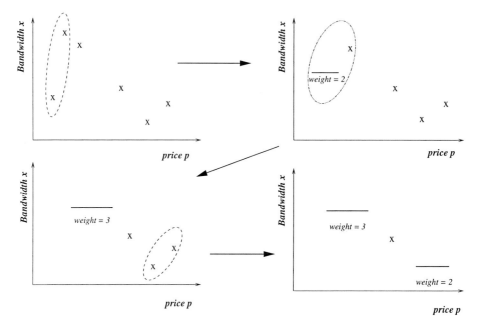

Figure 5.3: The Pool Adjacent Violators algorithm

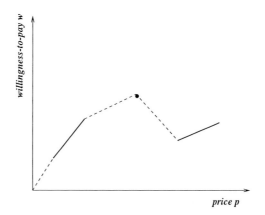

Figure 5.4: The curve of selections of willingness-to-pay on the (p, w) plane

finding the optimal choice. By means of such a grouping we can reduce the amount of computation to be performed without much reduction in the accuracy of the outcome. Such a grouping can be done rather easily. We can define K reference price values $p^{(0)}, \ldots, p^{(K-1)}$, where $p^{(i+1)} = p^{(i)} + \Delta$. Then we can transform the set of measurements available to a set of points $(p^{(i)}, x(p^{(i)}))$, where $x(p^{(i)})$ is the weighted average of the $x(p)$ of all of the original measurements for $p \in (p^{(i)} - \frac{\Delta}{2}, p^{(i)} + \frac{\Delta}{2})$; the associated weight $h(p^{(i)})$ will be the sum of the weights of all the above points. This procedure can clearly be done *on-line* while taking successive measurements. The appropriate value of the step Δ depends on the density of the prices for which there are available measurements, and can be determined on the basis of past experience. Alternatively, the reference prices can be set following the collection of an adequate number of measurements; in fact, if these measurements are not evenly distributed, then the reference prices need not be equidistant.

2. *Discount the weight of old points:* It is possible that some of the first selections made by the user are not that successful, and it is desirable that such points do not affect significantly the solution blocks of the antitonic regression algorithm. To this end, in our approach we assign to each point a *weight* which *decreases exponentially* with the 'age' of this point; when first recorded each point has a weight of 1 (unless the recorded point corresponds to a previously encountered value of price; in such a case, the new point is grouped, the weight of its group is updated (see below), and then increased by 1). By assigning such an exponentially decaying weight, the impact of the original points will diminish as new measurements emerge. When a new measurement is taken, the weight of *each* of the old points has to be multiplied by the same factor $e^{-\alpha \Delta t}$, where Δt is the time that elapsed since the previous measurement; the value of α should be small enough that each point has a considerable weight for some time. Other weights decreasing with the 'age' of the points could also be used; nevertheless, exponentially decaying weights have the property of being easily updated.

To summarise, the AA algorithm performs the following procedures:

1. Record pairs (w, x) and estimate price p as $p = w/x$.

2. Group points that correspond to values of p close enough to each other and update the exponentially decaying weights.

3. Perform antitonic regression, when a large enough number of recorded points has been gathered.

Once antitonic regression is performed, the recommended willingness-to-pay when the price is p equals $g(p) \cdot p$ if p falls within one of the solution blocks. If not, then the value sought can be found by means of linear interpolation on the (p, m) plane.

The proximity of the function $g(p)$ to the set of measurements can be estimated by means of the *normalised mean square error*, which is defined as follows:

$$\text{NMSE} = \frac{\sum_{p \in P} [g(p) - x(p)]^2 h(p)}{\sum_{p \in P} h(p)} \qquad (5.7)$$

Antitonic regression can be performed for a pre-specified large enough number of points; if the associated NMSE is not small enough then more measurements should be taken prior to activating the ABR agent until the accuracy of fitting is satisfactory. In fact, following activation of the AA, more measurements can be taken anyway. In such a case, the antitonic regression algorithm should *not* start from the beginning. On the contrary, upon recording of a new measurement, the solution blocks can be *updated* as follows: If the price corresponding to the new point does not fall into any of the intervals spanned by the solution blocks, then it suffices to run the Pool Adjacent Violators algorithm in order to group (in case of violation) the new point with the previously derived solution blocks, until no more violations exist. On the other hand, if the price corresponding to the new point does fall into an interval spanned by a solution block, this block should be decomposed into its constituent points; then it suffices to run the Pool Adjacent Violators algorithm starting with these points, the new one, and the rest of the previous solution blocks. These rules can be easily proved by the property of the algorithm that the order of considering violators is irrelevant. Thus one can proceed as though the new point (the one that triggered the updating of the blocks) was available from the beginning but was not yet involved in the pooling. In both of the aforementioned cases, there is an order of treating violations in the algorithm that would lead to the set of points and blocks where the update starts from. Thus, although the constituent points of all blocks should have been stored, those of a *single* block are actually used at a time.

Extensions

Networks

The AA algorithm described above is amenable to the case of *networks*. In general, when ABR connections share the resources of a network rather than of a single link, each connection is allocated bandwidth according to the *sum* of the prices in the links of its path [51, 84]. Thus (5.1) no longer applies, and users served by different paths face different prices. However, if we focus on a particular user U with limited market power, the Special Case of User Problem (5.5) still applies. This implies that the rest of the ABR agent approach is also applicable.

Non-concave utility functions

Throughout this section we have assumed that the utility function is concave. The approach presented can be extended to deal with *non-concave* utility functions. One such case of utility function is that depicted in Figure 5.5, indicating that an amount of allocated bandwidth below a certain threshold $x_{\min}$ is essentially useless. This case can be treated by approximating the non-concave part of the utility function with the dotted line also depicted in Figure 5.5. This approximate utility function implies that the user will ask for a *guaranteed* bandwidth amount (i.e. an MCR) equal to $x_{\min}$, while an additional amount (with diminishing marginal value) will be allocated to him from the capacity shared among the ABR connections.

We can also deal with the case of an arbitrary utility function by considering its *concave hull* $\hat{u}(x)$; see Figure 5.6. Indeed, first note that the net benefit function $u(x) - px$ cannot be maximised with respect to x on the non-concave part of $u(x)$. Therefore, the optimisation problem of (5.2) is equivalent to

$$\max_{w \geq 0} \left\{ \hat{u}\left(\frac{w}{w + W} C_{ABR}\right) - w \right\},$$

where the utility function $u(x)$ has been replaced with its concave hull $\hat{u}(x)$. Of course user preferences will be in accordance with the utility function $u(x)$. Since antitonic regression by definition fits a decreasing curve, the ABR Agent will approximate by means of such a curve the derivative of the concave hull $\hat{u}(x)$.

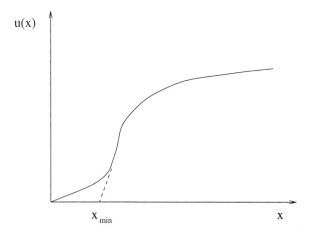

Figure 5.5: A non-concave utility function, and a simple approximation

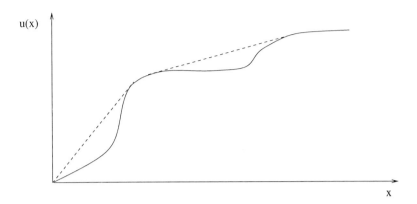

Figure 5.6: A non-concave utility function and its concave-hull

Charging for Web browsing

Throughout the section we have assumed that the parameter valued by the user (i.e. the argument of $u(\cdot)$) coincides with the parameter *charged linearly* by the network. That is, user utility is determined on the basis of the instantaneous peak rate x for each unit of which the user pays a price p. Moreover, we have assumed that this same parameter is also measurable by the AA. As explained earlier, these assumptions apply to the case of video-on-demand users, where the video is encoded with variable bit-rate. What if the user values the long-term mean rate m which is *not* the parameter shared and priced by the network provider and observed by the AA? For example, this applies to an ftp user, or to a user browsing the Web. We now argue that our approach is still applicable. For simplicity, we assume that the user transfers files or Web pages of size P, then thinks for some time T_{think}, then transfers another file or page, and so on. Clearly, there holds

$$m = \frac{P}{\frac{P}{x} + T_{\text{think}}} = f(x) \,,$$

because the denominator equals the total time between successive transfers. Then the user net benefit over an interval of unit duration is

$$u(m) - w = u(f(x)) - xp = u(f(w/p)) - w \,.$$

Comparing this with (5.5), we see that the corresponding optimisation problem is similar to those defined previously; it suffices to replace $u(x)$ by $v(x) := u(f(x))$. Furthermore it is easily seen that the function $v(x)$ is also increasing and concave in x, provided that $u(m)$ is increasing and concave in m. This follows from the monotonicity and concavity of $f(x)$. Therefore we can still apply antitonic regression, and define the ABR agent as in the case of video-on-demand, *without* having to take into account the expression of the function $f(x)$.

If the mapping between the parameter valued by the user and that priced by the network were not monotone and concave, then the function $v(x)$ can also be non-concave. In this case, the approach still applies, dealing with the concave hull of the utility function $v(x)$ as explained above.

5.2 Experiments with the ABR agent

Demonstration architecture

The major objective of the ABR demonstration of CA\$hMAN was to apply the theoretically justifiable charging schemes developed by the project (see Appendix B), and show visually the effects of sharing of bandwidth in economic terms and the benefit of employing the ABR agent defined in section 5.1. The demonstration platform implemented makes possible the comparison of the quality of service experienced by different users sharing a single ATM link, and can demonstrate that the user paying more will receive better quality. Moreover, the platform can show how the QoS of a connection deteriorates when the demand for bandwidth by other connections increases. Since there was no full-feature ABR hardware available within the time frame of CA\$hMAN it was necessary to emulate the functionality of both the ATM Adapter cards, and of the bandwidth allocation effected through flow control in the switches. The latter will be discussed below, because it is related to charging. As for the former, a software emulation was used, whereby the sending rate of the application is controlled at the application level rather than at the ATM level. A video application was used in order to allow for visual demonstration of the various effects.

A brief outline of the demonstration is as follows: In the beginning of the connection, each user declares the amount of money w he is willing-to-pay (per time unit) according to the bandwidth available to this connection and the QoS effected; at each time, the bandwidth available to each connection is specified by the Resource Allocation Module, on the basis of the willingness-to-pay of the corresponding users as well as of the other users connected, and of the total capacity available for ABR. The MPEG frames of each movie are selectively discarded by each Video Server in order to adapt to the permissible bandwidth while discarding the least important frames.

The complete architecture of the demonstration fulfilling the above scenario is shown in Figure 5.7. This consists of the following modules:

- Video Server: This module is responsible for sending MPEG-1 compressed video. It adapts the transmission rate according to the bandwidth allocated to the connection by the Allocation Module. This is achieved by means of selective frame discarding;

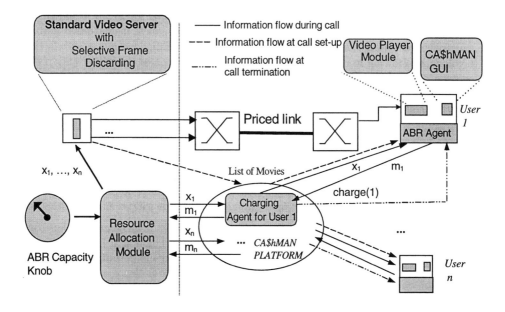

Figure 5.7: ABR demonstration architecture

that is, depending on the allocated bandwidth, an appropriate portion of the least important frames (in particular of the B frames, and if necessary of the P frames too) are discarded during a time-window, so that the allocated bandwidth just suffices for the transmission of the remaining frames. Multiple users retrieve movies from the same server. Hence the QoS received by these users will be primarily determined by their economic choices, as opposed to any hardware/software limitations of the server(s); this makes the impact of economic sharing of bandwidth more clear. Users are offered a selection of movies to choose from, together with an indication of how much this movie would cost under the price at the time of selection.

- Video Player Module: This module receives the MPEG-1 information as produced by the Video Sender. The resulting moving picture is shown on the screen.

- Resource Allocation Module: This module allocates bandwidth to the various ABR connections. This module emulates the allocation policy of an ABR switch. The module can be programmed to perform different allocation policies.

- ABR Capacity Knob: This entity controls the emulated capacity available for ABR traffic. It is used to increase or decrease the capacity made available by the network for ABR traffic. The value C_{ABR} is transferred to the Resource Allocation Module. Such a change can be effected either manually, or by means of a random process simulating arrivals and completions of connections with guaranteed QoS.

- Charging Agent: This module calculates the charge for each call, as the sum $\sum_t w_t \Delta t$ over the duration of the call.

- CA\$hMAN GUI: This is used for the input of user-related information, and for the presentation of information on movies and charging to the user.

- ABR Agent: Users are allowed to modify their willingness-to-pay at any time during the connection, on the basis of the video quality received. As already explained, the ABR agent is a software agent residing at the user-side in order to modify the user's selection of willingness-to-pay according to the varying conditions of the system.

- CA\$hMAN Management Platform: This platform (see also chapter 4) was utilised in order to enable passing of management information between the user-side and the Video Server Side; such information includes the movie list, the willingness-to-pay, the allocated bandwidth, and the final charge.

The architecture of Figure 5.7 can support a large variety of demonstration scenarios, through the willingness-to-pay parameters w_i and the ABR Capacity Knob, and enable an attractive visual demonstration of the results, including direct comparison of the performance different users receive simultaneously. For example:

- Two users sending the same video, declaring different w_i values. The user paying more receives better quality and is less affected by congestion (which is emulated through the ABR Capacity Knob).

- Initially there is only one user, who has declared a small willingness-to-pay w_i. He receives good quality of service until other users also enter the network. In order for the first user's quality to be maintained, he must increase his willingness-to-pay.

The demonstration architecture described above was also used for deriving qualitative conclusions regarding the effectiveness of the ABR agent. It was clearly observed that when it was desirable for the user to increase (decrease) the willingness-to-pay, the agent also recommended an increased (decreased) value. In the subsection to follow we present a quantitative assessment by means of simulation experiments and their results.

Experiments

Simulation model

A single-link system was simulated, where a varying capacity is shared by multiple ABR connections in the way described in section 5.1. In particular, C_{ABR} ranges between 60 and 120 Mbit/s. In each experiment, C_{ABR} is initialised at 80 Mbit/s, and is changed at big steps (between 5 and 40 Mbit/s) every 100 seconds of simulated time. These changes correspond to arrivals and departures of DBR VCs with high bandwidth requirements. In between these changes, C_{ABR} is also changed at smaller steps (namely of 1 Mbit/s), according to a random process simulating the Poisson arrivals and departures of 1 Mbit/s DBR calls with exponentially distributed duration.

User U was simulated separately from the other users, who were treated as a whole. In particular, in each experiment the choices of willingness-to-pay made by U under varying link states are simulated, and the points $(p = w/x, x)$ for user U are recorded. (Note that all quantities corresponding to amounts of money are expressed in the same monetary units, which are not further specified.) Bandwidth allocated to U is always calculated according to (5.1). The aforementioned points are subsequently used as the basis for the antitonic regression algorithm, following which the user is replaced (in selecting willingness-to-pay) by the ABR agent. The accuracy of the AA was assessed under various criteria; the results are presented in the next subsection.

For the users contending with U, it was sufficient to simulate the variations of their total willingness-to-pay W. During each experiment this is selected periodically according to the Gaussian distribution with mean $\bar{W}$ and standard deviation 0.75. The mean is re-selected every 10 selections according to the uniform distribution over a sliding interval of width 3. The mid-point of this interval depends on the value of C_{ABR}. When $C_{ABR} = 80$ Mbit/s then $\bar{W}$ is uniformly distributed in $[6.5, 9.5]$; if C_{ABR} changes then this window slides in the opposite direction, indicating that as C_{ABR} increases (resp. decreases), the price drops (resp. increases) and W has a tendency to increase (resp. decrease).

The behaviour of user U is simulated as follows: It is assumed that the utility function of U is $u(x) = 1 - e^{-x}$, where x is expressed in Mbit/s. Thus, the optimal willingness to pay $w^*(p)$ is known *analytically*. It follows easily from (5.6) that $x^*(p) = \max\{\log(1/p), 0\}$, thus leading to $w^*(p) = p\log(1/p)$ for $p \le 1$ and $w^*(p) = 0$ for $p \ge 1$. Nevertheless, to simulate actual user-behaviour, we have to introduce some noise in the user selections of willingness-to-pay, because a real user would not actually know the optimal choice accurately. Thus for the user U, we set $w(p) = w^*(p) \cdot Z$ where the factor Z is selected from the Gaussian distribution with mean 1 and standard deviation ranging between 0.1 and 0.3. In particular, the standard deviation of the inaccuracy factor Z equals $0.1 + 0.2e^{-\Delta t/4}$ where Δt is the time since the most recent large change of C_{ABR}. Thus the choices of U improve (i.e. are closer to the optimal) as time elapses since the last large change in C_{ABR}, because the link state ranges in a relatively restricted region and the user can 'learn' how to make better selections. Note that the inaccuracy involved does not vanish, because both W and C_{ABR} can still vary. Moreover, we have assumed that a good choice by U (i.e. a choice with Z close to 1) is valid for longer time; in particular, a new choice of w is simulated after time $(50 - 10|1 - Z|)$ secs. When such a choice is effected, a new value of W is also selected, the bandwidth allocated to U is calculated according to (5.1), and the corresponding point is recorded by the ABR agent. At the same time, price is updated as $p = (w + W)/C_{ABR} = w/x$; this value is employed in the subsequent selection of w. Note that the values of the various parameters of the simulation model have been tuned so that the assumption of 'limited market power' of U applies: typically W was 50-100 times larger than w.

The ABR agent performs antitonic regression with exponentially decreasing weights (points with weight less than 10^{-6} are ignored), and grouping of prices (see section 5.1). The value of the parameter α determining how fast the weights decrease was set at $\alpha = 1/1000$. The first selections of the agent are made after 100 points are recorded; the solution blocks are subsequently updated according to the rule described in section 5.1. The NMS Error (see (5.7)) of curve fitting was typically small, namely $\sim 4\%$ relative to the mean value of the measurements for x.

Experimental results

In this subsection we present the results from the simulation experiments. In particular the performance of the ABR agent is compared to that when user U acts optimally, and to the performance of a simple agent offering continuously a constant amount of money.

First we compare the willingness-to-pay selected by the ABR agent with the corresponding optimal selections which are known analytically. Figure 5.8 shows this comparison for an experiment whereby 120 choices of the ABR agent were tested. For reasons of clarity we compare the two series of selections every 5 steps; the accuracy of the selections of the AA is very good; the largest relative error with respect to the corresponding optimal point never exceeded 10% while it was typically much lower. Figure 5.9 shows a similar comparison from step 40 to step 80; this interval comprises an abrupt change of C_{ABR}. We notice that the AA does follow the corresponding variations of the optimal willingness-to-pay. Similar accuracy of the AA selections was observed in all other experiments. Figure 5.10 shows the final set of 350 points, 100 of which were generated by the simulated user U and the rest by the AA; the figure also shows the solution blocks of the antitonic regression.

The overall performance of the ABR agent was assessed in a series of experiments. For each experiment, the total accumulated utility $\sum_t u(x_t)\Delta t$ was calculated, together with the total money spent $\sum_t p_t \cdot x_t \Delta t = \sum_t w_t \Delta t$, and the total net benefit, which equals the difference between the previous two quantities. In all the experiments run, C_{ABR} undergoes identically distributed variations; the AA is activated (and offers selections of w) following antitonic regression over the set of the first 100 points. The quantities above were evaluated for subsequent intervals each comprising 20 selections of willingness-to-pay. Thus the ABR agent learns user behaviour from previous connection(s) of user U, and then it is employed in a subsequent connection.

In Tables 5.1 - 5.4 these measures are compared with the corresponding values that would have prevailed if the simulated user U always made the *optimal* choice. The numerical results of the table reveal excellent agreement between the performance of the ABR agent and the optimal performance. The overall performance of the ABR agent as well as the

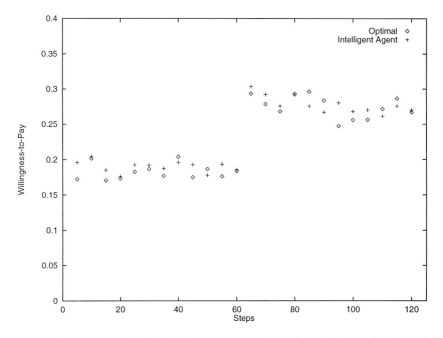

Figure 5.8: Comparing optimal willingness-to-pay with the selections of the ABR agent throughout an experiment

	Utility Accumulated	Money Spent	Net Benefit
ABR Agent	71.05	11.21	59.84
Optimal	70.72	10.67	60.05
Simple Agent	74.14	18.32	55.82

Table 5.1: Comparison of AA with optimal performance and with simple agent - Experiment 1

	Utility Accumulated	Money Spent	Net Benefit
ABR Agent	71.12	10.70	60.42
Optimal	70.97	9.95	61.02
Simple Agent	75.59	18.67	56.92

Table 5.2: Experiment 2

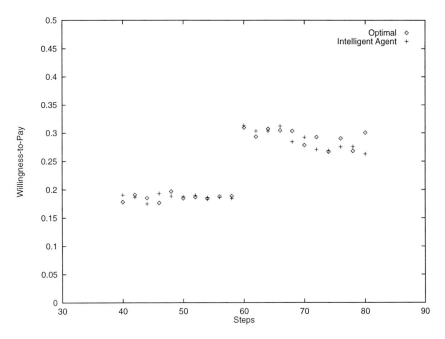

Figure 5.9: Comparing optimal willingness-to-pay with the selections of the ABR agent at a particular phase of an experiment

	Utility Accumulated	Money Spent	Net Benefit
ABR Agent	65.62	28.44	37.18
Optimal	65.72	28.50	37.22
Simple Agent	57.43	21.53	35.90

Table 5.3: Experiment 3

	Utility Accumulated	Money Spent	Net Benefit
ABR Agent	72.13	11.50	60.63
Optimal	70.97	10.21	60.76
Simple Agent	74.78	19.01	55.77

Table 5.4: Experiment 4

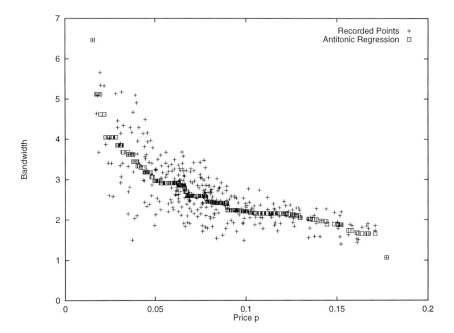

Figure 5.10: The set of points recorded by the end of an experiment, together with the curve fit by means of antitonic regression

optimal one were compared to that of a simple agent which always suggests a *constant* value as the willingness-to-pay; this value is the *time-average* of the optimal willingness-to-pay over 10 past experiments (in which all random events were identically distributed); this value equals 0.2547. It is seen from the corresponding results that the overall performance of the simple agent can be considerably inferior to that of the ABR agent, whose performance was *always* very close to optimal. The simple agent performs comparably to the AA only for experiments where the optimal willingness-to-pay is in a range close to the aforementioned constant selection.

One could argue that the simple agent can be improved by methods such as estimating time-averages in shorter time-scales. The ABR agent is preferable, since it is very *robust* in offering near-optimal selections while performing only simple computations. The AA was also observed to perform near optimally under other user utility functions, unlike the simple agent whose performance depends on the utility function.

5.3   Automated tariff renegotiation

Using CA\$hMAN's *abc* charging scheme for connections with quality-of-service guarantees (for example, ATM DBR or SBR connections), the user may be offered a choice of several different tariffs for a given peak rate. The user's best choice of tariff depends on the expected mean rate of the connection. The user may make a poor initial choice of tariff, or the mean rate may change significantly during the course of the connection. For lengthy connections the user may well want to renegotiate the tariff without re-starting the connection.

Manual renegotiation of tariffs is however a cumbersome task. The user of the connection has to continuously follow the development of charges to find out when one tariff is becoming better than the others. This is an ideal task for automation. Should the network attempt to automate the predictions of the user, thus making superfluous the incentive mechanism motivating the *abc* charging scheme? Crucial issues are which party (user or network) should take the consequences of making poor predictions, and the non-zero probability of tariff renegotiations being refused. Regarding the latter point, the simplifying assumption is made here that this probability is small enough not to significantly affect the strategies employed for renegotiations.

A simple on-line algorithm was implemented to assist the user in dynamically renegotiating tariffs for a given traffic contract. Although the heuristically motivated algorithm does not use predictions on the trends of the traffic trace, the charges attained by the algorithm were not much higher than the a posteriori computed theoretically minimal charges. The heuristic algorithm is easy to implement, its computational effort per charging interval is constant, and it might be integrated in an agent that assists the user in performing tariff selections.

In the following sections the algorithm is presented and results from comparative investigations of its properties are reported. One set of comparisons is made against results obtained in experiments, where experiment participants were provided with the opportunity of making tariff renegotiations using the CA\$hMAN charging management platform. The traffic selected for this purpose was the traffic that went through the ATM link connecting Telenor R&D to its Internet service provider. Another set of comparisons is made against the optimal tariff renegotiation strategies found by analysing the traffic statistics of the communication taking place in the experiments. This absolute lower bound on charges was obtained by a dynamic programming approach.

On-line heuristic for automatic renegotiation of tariffs

The heuristic is based on the following idea. Suppose there are only two different tariffs f_0 and f_1 available. When tariff f_0 is chosen, but tariff f_1 is better in a time interval $[t_i, t_j]$, an error of $f_0(t_i, t_j) - f_1(t_i, t_j)$ is incurred. If this error is smaller than $2c$, and if f_0 becomes again better than f_1 on $[t_j, t_k]$, especially if $f_0(t_i, t_k) - f_1(t_i, t_k) \leq 0$, then it would pay off to stay with tariff f_0 and not renegotiate at all. Therefore, if at the current time t_j, the error $f_0(t_i, t_j) - f_1(t_i, t_j)$ is smaller than $2c$ there is no renegotation, but a renegotiation is initiated as soon as the error becomes $2c$. It still remains to specify the start times t_i.

We formulate the heuristic for the case of two tariffs. The heuristic operates with a bucket that contains a *start_time* corresponding to t_i, and a field *fill* containing the accumulated error for the current tariff, starting from t_i. The bucket is declared "empty" when *fill* ≤ 0, and "overflowing" when *fill* $\geq 2c$. Also, *cur* denotes the index of the current tariff.

- Set current tariff index *cur* to an appropriate value (0 or 1). Set *bucket.fill* to 0 but do not set *bucket.start_time*.

- As long as the connection is charged, do:

- Read in the measurement data necessary to compute charges. The current time is t_j. The previous measurement time is t_{j-1}.

- Compute *error* as $f_{cur}(t_{j-1}, t_j) - f_{1-cur}(t_{j-1}, t_j)$. The error may be negative.

- If the bucket is empty and *error* ≥ 0, set *bucket.start_time* to t_{j-1}.

- If *bucket.start_time* is set, add *error* to *bucket.fill*.

- If the bucket has become empty, i.e. *bucket.fill* ≤ 0, empty the bucket by setting *bucket.fill* to 0 and unsetting *bucket.start_time*.

- If the bucket is overflowing, i.e. *bucket.fill* $\geq 2c$, renegotiate the tariff, update *cur*, and empty the bucket by setting *bucket.fill* to 0 and unsetting *bucket.start_time*.

If there are more than two tariffs, introduce as many buckets as there are tariffs, one for each of the non-current tariffs. The bucket corresponding to the current tariff will not be used. If several buckets are "overflowing" at the same time, choose the tariff corresponding to the bucket with the highest fill. When the renegotiation is decided, empty all buckets.

Note that the heuristic does not "know" anything about the future development of the trace. It uses solely historical data over a small time stretch. A heuristic using trend forecasts is expected to be even better.

Comparative investigations of algorithm properties

The results of comparative analyses of the experiment data are summarised in Table 5.5. The comparison is between manual renegotiation performed by the experimenter, optimal renegotiation performed off-line, a "no renegotiation" strategy which consisted of choosing (a posteriori) the best tariff for the given trace and sticking to it without renegotiation, and the renegotiation strategies resulting from applying the on-line algorithm.

In the experiments that provided the material for comparisons, the peak rate was set to $h = 3\text{Mbit/s}$. The renegotiation charge corresponded to between 5 and 10 seconds of duration charge for the source used. Several tariffs were available, offering different choices of duration charge a and volume charge b.

In Table 5.5

- The optimal charge is the cost of the theoretically optimal renegotiation strategy computed off-line,

- gap(manual) denotes the difference between the charges obtained by manual and optimal renegotiation sequences, in percent of the optimal value,

- gap(no-reneg) denotes the difference between the charges obtained by no renegotiation and by the optimal renegotiation sequence, in percent of the optimal value,

- gap(heur) denotes the difference between the charges obtained by the heuristic algorithm and by the optimal renegotiation sequences, in percent of the optimal value,

- n_{opt}, n_{man} and n_{heur} denote the number of renegotiations in the optimal, manual and heuristic algorithm renegotiation sequences.

Trace	Duration (h:min)	Number of tariffs	Optimal charge (Mbits)	gap (manual)%	gap (no-reneg)%	gap (heur)%	n_{opt}	n_{man}	n_{heur}
A	24:30	4	54914.2	3.67	5.37	2.08	64	41	63
B	47:58	4	218202	10.5	10.89	2.75	283	11	284
C	25:37	4	186188	4.46	4.17	1.41	145	14	147
D	116:38	4	245719	1.61	1.47	0.74	109	81	108
E	68:29	2	307479	4.74	4.73	2.96	392	5	386
F	66:39	2	391518	13.06	28.07	3.08	550	104	546
G	74:52	4	372276	5.06	5.11	2.49	483	61	495

Table 5.5: Comparisons of manual and heuristic algorithm renegotiation with optimal strategy

The charge achieved by the experimenter was at most 13% higher than the theoretically best achievable charge, and the experimenter usually performed many fewer renegotiations than the optimal strategy. However note that in most cases the best fixed tariff gives almost the same results as manual renegotiation.

In experiment F the two tariffs were deliberately set up such that no single tariff was near optimal. This forced the experimenter to actively negotiate between the two tariffs. As seen in the table, the experimenter actually succeeded in achieving a fair amount of the potential savings. A substantial contribution to this result was the success of the experimenter in catching a single large high-intensity period, lasting a significant fraction of a day. One should be very careful about drawing general conclusions on this basis.

If the experimenter had chosen not the best but the second-best tariff and stuck with it, the gap would in all cases have been larger than 20% (see [26]). To give the experimenters credit, one can say that manual on-line renegotiation achieves about as good results as the a posteriori choice of a single best tariff. One should also note that no single tariff was consistently best for all traces, even when applying the same tariff structure to all traces. So the task of choosing, a priori, a single best tariff for the next few hours is not trivial.

To further emphasise some of the information obtained, a subset of the results in Table 5.5 is displayed in diagrams. Figure 5.11 shows the performance of the heuristic algorithm by displaying the relative difference in overall charges obtained by the algorithm and obtained by the optimal strategy. The same differences are also plotted for selection of the a posteriori single best tariff, and for the case of manual tariff renegotiations.

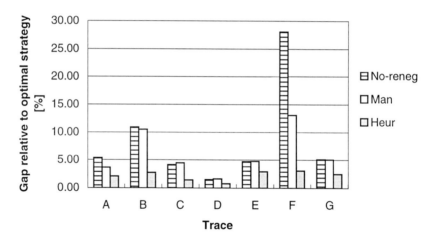

Figure 5.11: Increase in overall charge relative to optimal strategy

Figure 5.12 compares the numbers of renegotiations performed with the optimal strategy, the heuristic algorithm, and manual renegotiation.

As can be seen, the heuristic reduces the gap of the manual renegotiation sequence by at least a factor 2 in most cases. The heuristic renegotiates about as often as the optimal sequence. In fact, in many cases it mimics the optimal renegotiation sequence with a small time lag.

To summarise, it was experienced that the heuristic generally performs better than the human operators, and often very close to the optimal strategy, although the relative dif-

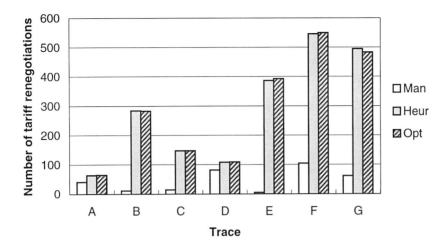

Figure 5.12: Comparison of numbers of renegotiations made

ferences in charges obtained are not large. The main advantage is thus represented by automation of the renegotiation process. The algorithm was built into the CA\$hMAN platform, giving user access to "computer aided" ATM service deployment.

5.4 Automated traffic contract renegotiation

Introduction

In the previous section, renegotiation was only applied to tariffs. The contracted peak rate was considered fixed. A quite different situation arises when a network operator offers the possibility of renegotiating the traffic contract (for example, the peak rate) for a charge c per renegotiation. The ATM service user may then try to renegotiate the contract whenever costs can be saved. We investigated an algorithm that could propose peak rate renegotiations for an ATM link carrying a large amount of adaptive (TCP/IP) traffic. We make the following assumptions:

- There is no knowledge about traffic characteristics and throughput preferences of the single connections carried. There is no knowledge of offered traffic, delays and buffer backlogs, because traffic is aggregated, and adaptive traffic backs off when encountering a bottleneck. The traffic transmitted, aggregated over certain intervals, is assumed to be known. Future capacity requirements are not known.

- Short-term delays are unimportant, and the probability of refusal of a traffic contract renegotiation is negligible.

- The charge for renegotiating the capacity is non-negligible, and the charges for communication are proportional to the capacity (peak rate).

- Restricting the capacity reduces the customer utility, through increased long-term delays experienced by the users of the connections carried through the link.

The task of deciding when and how to renegotiate capacity so as to balance communication charges and delay costs is non-trivial, and would be more or less impossible for a human operator. Instead, this functionality may be built into a (more or less) intelligent software agent, residing in the user domain, and acting on behalf of the ATM-user. The aim of the work presented in this section is to investigate and evaluate an algorithm for service deployment that may be built into such agents.

The section proceeds by presenting the exact meaning of delay that will be used in the analysis, and establishing the related optimisation problem. An outline of how this problem may be optimally solved in the case of complete knowledge of future traffic is given. We then propose an on-line algorithm. The results from the on-line algorithm are compared with the results from the optimal algorithm and with results from the "simple strategy" of keeping the peak rate fixed. The algorithms are evaluated in two scenarios: first, where delay values are computed by simulation, and second, where delays are measured from reproducible experiment traffic. Some parts of this work are also to be published in [25].

Delay and cost

For a given communication over a given type of communication service one may formulate the economic objective of obtaining the combined minimum of communication cost and delay cost. Delay is modelled by the fluid flow concept: offered traffic is seen as a constant flow inside the polling intervals (since nothing is known about the individual traffic sources), and the backlog buffer is virtual, but has a piecewise constant service rate, namely the contracted capacity. An example delay workload diagram may look like Figure 5.13.

For each interval of constant service rate there will be associated a cost related to the capacity, a cost related to the capacity renegotiation, and a cost related to the accumulated delay volume in the period. For a connection lasting a number of n intervals partitioned at the instants $t_0, t_1, \ldots, t_{n-1}$, the complete cost is expressed as:

$$C = \sum_{i=0}^{n-1} h_i(t_{i+1} - t_i) + nw_r + w_d \sum_{i=0}^{n-1} V_i \qquad (5.8)$$

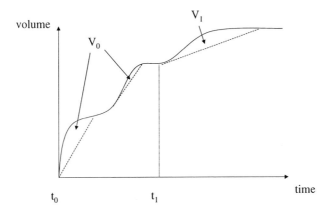

Figure 5.13: Volume/delay diagram for link delay model

The constant w_r denotes the charge made by the network for each renegotiation, and the constant w_d expresses the user's preference for small delays. The degrees of freedom in optimising the above object function lie in the choice of renegotiation instants t_i and corresponding peak rates h_i.

Optimal renegotiation strategy

In order to evaluate how well an on-line algorithm minimises the cost, an algorithm for computing optimal renegotiation schedules was implemented. The optimal algorithm assumes complete knowledge of future traffic offered to the link. The algorithm is based on the same idea as a dynamic programming algorithm developed by Grossglauser, Keshav and Tse [68] for renegotiated CBR service. In their setting the charge

$$C = \sum_{i=0}^{n-1} h_i(t_{i+1} - t_i) + nw_r$$

was to be minimised under the condition that buffer occupancy never exceeds a given bound. In our setting the charge

$$C = \sum_{i=0}^{n-1} h_i(t_{i+1} - t_i) + nw_r + w_d \sum_{i=0}^{n-1} V_i$$

is to be minimised without conditions on buffer occupancies. The algorithm of [68] can be easily adapted to the above minimisation problem. It operates with the asumptions that renegotiation decisions can be made only at equidistant time slots, that peak rates can only be chosen from the discretised values $\{0, \delta, 2\delta, \dots, K\delta\}$ for some bit rate δ, and that offered traffic rates take the same discretised values $\{0, \delta, 2\delta, \dots\}$ without upper bound.

Heuristic algorithm for capacity renegotiations

An on-line algorithm for capacity renegotiations has to deal with two uncertainties; first, uncertainty about the future trace; and second, uncertainty about presently offered traffic and delays. The only information the algorithm can use is traffic observations from the past gathered at fixed polling intervals. Note that offered traffic is not equal to observed traffic, especially when offered traffic exceeds the present link peak rate.

In order to deal with the unknown future, the on-line algorithm observes the past. If the "cost savings" by renegotiating to a new peak rate exceed a certain bound, a renegotiation to this peak rate is proposed. In order to deal with the unknown delay the on-line algorithm makes a guess about offered traffic. More specifically, if the observed traffic rate in the last interval is "well below" the present peak rate (i.e. $\leq$ peak-rate $-\delta$), then offered traffic is assumed to be equal to observed traffic. If offered traffic is "near" the present peak rate (i.e. $>$ peak rate $-\delta$), offered traffic is assumed to be peak rate $+\delta$.

The so-called *critical region* heuristic depends on a parameter c_r (cost per renegotiation), a parameter c_d (unit delay cost), and a discretisation of peak rates δ. At each polling interval the platform calls the critical region heuristic and passes it the traffic rate observed in the last interval. The heuristic will either propose to stay with the present peak rate or propose renegotiation to a peak rate in the set $\{\delta, 2\delta, \dots, K\delta\}$. The parameters c_r and c_d should not be confused with w_r and w_d of the objective function (5.8). In the performance analysis c_r and c_d are varied to study the behaviour of the heuristic, whereas w_r and w_d stay fixed. We describe one step of the so-called critical region heuristic.

The internal data structure consists of an array of critical regions indexed by the possible peak rates. A critical region for a peak rate consists of a field *started* and a field *target time*. *Starting* a *critical region* means to set *started* to true and set its *target time* to a certain time past the present time. *Stopping* a critical region means setting *started* to false. As soon as the present time exceeds the *target time* for a started critical region, a renegotiation to the associated peak rate is proposed.

One step of the critical region heuristic:

- If the observed traffic rate is $>$ (present peak rate $-\delta$), and the critical region belonging to (present peak rate $+2\delta$) is not yet started, *start* it now and set its *target time* to: present time plus the square root of $2c_r/(c_d * \delta)$. The reason behind this setting is that we assume offered traffic to be (present peak rate $+\delta$) from the start of the critical region and for some time in the future. Under this assumption the delay cost ($c_d \times$ assumed delay) incurred between start time and target time will exceed the cost for one renegotiation.

- If the observed traffic rate is $>$ (present peak rate $- \delta$), and the present time exceeds the *target time* of the critical region belonging to (present peak rate $+ 2\delta$), propose a renegotiation to (present peak rate $+ 2\delta$), *stop* all critical regions, and exit.

- If the observed traffic rate is $\leq$ (present peak rate $- \delta$), *stop* the critical region belonging to (present peak rate $+ 2\delta$).

- For all critical regions belonging to peak rates $k\delta$ with $k\delta <$ present peak rate and $k\delta \geq$ (observed traffic rate $+ \delta$) do the following.

  - If the critical region is not started, *start* it now and set its *target time* to present time plus $2c_r /$ (present peak rate $- k\delta$). The reason for this setting is that the schedule renegotiating to $k\delta$ at start time of the critical region and then renegotiating back again will become cheaper than the schedule waiting until *target time*, when offered traffic rates stay below $k\delta$ between start and target time.

  - If the present time exceeds the *target time* of the critical region, propose a renegotiation to $k\delta$, *stop* all critical regions, and exit.

- *Stop* all critical regions belonging to peak rates $k\delta$ with $k\delta <$ (observed traffic rate $+ \delta$).

The workings of the algorithm are illustrated in Figures 5.14 and 5.15.

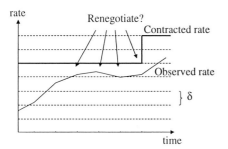

Figure 5.14: Increasing load

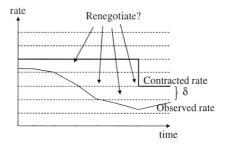

Figure 5.15: Decreasing load

Environments for renegotiation strategy evaluation

The approach taken for evaluation of the algorithms is to let them work on traffic trace samples. The samples were obtained by making measurements with the CA\$hMAN charging management platform on the traffic on the ATM link connecting Telenor R&D to its Internet service provider. Link speeds at measurements were set to an ATM payload rate of 10 Mbit/s. For the material used in the analyses, the traffic was well below this limit.

It is assumed that traffic is flexible, translating communication restraints into communication delays. The algorithm was analysed in two environments, by simulation and by experiments.

Simulation environment

In the simulation environment, the backlog delay buffer can be modelled by a leaky bucket, and offered traffic can be read directly from original statistics. The simulation environment thus provides for speedy evaluations compared to the experiments performed in real time. The optimal renegotiation strategy can only be worked out in a simulation environment, and most comparative investigations are therefore performed by simulations.

Experimental environment

As a validation of operational properties, algorithms are in addition run in real time in an ATM network fed by computers recreating the original traffic trace by TCP/IP traffic over ATM. The use of given traffic samples allows the computation of backlog delay volumes aggregated during experiments with the algorithms. Such evaluations are of course impossible using actual traffic, because introducing restrictions on link speeds will modify the offered load, and the information needed to compute delay costs will be lost. The two environments serve to investigate how theoretical results relate to an environment where rate adaptations are not perfect, and where other random effects, such as scheduling delays, can be observed.

The experiment system is depicted in Figure 5.16, and consists conceptually of a non-adaptive source generating traffic as observed from the original unconstrained data transfer, a backlog buffer storing information that cannot be immediately sent, and an adaptive source that uses a TCP connection in order to get realistic rate adaptation. Generated traffic goes through an ATM network consisting of one link, where actual transmitted data at the ATM level is measured in a charging platform. This platform also controls link rates of the connection to be charged, where level and duration of link rates are governed by the agent which takes renegotiation decisions on the basis of usage data provided through the platform.

Time granularity of the agent is approximately five seconds, i.e. decisions on renegotiations are made with this period. The data source is piecewise constant with the same period as the agent. Traffic fluctuations over smaller time scales would not have influenced the working of the renegotiation heuristic, because the heuristic sees only traffic aggregated over five seconds. For the performance analysis of the heuristic, however, the short-term statistical variations in the measured delays should have been taken into account by using a more detailed source model. On the other hand, the goal in the design of the heuristic was to weigh long-term delays against communication and renegotiation charges. Short-term delays can be taken into account by either reducing the reaction time of the heuristic to

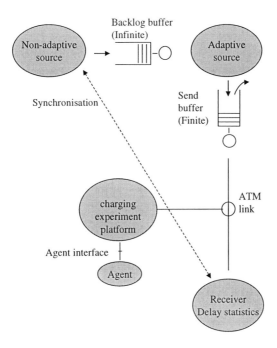

Figure 5.16: Experiment system

something less than 5 seconds, or by decreasing the granularity of the peak rates to be negotiated, such that peak rates lie sufficiently high above the observed aggregated mean rates. This was not investigated further.

One important difference between the experimental environment and the simulations is the nature of rate adaptations. In TCP this adaptation is normally made by probingly increasing the send rate until packet losses occur, whereafter the send rate is reduced before a new increase. The output rate of a TCP source towards a fixed bottleneck should therefore oscillate. In the experiments, the bottleneck is moved to inside the sending computer, but it still turns out that the amount of capacity absorbed by the rate adaptation is a significant portion of the available capacity. By testing the link utilisation using a greedy TCP source, it was experienced that in the range of bit rates used in the experiments, 20% of the capacity consistently remained unavailable for transmission of user data. As the algorithms work on measured utilisation of the ATM links, situations may arise where algorithms fail to raise capacity because links cannot be sufficiently loaded. In most experiments, the observed rates passed to algorithms were thus increased by a factor 1.25 from the measured value. In the simulation and experiment platforms delays were computed differently. The simulation computes delay volumes from the statistical trace directly, whereas the experiment platform sums up (delay × volume) for each packet received. Delay is here the time spent in the software backlog buffer. Transfer time over the link was virtually zero. A small test with constant link rates was performed to compare delay values from the two environments. To account for the reduced throughput through the ATM link, the constant bit rate in the experimental environment was a factor of 1.25 higher than the constant bit rate in the simulation. The test showed that experimentally measured delays vary little (when using the same link rate) and that experimental and simulated delay values conform in the range of non-negligible delay values.

Observations and results

Experiments were conducted on several different traffic trace samples, with different c_r, c_d parameters (controlling step sizes in the critical region heuristic) and different link rate discretisations δ. The largest observed rate in any of the used samples was 5 Mbit/s. It was experimented with $\delta = 1$Mbit/s and $\delta = 0.5$ Mbit/s. The traffic trace samples had been collected during busy hours and morning hours with less traffic. We compared the performance of the critical region heuristic with the optimal algorithm and with the strategy of not renegotiating at all.

The outputs of the different algorithms can be evaluated by two numbers, the *charge*, which is defined as the communication cost of the schedule plus w_r times the number of renegotiations, and the *delay*, which is defined as the sum of the V_i in Figure 5.13. Throughout the analysis, w_r has a value of 80963.4 (cells), corresponding to the communication charge of a 1Mbit/s link for the length of 6 polling intervals (of length $t = 5.18$ sec). With this cost it does not pay off to renegotiate inside each polling interval.

Figures 5.17 to 5.19 illustrate the results for one of the experiments. The underlying traffic sample was 35 minutes long and collected during the busy hour of a working day. The peak rate discretisation used by the heuristic and optimal algorithms was set to 0.5 Mbit/s. The critical region heuristic was run with $c_r \in \{80963.4, 121445\}$ and $c_d \in \{0.5148, 4.6332\}$. With this parametrisation the heuristic waits for approximately 24 or 36 polling intervals before proposing a peakrate 0.5 Mbit/s lower than the present peak rate (and correspondingly less for proposing even lower peak rates), and it waits for one to four polling intervals before proposing an upward renegotiation by 1 Mbit/s. The critical region was moreover run for $c_r = 6746.95$ and $c_d = 0.19305$. With this parametrisation the heuristic waits two steps before proposing a peak rate 0.5 Mbit/s lower than the present peak rate, and two steps before proposing an upward renegotiation.

Figure 5.17 shows the results of the simulation for this setting of c_r, c_d parameters. Each run produces a point in the (charge/delay) plane. Points belonging to schedules produced with the same c_r value have the same tag. It is however, easy to distinguish which of the two points belongs to which of the two possible c_d-values. In general, the larger c_d, the smaller the delay. Moreover, Figure 5.17 shows the simulated results for the no-renegotiation strategy with constant bit rates in $\{2.5, 3.125, 3.75, 4.375\}$ Mbit/s. The critical region heuristic with $c_r \in \{80963.4, 121445\}$ was able to improve both the charge and the delay as compared to the constant bit rate schedule of 3.125 Mbit/s.

Figure 5.18 shows the results of the experiment for the same setting of c_r, c_d parameters. Each parameter setting was tested four times. Comparing the results with Figure 5.17, one sees that the points have approximately the same relative position with respect to each other. This finding was confirmed also for other traffic samples and parameter settings, and validates the usefulness of simulation in comparing charge/delay values.

Figure 5.19 shows simulation results for the same values of c_r, but more values of c_d. Also shown are the results from optimisation. For the purpose of illustration all (charge/delay) points produced by the critical region heuristic for fixed c_r but varying c_d are connected by one line. For small c_d values, delay can vary unpredictably, but charge in general decreases for decreasing c_d. The critical region heuristic with $c_r = w_r$ and appropriately chosen c_d performs better than the constant bit rate schedule of ≥ 2 Mbit/s (charges $\geq 9e + 06$). As a preliminary result, which is also confirmed by experiments made with other traffic samples, it was found that

- For any constant bit rate schedule, the critical region heuristic with $c_r = w_r$ and appropriately chosen c_d produces better charge/delay values.

- For bursty traffic, the critical region heuristic with $c_r = w_r$ is able to close part of the gap between the constant bit rate schedules and the optimal schedule, which uses knowledge of the whole trace.

- The critical region heuristic with a peak rate discretisation of 0.5 Mbit/s performs considerably better than with a discretisation of 1 Mbit/s.

- For small c_d values, delay can vary unpredictably with small variations in c_d.

Conclusion

Our goal was to design an algorithm that is able to assist the user in renegotiating the capacity of an ATM link with flexible traffic (e.g. TCP/IP) by making a tradeoff between communication charges, renegotiation costs and the user's sensitivity to long-term delays. The algorithm operates solely on observed send rates and does not need any information about buffer backlogs. The algorithm was tested by simulation and in an experimental environment, with a traffic source imitating previously collected aggregate traffic over an ATM link, such that delay values could be computed. The algorithm's performance in terms of charge and delay was compared to the performance of an optimal off-line renegotiator (with knowledge of the complete trace) and of a simple constant bit rate strategy. The heuristic described and tested in this section is clearly able to improve on the strategy of

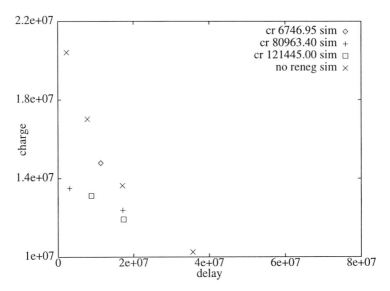

Figure 5.17: Simulation results

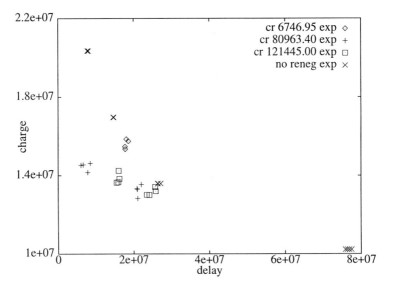

Figure 5.18: Experimental results

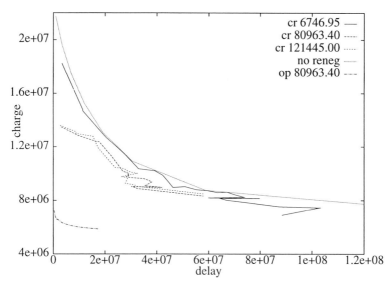

Figure 5.19: Comparison of simulation with optimal algorithm

maintaining a constant link rate sufficiently high above the traffic mean rate. This means that for any sufficiently large constant link rate there exist parameter values that made the on-line renegotiation algorithm produce schedules with significantly lower charge and less delay than the constant bit rate solution.

Further improvements can be thought of. For instance one can imagine integrating the capacity renegotiation agent with the tariff renegotiation agent described in the previous section. Tariff renegotiation could be applied in intervals of constant peak rate. It is, however, difficult to assess the benefit of these two algorithms working together. The idea could be applied to a situation in which the network refuses traffic contract renegotiations with a certain non-negligible probability, but usually accepts tariff renegotiations.

We assume the heuristic can also be applied to the renegotiation of traffic contracts for end-to-end guaranteed services for users that are more delay-sensitive than the operator of an ATM link. In this case the agent might additionally have access to user's preferences for throughput or it can even measure delay on-line. The performance of the on-line heuristic described in this section will have to be assessed anew in this situation, preferably through experiments with real users.

Chapter 6

Open issues

The CA$hMAN trials of ATM charging schemes focused on a simple scenario involving two parties (user and network) with usage-based charging for various ATM bearer services. The charging schemes, based on duration and volume charges, were designed to reflect resource usage and convey appropriate incentives to users in as simple a way as possible. Some of CA$hMAN's work addressed the need for user interfaces and software agents to help users to understand and interact with these charging schemes.

For these charging schemes to be implemented in real networks some wider issues need to be tackled. In this chapter we discuss some of these unresolved issues. Although these issues will apply generally to any usage-sensitive charging scheme, we make specific reference to possible approaches for the CA$hMAN *abc* scheme. We discuss the following issues:

- Service providers may offer transport services and value-added services over an ATM network. The service provider might buy ATM bearer capacity from a network provider on a usage basis, but might not want to pass these charges on directly to the customer. The service provider might indeed want to charge the customer on a usage basis, but in a way that is understandable and related to the service being offered. How can such service-level charging schemes be formulated and how do they relate to the underlying ATM-level charging? To what extent are appropriate usage incentives passed on to the end-customer?

- How can the incentives of usage-based charging be transferred between network operators? Is it feasible to base interconnect charging on the same time and volume-based charging as is used for end-customers? Are there simpler schemes for interconnect charging that still transfer incentives between networks?

- How should relative prices of different transport services be set? How are these relativities affected by resource usage costs and by customer utilities?

- Usage-based charging for ATM may require tariff and measurement information to be passed between networks. Such requirements need to be included in agreed telecommunications standards for broadband multiservice networks.

- How could CA$hMAN pricing models be implemented in IP networks?

6.1   Service-level charging

As far as offering services over ATM is concerned, several levels can be distinguished. In the first place we can consider the *ATM bearer services*, i.e. 'real ATM connections'. These connections are characterised by ATM layer transfer capabilities such as DBR, SBR, ABR, and by characteristics such as point-to-point, point-to-multipoint, switched, semi-permanent, etc. Secondly, we have the *ATM adaptation bearer services* (such as LAN-interconnect over ATM, circuit emulation over ATM, frame relay over ATM). These are non-ATM *transport* services that make use of an underlying ATM network. Finally, there are *value-added services*, such as videoconferencing, Internet access, and full-service ISDN interworking. These services are offered by a service provider that uses ATM as an underlying transport technology.

In fact, it could be stated that the first level corresponds to the *ATM level*, whereas the second and third levels are offered at the *service level*. Clearly these different levels impose different requirements on the charging scheme to be used. Therefore an essential distinction should be made between charging schemes meant for these different levels. Charging at the ATM level has been examined extensively within the framework of the CA$hMAN project. In this section we consider how service-level charging might be based upon CA$hMAN charging schemes used at the ATM level.

Charging native ATM bearer services

It seems at present that native ATM bearer services are unlikely to be used much by individual customers, but rather by customers who are service providers, system operators of major companies, etc. As they have experience in the field of networking they might accept the use of charging algorithms with a degree of complexity. In order to choose appropriate traffic contracts at the ATM level they need to have an understanding of peak rates, burst sizes, and so on. CA$hMAN charging schemes demand in addition a choice of tariff which requires, at the most, an estimate of a connection's mean rate.

If residential customers make use of ATM services, then additional effort must be put into helping users to make a good choice of tariff. One approach is to adopt a simple user-friendly interface and offer only a few standard tariff options. An alternative approach is to use software agents in the user domain which help the user to negotiate, and possibly renegotiate, traffic and tariff contracts. These approaches were explored in the CA$hMAN platform and user trials (see chapters 4 and 5).

Charging at the service level

Consider an end-customer who buys high-level services from a service provider, who in turn buys ATM capacity from a network provider. The service provider must provide a user interface that presents to the user a service-level view of tariff and quality of service options. This interface is represented by the charging agent in Figure 6.1.

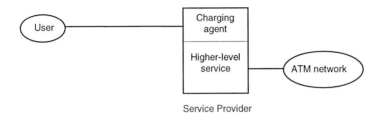

Figure 6.1: Agent for service-level charging

This charging agent translates between ATM traffic contracts and a service-level representation of quality of service. In addition, if the service provider is paying for ATM connections on a per-connection usage basis, then the charging agent has to translate between ATM connection tariffs and a service-level view of charges.

An agent for service-level charging needs the following functionality:

1. It should interpret an ATM traffic contract in terms of the service-level QoS - a function which requires detailed knowledge of the characteristics of the service (or user application). Some examples might be:

   - Web browsing. This is essentially a file transfer operation. The important QoS characteristic is the total time to transfer a Web page, which depends on the mean rate of the connection, which in turn will depend mainly on the PCR, SCR (for an SBR connection), or MCR (for an ABR connection).

   - Real-time video. Important QoS characteristics are the image size and video frame rate, which are related to the PCR and SCR (for an SBR connection) but in a possibly complex way that depends on the characteristics of the video source and the video encoding methodology used.

2. Secondly the agent should provide some estimate of the cost of the connection, on the basis of the ATM tariff and the expected traffic characteristics. Important components of the traffic characteristics (such as the mean rate) may not be easily predictable at the start of the connection, but a user agent might aim to use historical data to help the prediction.

3. Finally the agent should present to the user a graphical interface that is easy to understand and to use, for example using slider bars.

In practice many service providers might wish to provide very simple tariffs, even if these do not track the underlying ATM-level charging. Consider some examples of video applications:

- For a service provider who offers a video playback service, the characteristics of the video data are known in advance. The service provider can offer a simple duration-based tariff which, on average over many connections of many customers, will absorb the varying ATM-level charges. The communications charges are, in any case, likely to be bundled in with content charges.

- For a video-telephony service a simple duration-based charge would remove user incentives to constrain mean data rates. However the service provider might consider that the resulting inefficiency (and higher average charges) are more acceptable to users than charges which fluctuate in an unpredictable way.

For other services, such as Internet access, the service provider might consider that charging for both duration and volume generates essential customer incentives. Service-level tariffs would then need to have the same form as ATM-level tariffs. The service provider's charging interface could nevertheless aim to simplify things by, for example, offering a limited number of tariff choices and by using a helpful graphical interface. This functionality has much in common with the user agents that were discussed in chapter 5.

Content charges

Communications tariffs may be used to collect charges for content that is provided within connections. With CA$hMAN's unified charging scheme, content charges might be included within any component of the tariff - the subscription charge, duration charge, volume charge, or connection set-up charge. Any of these choices might be appropriate depending on the nature of the content. Hence this charging mechanism presents considerable flexibility for charging appropriately for content and integrating content charges with connection charges.

6.2   Interconnect charging

As a result of diversity and competition in telecommunications an increasing proportion of traffic traverses networks run by different operators. Charging and accounting arrangements are an important part of the interconnect agreements that apply to such traffic.

Network operators therefore have a customer role as users of interconnect services provided by other operators together with their associated charging schemes.

Interconnect charges should reflect resource usage by the relevant traffic, in order to provide the right incentives to the network operators and to end-customers. The charging schemes experienced by end-customers should be compatible with interconnect charging in order that appropriate incentives are transmitted.

In an ATM environment interconnect arrangements will necessarily have an increased complexity. Suitable traffic and tariff contracts must be communicated at the interfaces between networks, service guarantees made to the originating customer must be upheld across the connection, and accounting data must be collected and exchanged and agreed between the networks concerned.

Interconnect and the commercial environment

Interconnect agreements have in the past been formed between network operators who were monopoly suppliers. The introduction of privatisation and competition is generally accompanied by strong regulatory powers, which might be relaxed as competition develops. Interconnect agreements may be subject to regulation or influence at a variety of different levels, including state authorities in the US, national regulators, the European Commission, World Trade Organisation agreements, and the ITU.

Interconnect agreements have typically been based on revenue-sharing models. In an open competitive market for interconnect one would expect to see the development of customer/supplier relationships with more flexible and varied charging models.

Within each country increasing competition may lead to the emergence of many small network operators and service providers and the end of dominance by the national PNO. This may lead to a much more volatile and fragmented market where it is more difficult to maintain stable tariffs. On the other hand telecommunications carriers are grouping together in new global consortia. It is to be expected that each such consortium will want to route traffic between its own partners rather than use competitors. One way that a consortium might encourage this would be by offering matching tariffs that provide customers with efficient and cost-effective end-to-end services.

Influences on interconnect charging

What factors will influence the charging schemes to be adopted for interconnect and the tariffs that will be set in an open and competitive market?

Network cost

Tariffs should be capable of reflecting network costs. Competitive pressure should lead to higher charges for connections that use inherently expensive network resources (for example international routes, or intelligent network switching and database facilities).

Capacity usage

Economic theory suggests that competition should drive operators to adopt usage-sensitive charging schemes that appropriately transmit incentives to interconnecting networks and to customers. Each operator will want to take account of usage costs (which may include downstream interconnect charges) and reflect these costs back to its customers (who may be other networks or service providers). In principle this should favour the adoption of charging schemes which properly transmit usage-related incentives through networks and back to customers, even though no individual operators need to be concerned with overall network efficiency. However it remains to be seen how far this can be achieved through competition given the complex technical and commercial nature of global telecommunications.

Matching tariffs

There are several different ATM transport capabilities (ATCs). These have varying numbers of traffic contract parameters, which can vary over substantial ranges. Hence there is a vast range of possible ATM contracts which can be offered. Each carrier will presumably offer distinct tariffs for only a subset of this possible range - it is unlikely to be worthwhile to offer many services with subtle tariff distinctions.

In general interconnecting operators may not offer distinct tariffs for the same choices of ATCs and traffic contract parameters. However the end-user has a specific contract with the operator that is providing his service, which he expects to be applied to his entire end-to-end connection. Any mis-match in tariffs could have an impact on prices to end-users. Operators within a global consortium will have a strong incentive to offer matching tariffs.

Methods for interconnect charging

Interconnect charging agreements have typically been on an aggregated basis, for example the use of total paid minutes commonly used for international connections. In a multiservice environment interconnect charges need to reflect the widely differing capacity usage of individual connections. This might be achieved by accumulating individual connection charges or through some means of bulk charging that reflects total capacity usage. Both of these approaches can be achieved by extension of the simple duration and volume charging scheme, as described in the following sections.

Per-connection charging

A useful property of the linear time and volume charging scheme is additivity of tariff parameters for a connection traversing several interconnected components in sequence. Consider the scenario in Figure 6.2, where the customer originates a connection to Operator 1 and the connection is then routed through Operator 2.

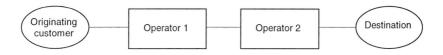

Figure 6.2: Connection through two interconnecting network operators

Assume that the fee that Operator 1 pays to Operator 2 for completing the connection takes the form

$$a_2 T + b_2 V + c_2$$

where T and V are the duration and volume of the connection. Then Operator 1 can offer tariffs of the form

$$(a_1 + a_2)T + (b_1 + b_2)V + (c_1 + c_2)$$

where (a_1, b_1, c_1) constitutes the tariff for using the network of Operator 1.

Of course an operator may not wish simply to pass on interconnect charges unchanged, but this additivity does provide for accounting transparency which would, for example, facilitate accounting arrangements based on revenue-sharing models.

The choice of interconnect charging arrangement has consequences for the interface between the two networks. With per-connection charging the interface must enable the agreement of tariff parameters (in addition to traffic contract parameters) at the start of each connection. In addition the networks must exchange accounting data comprising duration, volume, and tariff choice for each connection.

Bulk charging

When interconnect charging is done on a per-connection basis the total charges for an aggregate traffic flow may not closely reflect the resource usage (in terms of switching and transmission capacity) of the interconnecting operator. This is because the required capacity is determined by the maximum simultaneous total capacity requirements of individual connections. With per-connection charging the total charge is the same for several consecutive connections as it is for several simultaneous connections. This may become a significant issue when a single operator generates a large traffic flow via an interconnecting operator.

Where the traffic flow is routed through the interconnecting operator to a single destination (to a third operator, say) then another possibility is to provide a PVC. This is simpler for the interconnecting operator, but the onus is then on the originating operator to forecast the required interconnect capacity. This solution is also likely to be less efficient than using switched connections since there is no scope for sharing the required transmission capacity with other traffic.

An alternative possibility is to charge for bulk use of capacity. This aims to reflect the resource usage cost of the interconnecting operator and also to avoid some of the overheads of charging on a per-connection basis. There have already been proposals (e.g. [8]) to base telephony interconnect charging on the actual capacity required to carry the total traffic. If in addition this capacity has to be agreed in advance this has the effect of shifting, from supplier to purchaser, the risk involved in predicting the required capacity.

Bulk charging could naturally be applied to a class of connections that are not distinguished (by charge) according to their route through the network. Several applicable scenarios can be envisaged:

1. A bulk charge for all traffic using a single route through the network, or several equivalent routes to the same destination. An example would be an international carrier charging for all traffic to one country.

2. More generally, a class of traffic for which the carrier does not wish to discriminate by destination. An example might be terminating international traffic within a national network.

3. The originating carrier sends traffic over a fixed path, with a single entry and exit point, through the interconnecting carrier's network. Bulk charging may be a desirable alternative to using a PVC where transmission capacity can be multiplexed.

A natural approach to bulk charging is to extend the linear time and volume scheme as follows:

The charge for traffic in a time period T is

$$aT + bV_T + cN_T$$

where V_T is the total volume of the interconnect traffic in T, and N_T is the total number of connections in T. This bulk charge could be levied in successive periods (e.g. of $T = 1$ hour), or could be applied solely within some defined peak periods (e.g. a daily busy hour).

The tariff parameters a, b, c are for agreement between the operators, but could have the following interpretation:

- a is a capacity rental charge which should relate to the maximum bulk capacity required.

- The volume charge b and connection charge c could be the same as would be applied in per-connection charging.

Since different traffic classes (e.g. SBR and ABR) would be charged at different rates, they would need separate bulk charges.

The bulk charging scheme described above is essentially a combination of capacity and volume charges, and as such it could represent a compromise where the risk entailed in predicting capacity is shared between supplier and purchaser. The capacity element of the charge (the tariff parameter a) might be agreed in advance, which would imply the need to impose a capacity limit on the interconnect traffic. Alternatively this charge might be calculated retrospectively on the basis of some measurement of total capacity requirement.

6.3   Relative prices of services

The abc scheme described in chapter 2 enables charges to reflect the influence of source traffic parameters, such as peak cell rate, on resource usage costs. However the scheme does not determine how to set relative charges for connections with different QoS levels, or how to set relative charges between guaranteed and elastic services.

Courcoubetis et al [48] have considered the case where priority queueing is used to give a preferential delay guarantee to one class of traffic. This leads to an admissible operating region (in terms of the numbers of connections of each traffic class in the system) having several linear constraints. The optimal operating point will be on one of the linear boundaries, but this point will be determined by issues such as the price sensitivity of demand for each traffic type. This is generally the case where distinct service levels are offered to traffic classes sharing the same resources - it is not possible to unambiguously assign usage costs to connections of each traffic class, and setting relative prices requires (in principle) a knowledge of user utilities [106].

Lindberger [88] discusses relative prices of guaranteed and elastic services (in the ATM context, elastic services comprise UBR and ABR bandwidth exceeding the MCR). Using an argument based on the increase in efficiency when guaranteed and elastic services share the same resources, in a stationary traffic context, he concludes that the charge for elastic connections should be at least 50% of the charge for guaranteed service connections. However Walker et al [116] argue that user demand sensitivity for high-volume services such as video will generate price differences of several orders of magnitude.

Optimising relative prices

It is possible in principle to apply an optimisation procedure to determine relative prices. Consider two classes of traffic which share the same resources: for example DBR and SBR connections might share the same switching and transmission resources but with different buffers. Assume that connections within each traffic class (DBR or SBR) are homogeneous - they have the same traffic and QoS parameters. The first step is to determine the linear constraints bounding the admissable operating region. If prices (per unit time) p^D and p^S are assigned to DBR and SBR connections respectively, then the revenue per unit time is

$$p^D x^D(p^D) + p^S x^S(p^S) \qquad (6.1)$$

where $x^D(p^D)$ and $x^S(p^S)$ are the user demand functions, that is the expected rate of connections per unit time as a function of the price. The optimisation then consists of setting prices so as to maximise expression (6.1) over the operating region. This procedure can be extended to more general situations, such as non-homogeneous traffic types, multiple QoS levels, guaranteed and elastic services.

This framework allows us to explicitly calculate relative prices, as follows. It can be verified that in the situation of DBR and SBR sharing resources, the admissible region can be characterised by two linear constraints, typically of the form $\alpha x^D \leq C$ and $\beta x^D + \gamma x^S \leq C$. Assuming a local linearisation of the relation between demand and prices:

$$x^D = a - bp^D \quad \text{and} \quad x^S = c - dp^S,$$

and associate Lagrange multiplier λ (μ, respectively) with the first (second) constraint of the admissible region, so that the optimisation becomes to maximise:

$$L(p^D, p^S, \lambda, \mu) = p^D \cdot x^D(p^D) + p^S \cdot x^S(p^S) - \lambda(\alpha x^D - C) - \mu(\beta x^D + \gamma x^S - C) - f(C).$$

Then calculations yield

$$p^D = \frac{a + \lambda\alpha b + \mu\beta b}{2b} \quad \text{and} \quad p^S = \frac{c + \mu\gamma d}{2d}.$$

Now there are four possibilities. In the first place, the optimal quantities can lie in the interior of $S(C)$. When resources are abundant $\lambda = \mu = 0$; prices are simply $p^D = a/2b$ and $p^S = c/2d$. The second possibility is that the optimum is such that the first constraint is satisfied with equality and the second with strict inequality, corresponding to $\lambda > 0$ and $\mu = 0$. The SBR user should pay $c/2d$. To find λ, in this case, express p^D as a function of C and α by means of the equation $\partial L/\partial \lambda = 0$, and then solve for λ in $\partial L/\partial p^D = 0$. The third case is such that the optimal quantities lie on the second constraint, where the first is satisfied strictly; then $\lambda = 0$ and $\mu > 0$. In the last case, both resources are scarce, $\lambda > 0$ and $\mu > 0$.

Practical considerations

User demand functions

It is unlikely that network providers can estimate user demand functions with any precision. These functions will differ considerably between users, and will vary in response to commercial and marketing activities. Nevertheless the optimisation procedure described above makes clear the relationship between price-setting and user demand. Setting relative prices carries an implicit assumption about user demand functions, so a network provider should find some value in making this explicit - by making sensible assumptions about user demands and calculating the resulting price relativities.

Substitution effects

For many connections users may have flexibility in their choice of service - they might choose between different traffic contract parameters, QoS classes, and ATCs on the basis of relative prices. These substitution effects can be taken into account in the optimisation procedure by suitable definition of user demand functions, assuming that quantified estimates of the effects can be obtained.

Competition

Simple models of competition can be incorporated into this price-setting procedure, for example by allowing user demand functions to depend on the price relativity between one network and its competitor.

A rough model to investigate the effect of competition is the following. Where before we assumed just one network with capacity C, we now consider n competitors, each of them having capacity C/n. Let $p^D(x^D)$ be the price the customers are willing to pay if the supply is x^D; $p^S(x^S)$ analogously. Then the optimisation problem of the ith supplier becomes (if we assume a linear relation between prices and demand)

$$\max_{x_i^D, x_i^S} \left\{ p^D \left(\sum_{i=1}^n x_i^D \right) x_i^D + p^S \left(\sum_{i=1}^n x_i^S \right) x_i^S \right\} - f \left(\frac{C}{n} \right).$$

Calculations yield that the prices become

$$p^D = \frac{a}{(n+1)b} + \frac{n}{n+1}(\lambda \alpha + \mu \beta) \quad \text{and} \quad p^S = \frac{c}{(n+1)d} + \frac{n}{n+1}\mu \gamma.$$

The striking result is that the profits of all companies leak away as n grows large: prices become $\lambda \alpha + \mu \beta$ and $\mu \gamma$, respectively, exactly equal to the costs.

Timescales

What factors should be taken into account when computing optimal price relativities? This depends to a large extent on the relevant timescale. The revenue-maximising approach (expression (6.1)) applies over a short timescale during which capacity is fixed and user demand functions are constant. If capacity costs can be quantified then variable capacity can also be taken into the optimisation by maximising the difference between revenue and capacity cost. Over longer timescales there are dynamic effects which invalidate this approach - for example, user demand functions will change owing to competitor actions.

6.4   Standards activities

As described in chapter 1.3, various standards have been (and are still being) defined for ATM networks. The ATM Forum, with strong industry representation, has led the way in defining the detailed operation of ATM protocols, including the initial definition of ATM service classes. ITU-T, as the primary body for telecommunications standardisation, has defined a range of standards for ATM network design, operation, and interworking. Although important aspects such as traffic contract parameters and quality of service parameters have been defined carefully, there has been virtually no definition of standards for charging in ATM networks. Standards for ATM charging are now being addressed within ITU.

Standards and ATM charging

CA$hMAN has developed charging schemes for ATM and implemented these schemes on an experimental platform. For such schemes to be implemented in commercial networks, measurement information must be provided by such networks. In addition, charging information needs to be communicated between users and the network, and also between different networks.

To ensure that such information is available in commercial equipment, standards that describe the charging capabilities of networks and network elements must include this information. For this reason, CA$hMAN participants have supported the development of standards for ATM charging within ITU-T.

ITU-T activity on ATM charging

Through the active participation of Royal KPN in ITU-T, CA$hMAN work has been the major driving force behind initiating the first standardisation activity on ATM charging and drafting the first Recommendations. This activity has been required in two of ITU's Study Groups.

ITU-T Study Group 3 deals with tariffs and accounting, and is developing a Recommendation on charging and accounting principles for ATM. This Recommendation is expected to focus on duration and volume as the basic parameters for charging ATM connections, and will detail the need for such parameters to be measured. It will also address the exchange of charging information between network operators and between customers and network operators.

One concept that is presently being considered for this new draft Recommendation is a "Chargeable Cell Rate". This would apply to interconnect accounting and would represent the reservation-based element of the charge (as opposed to the charge for measured usage). The Chargeable Cell Rate would be a nominal charging rate, based on the ATC and traffic descriptor for each connection, and intended to simplify the problem of aggregating charges over connections with different characteristics. The CCR would be operator-specific.

ITU-T Study Group 13 is studying the network capabilities required to support charging in ATM networks, and will define how the network should provide the parameters and measurements specified by Study Group 3.

As a result of inputs based on the knowledge built up by the CA$hMAN project, ITU-T has been able to develop in a short time the essential content for new Recommendations on ATM charging. From CA$HMAN experience the parameters which play a role in ATM charging schemes and need to be standardised were well understood. Metering of time and volume and registration of the ATM traffic contract parameters are now part of a draft Recommendation. CA$hMAN experience of experimental implementation of charging schemes will also assist the Study Group 13 work on network capabilities for charging.

6.5   IP charging

In the current Internet, the rate at which a source sends packets is controlled by TCP, the transmission control protocol of the Internet [76], implemented as software on the computers that are the source and destination of the data. The general approach is as follows [43]. When a resource within the network becomes overloaded, one or more packets are lost; loss of a packet is taken as an indication of congestion, and the sender slows down. The TCP then gradually increases its sending rate until it again receives an indication of congestion. This cycle of increase and decrease serves to discover and utilise whatever bandwidth is available, and to share it between flows.

The approach has worked well in the past, when most flows have implemented reasonable versions of TCP, producing broadly similar bandwidth allocations for flows sharing similar resources. But the approach is breaking down, for two related reasons. First, there is an incentive to modify the TCP algorithm so that it strives more aggressively for a larger share of available bandwidth, or even to avoid using any form of congestion control. Secondly, applications are becoming more heterogeneous, with widely differing, and constantly evolving, statistical characteristics and sensitivities to delay.

The possibility that unresponsive flows could contribute to congestion collapse in the Internet is discussed by Floyd and Fall [58], where it is observed that it is no longer possible to rely on end-nodes to use end-to-end congestion control, or on developers to incorporate end-to-end congestion control in their applications. This observation, together with the heterogeneity of applications, has motivated work (reviewed in [43, 58, 71]) on various measurement and scheduling mechanisms that might be implemented within the network itself to restrict the bandwidth of flows and to discriminate between the services that are provided to different users.

Our aim here is to describe a different approach. Our premise is that if the resource implications of their actions can be made known to end-nodes, then the end-nodes themselves may be best placed to determine what should be their demands upon the resources of the network.

The issue at stake here is important in both theory and practice. The optimal allocation of resources depends upon the utilities the various users attach to their several flows through the network, as well as upon the properties of the resources within the network. It is possible that it is easier to achieve an efficient allocation by conveying information on congestion from the network to intelligent end-nodes rather than by requiring users to classify their flows into predefined categories and conveying this information from users to the network. Certainly the development of ATM traffic classes [13] illustrates some of the drawbacks of an approach that requires the definition of a set of service categories before the applications that might use these categories have been developed or have become widespread.

It is shown in Appendix B that, if users' utilities are concave functions of their attained throughput, then their aggregate utility is maximised by the network allocating scarce network resources according to a weighted *proportional fairness* criterion: loosely, the network shares resources in proportion to how much the users choose to pay. It has also been shown [85] that a weighted proportionally fair allocation could be achieved by simple rate control algorithms, using increase and decrease rules similar to those described by Chiu and Jain [42] and Jacobson [76] and implemented in TCP. Crowcroft and Oechslin [53] have proposed ways of setting parameters of the TCP protocol to achieve weighted proportional fairness, and have presented results from simulations and prototypes. This work has demonstrated the possibility of a charge-aware TCP, with congestion control *parameters* alterable by end-nodes in an incentive-compatible manner. Here we take a step further: we investigate the possibility that end-nodes or developers may be allowed uninhibited access to the *algorithms* used for congestion control while still maintaining incentive-compatibility (this section is based on [65]).

We use a simple slotted model of a resource to illustrate how network shadow prices [85] may be identified, at least statistically, on the sample path describing load on the resource.

Sample path shadow prices

In this section we explore a very simple resource model. The aim of our discussion is to show that the shadow price of a resource, the key variable of the model of section 2 of Appendix B, is straightforward to identify, at least statistically, on the sample path describing the load on the resource.

Suppose that time is slotted, and that a resource has capacity per slot to cope with N packets, with any excess lost. Let the load upon the resource per slot, Y, be generated by adding together a number of independent Poisson random variables $X_1, X_2, \ldots, X_m$, with means $x_1, x_2, \ldots, x_m$ respectively. Then Y has a Poisson distribution with mean $y = \sum_1^m x_r$. Let the cost to the system be the number of packets lost. Then the expected cost per slot $C(y)$, is given by

$$
\begin{aligned}
C(y) &= \mathbf{E}(Y - N)^+ \\
&= \sum_{n \geq N}(n - N)e^{-y}\frac{y^n}{n!}
\end{aligned}
$$

whose derivative with respect to y, $p(y)$, satisfies

$$
\begin{aligned}
p(y) &= \sum_{n \geq N}e^{-y}\frac{y^n}{n!} \\
&= \mathbf{P}\{Y \geq N\}.
\end{aligned}
$$

Suppose next that whenever the number of packets arriving in a slot exceeds N, a mark is placed on *each* of these packets. (We shall not distinguish between packets which are lost and those which are merely marked: we treat them all as marked packets.) Conditional on the event $Y = n$, X_r has a binomial distribution with parameters n and x_r/y. Thus the expected number of marks per unit time placed on packets from the rth flow is

$$
\begin{aligned}
\mathbf{E}(X_r I\{Y > N\}) &= \sum_{n > N}\mathbf{E}(X_r \mid Y = n)\mathbf{P}\{Y = n\} \\
&= \sum_{n > N}\frac{x_r}{y}ne^{-y}\frac{y^n}{n!} \\
&= x_r\sum_{n \geq N}e^{-y}\frac{y^n}{n!} \\
&= x_r p(y)
\end{aligned}
$$

as required by the model of section 2 of Appendix B.

Thus, for Poisson statistics, the marking of every packet when a resource is overloaded produces an expected charge per unit of flow, $p(y)$, precisely equal to the shadow price at the resource, and the expected charge per unit time to flow r, $x_r p(y)$, is precisely the fair charge to this flow under the model of Appendix B.

Now for statistics more general than Poisson, we cannot expect such precise identities. In particular, under more general flow statistics, the resource implications of additional flow may not be easily summarised by variation of a single real number, such as the rate of a Poisson process. Yet we can show that the key relationship, between the expected increase in system cost caused by a given load increment and the expected charge to that load increment, is more fundamental.

Suppose that the load Y on the resource is a positive random variable, and that we wish to assess the impact of an additional load, X, where X is a non-negative random variable, not necessarily independent of Y. Then the increase in the number of packets lost is

$$[X + Y - N]^+ - [Y - N]^+ = XI\{X + Y > N\} - (N - Y)I\{X + Y > N > Y\}.$$

Thus

$$\mathbf{E}[X + Y - N]^+ - \mathbf{E}[Y - N]^+ \leq \mathbf{E}(XI\{X + Y > N\}). \tag{6.2}$$

Further, if N, Y and X are integral, and if the additional load is a *small* increment, satisfying $\mathbf{P}\{X = 0 \text{ or } 1\} = 1$, then the event $\{X + Y > N > Y\}$ is impossible, and we have that

$$\mathbf{E}[X + Y - N]^+ - \mathbf{E}[Y - N]^+ = \mathbf{E}(XI\{X + Y > N\}). \tag{6.3}$$

Thus, for *small* increments, we have our desired identity between the expected increase in system cost caused by the additional load and the expected charge to the additional load. It is worth emphasising that the inequality (6.2), and the consequent equation (6.3) for small increments, do not require any distributional assumption on the increment X, not even independence of the load Y.

We can extend the simple model described above to allow a queue with finite buffer. Let Y_{t-1} be the number of packets that arrive at the resource in the slot $(t - 1, t]$, and let Q_t be the queue size at time t. Then the recursion

$$Q_t = \min\{N, Q_{t-1} - I\{Q_{t-1} > 0\} + Y_{t-1}\}$$

describes a queue with a buffer capacity of N that is able to serve a single packet per slot; the number of packets lost at time t is

$$[Q_{t-1} - I\{Q_{t-1} > 0\} + Y_{t-1} - N]^+.$$

The impact of an additional packet upon the total number of packets lost is relatively easy to describe. Consider the behaviour of the queue *with* the additional packet included in the description of the queue's sample path. Then the additional packet increases the number of packets lost by one if and only if the time of arrival of the additional packet lies between the start of a busy period and the loss, within the same busy period, of a packet; otherwise the additional packet does not affect the number of packets lost.

Thus the sample path shadow price of a packet is one or zero according to whether or not its time of arrival lies between the start of a busy period and a packet loss within the same busy period (the interval that plays an important role in the definition, in Appendix A.2, of an effective bandwidth. Unfortunately it will often be difficult to determine the shadow price of a packet while the packet is passing through the queue; it will, in general, be unclear whether or not the current busy period will include a later packet loss.

In [65] several marking mechanisms are discussed which approximate the ideal marking behaviour, including adaptations of the *Random Early Discard* and *Explicit Congestion Notification* mechanisms proposed by Floyd and Jacobson [59, 57]. In particular these mechanisms may be used to ensure that, in total, the correct number of packets are marked. By this means we ensure that the proportion of packets marked at a resource is equal to the probability that the removal a randomly chosen packet would reduce by one the number of packets lost at the resource.

Discussion

In [65] a study is conducted of how these sample path shadow prices may be used to transfer information and incentives to end-nodes: the study investigates the behaviour of a system comprising a resource and end-nodes equipped with various transmission control algorithms designed to achieve different user objectives. It is suggested there that by appropriately marking packets at overloaded resources, end-nodes are provided with the necessary information to make efficient use of the network. This may be enough in a network with cooperative end-nodes: otherwise it is suggested that a fixed small charge for each mark ensures that end-nodes also have the correct incentive to use the network efficiently. Thus the marks we have described provide a rational basis for a usage-related charging scheme. If usage-related costs are not a large proportion of network costs, then one might expect that these usage-related charges would be small in comparison with non-usage-related charges such as connection and subscription charges. Nonetheless even small usage-related charges should influence developers to incorporate end-to-end congestion control in their applications, and thus lead to a substantial improvement in the efficiency of network operation.

The approach of this section has not explicitly considered the market structure within which the network operates. (See [64] for an analysis of Odlyzko's [100] "Paris Metro Pricing" proposal within an economic model of competition.) The model of section 2 of Appendix B is readily extended to allow routing choices [85], and this provides some insight into how a geographically structured competitive environment might operate. An oft-expressed concern about congestion-related pricing is that a monopolist might deliberately allow congestion in order to increase revenue. This is really a concern about monopoly rather than congestion pricing: we simply note that even an unregulated monopolist would have an incentive to balance charges between, for example, connection, subscription and usage components so as to maximise the efficiency of the network. The key point here is familiar from economic theory [115]: if a monopolist has sufficient freedom over pricing then it can maximise net benefit *and* appropriate this benefit for itself.

Shenker *et al.* [107] provide a valuable discussion of architectural issues of pricing IP networks, and in particular the topics of multicast and receiver charging. We note that the marks carrying shadow prices can be distributed to the receivers of a multicast quite naturally. Consider a point in the network where a packet is replicated to produce, say, k daughter packets. If the packet to be replicated carries a mark, then assign this mark to just one of the daughter packets, randomly selected from amongst the k possibilities. (The random distribution may be uniform or weighted in accordance with any other information available concerning, for example, subsequent replications.) The shadow price of each scarce resource is thus shared over the users benefiting, and end-nodes have incentives to join multicasts rather than to use inefficient unicasts.

Appendix A

Pricing for guaranteed services

A.1 Overview

Connections that are offered strong service guarantees, and are subject to connection acceptance control, should be charged on the basis of their resource usage in order to generate appropriate incentives. How can such charges be defined in a way that is feasible to implement and manage? We consider charges based on effective bandwidth models for resource usage. Section 2 provides an introduction to the concept of an effective bandwidth.

Effective bandwidth depends on the traffic characteristics of the source and on network conditions. The influence of network conditions can be represented by two parameters, one representing space (such as buffer and link capacities) and one representing timescales.

Also in section 2 we describe why appropriate charging schemes should be based on tariffs that depend both on static parameters that are policed and on dynamic parameters that are measured. The tariffs offered to users are obtained from bounding approximations to the effective bandwidth function expressed in terms of the static and dynamic parameters.

In section 3 we present a simple charging mechanism where charges are linear combinations of the duration and volume of the connection. Users can minimise their charge by choosing tariffs corresponding to their expected mean rates. This charging mechanism forms the basis of the unified *abc* charging scheme that was presented in chapter 2, and which has been implemented and studied in CA$hMAN trials.

Section 4 describes models based on more general linear functions of measurements. A tax band charging scheme is described, and numerical results are presented of a comparison between this tax band scheme and the simple time and volume scheme.

Section 5 considers issues of accuracy and fairness in charging. It is not essential for charging to use an absolutely accurate measure of effective bandwidth. However charges should, to a reasonable degree, be proportional to actual effective bandwidth - that is, the ratio (charge)/(effective bandwidth) should have a low variability across different connections.

167

This ensures fairness, which preserves appropriate user incentives. The simple charging scheme has been tested by experimental analysis and found to provide a good level of fairness.

In order to ensure QoS guarantees and efficient network operation, connection acceptance control (CAC) needs to have accurate estimates of the resources required by connections. Hence CAC naturally has a close relation with charging. Section 6 describes a CAC that uses bounding tangents to the effective bandwidth function, as does the simple charging scheme. This CAC might use the same functions as are used for tariffs. However the impact of charging is on a longer time scale than CAC and thus may not need to use the same parameters.

The work presented in this Appendix is drawn largely from the papers [48], [47] (accuracy and fairness), and [50] (accuracy of effective bandwidth and investigation of link operating point parameters s, t); related software regarding the latter is available from [110].

A.2   Effective bandwidth

The concept of an effective bandwidth provides a notion of network resource usage appropriate for a multiservice broadband network, but this concept does not lend itself naturally to be used as a charging mechanism. This section introduces the effective bandwidth concept and describes a methodology for defining charging schemes with the property that the expected charge for a connection bounds the effective bandwidth of the connection. The following section will explicitly present one such simple charging scheme.

Effective bandwidths as a measure of resource usage

Suppose the arrival process at a broadband link is the superposition of independent sources of J types: let n_j be the number of connections of type j, and let $\mathbf{n} = (n_1, \dots, n_J)$. We suppose that, after taking into account all economic factors (such as demand curves, price sensitivity, competition, and so forth), the proportions of traffic of each of the J types remain close to those given by the vector $\mathbf{n}$, and we seek to understand the relative usage of network resource that should be attributed to each traffic type.

We take a discrete time model and let $X_{ji}[0, t]$ be the total load produced by the ith source of type j in epochs $1, \dots, t$. We assume this is equal in distribution to $X_j[0, t]$ and that the increments of $\{X_{ji}[0, t], \ t \geq 0\}$ are stationary. Then the *effective bandwidth* of a source of type j is defined as

$$\alpha_j(s, t) = \frac{1}{st} \log \mathbf{E} \left[e^{sX_j[0,t]} \right] , \qquad (A.1)$$

for some choice of a *time parameter* t and *space parameter* s. The effective bandwidth has the property that it increases from the mean to the peak value of $X_j[0, t]/t$ as s increases from 0 to ∞.

Parameters s, t are system-defined parameters which depend on the characteristics of the multiplexed traffic and the link resources (capacity and buffer). Specifically, the time parameter t (measured in, for example, msec) corresponds to the most probable duration of the busy period of the buffer prior to overflow [52, 93, 119]. The space parameter s (measured in, for example, kb^{-1}) corresponds to the degree of multiplexing and depends, among others, on the size of the peak rate of the multiplexed sources relative to the link capacity. In particular, for links with capacity much larger than the peak rate of the multiplexed sources, s tends to zero and $\alpha_j(s, t)$ approaches the mean rate of the sources, while for links with capacity not much larger than the peak rate of the sources, s is large and $\alpha_j(s, t)$ approaches the maximum value of $X_j[0, t]/t$.

Let $L(C, B, \mathbf{n})$ be the proportion of workload lost, through overflow of a buffer of size $B > 0$, when the server has rate C and $\mathbf{n} = (n_1, n_2, \dots, n_J)$. A key definition is the *acceptance region* $A(\gamma, C, B)$. This is the subset of $\mathbf{Z}_+^J$ such that $\mathbf{n} \in A(\gamma, C, B)$ implies $\log L(C, B, \mathbf{n}) \leq -\gamma$. A point in A corresponds to a traffic mix under which the proportion of workload lost is below the maximum acceptable level, and hence such a traffic mix can be 'accepted' by the system.

If the boundary of the region A is differentiable at the point $\mathbf{n}$, then the tangent plane determines a half-space which is well approximated, when C, B, and $\mathbf{n}$ are large [36, 52, 82, 109], by

$$\sum_j n_j \alpha_j(s, t) \leq C + \frac{1}{t}\left(B - \frac{\gamma}{s}\right) \tag{A.2}$$

where (s, t) is an extremising pair in the equation

$$-\gamma = \sup_t \inf_s \left[st \sum_{j=1}^J n_j \alpha_j(s, t) - s(Ct + B) \right]. \tag{A.3}$$

The effective bandwidths $\alpha_j(s, t), j = 1, \dots, J$, thus determine the relative usage of network resource by traffic types j, for local variations of the traffic mix $\mathbf{n}$, where the amount of resource is given by (A.2).[1] The asymptotics behind this approximation assumes only stationarity of sources, and illustrative examples discussed in [82] and [104] include periodic streams, fractional Brownian input, policed and shaped sources, and deterministic multiplexing. Note that the QoS guarantees are encoded in the effective bandwidth definition through the value of γ which influences the form of the acceptance region.

Investigations with real traffic [50] have shown that the above effective bandwidth definition can accurately quantify resource usage. This work also investigated the parameters s, t for

---

[1] For a rigorous mathematical treatment of the effective bandwidths and the asymptotics the reader is referred to [52], and, for the case of several resources, [118].

real traffic and showed how they can be used to explain the phenomena which occur at a multiplexer and are related to the time scales of buffer overflow and traffic burstiness.

We must stress now the network engineering implications of the above results. For any given traffic stream, the effective bandwidth definition in (A.1) is nothing more than a template that must be filled with the system operating point parameters s, t in order to provide the correct measure of effective usage which is appropriate in the particular situation. Hence, one should extend the definition of the operating point of the network to include, besides the description of the traffic mix $\mathbf{n}$, also the pair s, t. This last component is the 'complete information' we need from the network in order to determine the effective bandwidth of a traffic stream.

Experimentation [50] has shown that the values of s, t are to a large extent insensitive to small variations of the traffic mix. Furthermore, in networks multiplexing a large number of users, the relative values of the traffic mix $\mathbf{n}$ at each link change slowly during the day, and hence the values of s, t could be successfully approximated (for example, by assigning constant values in the various time zones of interest). The values for s, t can be computed either by solving (A.3) or using online measurements. This requires the computation of the logarithmic moment generating function of the traffic as seen by the network, and is by no means hard since it can be done off-line, using traffic traces [50] (related software is available at [110]).

There is a considerable literature on the performance modelling of ATM networks (good overviews are provided by Roberts et al. [54, 78]); however the above brief introduction to effective bandwidths will suffice for our development of charging schemes.

Relation with charging

It is often the case that a reasonable local approximation of the region A can be made in terms of a finite number of tangent hyperplanes at some boundary points $n^1, ..., n^R$. Each such linear constraint is of the form of (A.2) where the s, t are determined by the corresponding traffic mix at the boundary point. To illustrate our point assume, with no loss of generality, that an approximation of the acceptance region is given by the two constraints

$$\sum_{j \in J_1} n_j \alpha_j(s_1, t_1) \ \leq K_1 \tag{A.4}$$

$$\sum_{j \in J_2} n_j \alpha_j(s_2, t_2) \ \leq K_2 \tag{A.5}$$

where

$$K_1 := C + \frac{1}{t_1}\left(B - \frac{\gamma}{s_1}\right), \qquad K_2 := C + \frac{1}{t_2}\left(B - \frac{\gamma}{s_2}\right).$$

and the s_i, t_i are the appropriate extremising values at the corresponding boundary points.[2]

Assume that a network operator charges f_i per unit time for a connection of type i, $i \in J$. The revenue $\sum_{j \in J} n_j f_j$ is maximised by operating, if possible, at some point on the boundary defined by (A.4) and (A.5). The operating point will be determined by factors such as the demand, which is determined by the price sensitivity of the two types of traffic.

However, whatever the nature of the demand, there will be shadow prices λ_1 and λ_2 associated with relaxation of the constraints (A.4) and (A.5) respectively. If (A.4) is active (i.e. the network operates at capacity constrained by K_1), then it will be appropriate to charge type $i \in J_1$ connections an amount which bounds $\lambda_1 \alpha_i(s_1, t_1)$. If (A.5) is active, then it will be appropriate to charge $i \in J_2$ connections an amount which bounds $\lambda_2 \alpha_i(s_2, t_2)$. If both (A.4) and (A.5) are active, then a connection $i \in J_1 \cap J_2$ should incur a total charge which bounds $\lambda_1 \alpha_i(s_1, t_1) + \lambda_2 \alpha_i(s_2, t_2)$.

From the above discussion it follows that if one assumes that the operating point of the link is on the boundary of the acceptance region, the usage-based component of the charge of a connection should be a linear function of the effective bandwidths of the connection corresponding to the active constraints of the form (A.2). There are many indications that any economically justifiable operation of the system will require the operating point to be on the boundary, for example see [89] for the case of social welfare maximisation.

Charges based upon effective bandwidths and user incentives

We have argued above that effective bandwidths can provide a way to assess resource usage, and hence can be used for constructing the usage-based component of the charge. Given that effective bandwidths are to play a part in charging, there are two extreme methods by which this can be done.

Consider sources of type j, where 'type' is distinguished by parameters of the traffic contract and possibly some other static information. The network could form the empirical estimate $\tilde{\alpha}_j(s, t)$ of the expectation appearing in formula (A.1), as determined by past connections of type j. Would it be reasonable simply to charge each newly admitted connection of type j an amount per unit time equal to $\tilde{\alpha}_j(s, t)$? Of course it would, and in fact this is precisely the charging method adopted by an all-you-can-eat restaurant. At such a restaurant each customer is charged not for his own food consumption, but rather for the average amount that similar customers have eaten in the past. But all-you-can-eat restaurants encourage diners to over-eat and small customers with small appetites are likely to feel they are over-charged.

The problem with adopting a charging scheme in which a connection is charged at a rate per unit time which is determined wholly in terms of parameters that are known at call setup, is that there is no feedback mechanism to penalise customers who use more than the

---

[2]In the case of a two-class priority system, for appropriate s, t, the acceptance region is of the form (A.4),(A.5), where $J_2 \supset J_1$, and $J_1, J_2 \cap \bar{J}_1$ are the high and low priority traffic respectively, [48].

typical amounts of resources used by others of their type. Each customer may as well use the maximum of network resources that the contract allows, which will result in $\tilde{\alpha}_j(s,t)$ eventually becoming the largest effective bandwidth that is possible subject to the agreed policing parameters. Customers who have connections of type j, but whose traffic does not have the maximal effective bandwidth possible for this type, will not wish to pay as if they did, hence will seek network service providers using a different charging method.

At another extreme, one might charge a customer wholly on the basis of measurements that are made for his connection, i.e., charge the value of the effective bandwidth of the traffic actually sent. This has a conceptual flaw, which can be illustrated as follows. Suppose a customer requests a connection policed by a high peak rate, but then happens to transmit very little traffic over the connection. Then an *a posteriori* estimate of quantity (A.1) will be near zero and the charge near zero, even though the *a priori* expectation may be much larger, as assessed by either the customer or the network. Since tariffing and connection acceptance control may be primarily concerned with expectations of *future* quality of service, the distinction matters. This is the case because such a charging scheme does not account for the resources reserved for the duration of the call at call setup, which is unfair for the network operator.

Our approach lies part way between the two described above. We construct a charge that is based on the effective bandwidth, but which is a function of both **static parameters** (such as the peak rate h, or other parameters of leaky bucket regulators) and **dynamic parameters** (these correspond to the actual traffic of the connection, the simplest ones being the duration and volume of the connection); we *police* the static parameters and *measure* the dynamic parameters; we bound the effective bandwidth by a linear function of the measured parameters, with coefficients that depend on the static parameters; and we use such linear functions as the basis for simple charging mechanisms. This leads to a charge with the right incentives for customers, which also compensates the network operator for the amount of resources reserved.

Charges that are linear in time and volume

Suppose that a connection lasts for epochs $1, \dots, T$ and produces loads of $X_1, \dots, X_T$ in these epochs. Imagine that we want to impose a *per unit time* charge for a connection of type j that can be expressed as a linear function of the form

$$f(X) = a_0 + a_1 g(X), \qquad\qquad (A.6)$$

where $g(X)$ is the measurement taken from the observation of $X = (X_1, \dots, X_T)$ corresponding to $(1/T) \sum_{i=1}^{T} X_i$. In other words, the total charge is simply a function of the total number of cells carried, and, through a_0, the duration of the connection[3]. This is

---

[3]In [48] we generalise this approach for charges that are linear in arbitrary measurements. An example of such a charging scheme is discussed in section 4 of this Appendix

practically the simplest measurement we could take, and leads to charging schemes based on just time and volume.

We argued above that the usage-based charge of a connection should be proportional to the effective bandwidth of the connection evaluated at the active constraints of the acceptance region. Hence a challenging task is to encode such a charge as the function f in (A.6). For simplicity we assume the case of a single active constraint, and hence the usage-based charge of the connection should be proportional to $\alpha(s, t)$, for appropriate s, t.

Let $\bar{\alpha}(m, \mathbf{h})$ be an *upper bound for the greatest effective bandwidth possible subject to appropriate constraints*, i.e.,

$$\bar{\alpha}(m, \mathbf{h}) := \max_{\substack{X \,:\, \mathbf{E}g(X) \,=\, m \\ X \,\in\, \mathcal{X}(\mathbf{h})}} \left\{ \frac{1}{st} \log \mathbf{E} \left[e^{sX[0,t]} \right] \right\}, \tag{A.7}$$

where $\mathcal{X}(\mathbf{h})$ is the set of processes that satisfy the static contract parameters $\mathbf{h}$. Consideration of $\bar{\alpha}(m, \mathbf{h})$ is partly motivated by the remark that this is what we would charge to a customer with mean rate m who makes maximal use of his service contract. An important property of $\bar{\alpha}(m, \mathbf{h})$ is that it is concave in m.

We define now our tariffs in terms of the charging function f parameterised with $m, \mathbf{h}$. Mathematically, this corresponds to the tangent hyperplane of $\bar{\alpha}(m, \mathbf{h})$ at m:

$$f(m, \mathbf{h}; X) := \bar{\alpha}(m, \mathbf{h}) + \lambda_m(g(X) - m), \tag{A.8}$$

which is of the form $a_0 + a_1 g(X)$, where $a_0[m, \mathbf{h}] = \bar{\alpha}(m, \mathbf{h}) - \lambda_m m$, $a_1[m, \mathbf{h}] = \lambda_m = \frac{\partial}{\partial m} \bar{\alpha}(m, \mathbf{h})$. These coefficients depend on the customer's choice of m. We can show that the expected value of the charging rate for this connection is $\mathbf{E}f(m, \mathbf{h}; X) \geq \bar{\alpha}(\mathbf{E}g(X), \mathbf{h})$ with equality if $m = \mathbf{E}g(X)$ (the actual mean rate of the connection). Hence the customer minimises the expected charge for his connection if he chooses the tariff $f(\mathbf{E}g(X), \mathbf{h})$.

As we intended, the coefficients $a_0[m, \mathbf{h}], a_1[m, \mathbf{h}]$ depend upon both static information, as well as the customer's expectations about measurements that will be taken during the duration of the call. Some other desirable properties of our charging function f include

- The expected charging rate for a connection, $\bar{\alpha}(\mathbf{E}g(X), \mathbf{h})$, is conservative, in the sense that every connection is charged at an expected rate which is at least its effective bandwidth.

- Such over-charging as takes place is *minimal with respect to the information available*. That is, $\bar{\alpha}(\mathbf{E}g(X), \mathbf{h})$ is equal to the effective bandwidth of a connection that has the maximum effective bandwidth amongst connections having the same mean rate and which are parameterised by the same static parameters. It would not be possible to charge less and still be conservative in respect to all possible connections.

Note that the dependence of the charge on m provides the customers with the right incentives for avoiding the 'all-you-can-eat restaurant' effect mentioned before.

The results of this section were of merely theoretical interest since the construction of f is directly related with knowing the function $\bar{\alpha}(m, \mathbf{h})$ which is in general extremely hard to compute. In the next section we propose some simple approximations for $\bar{\alpha}(m, \mathbf{h})$ which serve our purpose. For a more detailed reference on this subject we refer the reader to [48].

Approximations for $\bar{\alpha}(m, \mathbf{h})$

We start first with a simple approximation for $\bar{\alpha}(m, \mathbf{h})$, which is an upper bound on the actual value. This approximation is extremely valuable since it indicates the relation of the various time scales involved in the overflows of the buffers.

Let m be the mean rate of the process, and $\bar{X}[0, t]$ be the maximum amount of traffic produced in $[0, t]$ [4]. Since the process is subjected to policing, we have $\bar{X}[0, t] < \infty$. The constraint $0 \leq X[0, t] \leq \bar{X}[0, t]$, together with the convexity of the exponential function implies that

$$\alpha(s, t) \leq \frac{1}{st} \log \left[1 + \frac{tm}{\bar{X}[0, t]} \left(e^{s\bar{X}[0,t]} - 1 \right) \right].$$

If the source is policed by parameters (ρ_k, β_k), $k \in K$, we have

$$\bar{X}[0, t] \leq H(t) := \min_{k \in K} \{ \rho_k t + \beta_k \}, \tag{A.9}$$

and so

$$\bar{\alpha}(m, \mathbf{h}) \leq \frac{1}{st} \log \left[1 + \frac{tm}{H(t)} \left(e^{sH(t)} - 1 \right) \right]. \tag{A.10}$$

We call this the 'simple' bound. The above equation is illuminating for the effects of leaky buckets on the packet losses. Each leaky bucket (ρ_k, β_k) constrains the burstiness of the traffic in a particular time scale. *The time scale for burstiness that contributes to the overflow of the buffers in the network is determined by the index k which achieves the minimum in (A.9)* (remember that t is defined by the global operating point of the network, and is equal to the time it takes to overflow the buffers in the network, see [52, 93, 119]).

If $t = 1$ the bound (A.10) reduces to

$$\bar{\alpha}(m, \mathbf{h}) = \frac{1}{s} \log \left[\left(1 - \frac{m}{h} \right) + \frac{m}{h} e^{sh} \right], \tag{A.11}$$

appropriate for the case where buffers in the network are small and the argument minimising expression (A.9) corresponds to the peak rate h. We refer to this as the 'peak'

---

[4]Formally $\bar{X}[0, t]$ is the possibly infinite essential supremum of the set $\{x : P\{X[0, t] > x\} > 0\}$.

approximation. Charges based on this bound have been considered in [81] and are discussed in the next section.

A last, but more accurate, approximation can be obtained in the case where a connection is policed by a single leaky bucket (ρ, β). Then the worst case traffic (for given values of s, t) consists of blocks of an inverted T shape being either periodic or having random gaps. We call this the 'inverted T' approximation.

There are other approximations of $\overline{\alpha}(m, \mathbf{h})$ that involve more complex measurements than simply time and volume. These are considered in [48] and some of them are discussed in section 4.

A.3   A simple charging mechanism

In this section we present a charging mechanism based on the simple bound to the effective bandwidth function that was developed in the preceding section.

Consider an on/off source with a known (and possibly policed) peak rate h, but with a mean rate that may not be known with certainty, even to the user responsible for the source. Assume, however, that the user has a prior distribution G for the mean rate M of the connection. The distribution G may represent very vague information, or might be constructed by recording past observed mean rates. Then the expected mean rate of the connection is

$$\mathbf{E}_G M = \int_0^h x \, dG(x).$$

If the network knew the prior distribution G for the mean rate M, then the network would determine the effective bandwidth of the connection as

$$\frac{1}{s} \log \mathbf{E} e^{sA} = \frac{1}{s} \log \mathbf{E}_G \mathbf{E}(e^{sA} \mid M) = \frac{1}{s} \log \mathbf{E}_G \left[1 + \frac{M}{h}(e^{sh} - 1) \right]$$

$$= \frac{1}{s} \log \left[1 + \frac{\mathbf{E}_G M}{h}(e^{sh} - 1) \right]. \qquad (A.12)$$

But expression (A.12) is just the effective bandwidth if M is not random, but identical to its mean value under G. We see that since the source is on/off with known peak rate the network need only know $\mathbf{E}_G M$, the user's expected mean rate; further detail about the distribution G does not influence the effective bandwidth, and would be superfluous for the network to even request.

How, then, should the network encourage the user to assess and to declare the user's expected mean rate? We next investigate whether the charging mechanism might be used to provide the appropriate amount of encouragement.

Suppose that, before a connection's admission, the network requires the user to announce a value m, and then charges for the connection an amount $f(m; M)$ per unit time, where

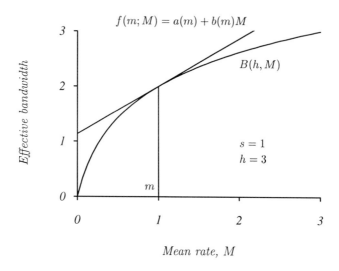

Figure A.1: Effective bandwidth as a function of mean rate

M is the measured mean rate for the connection. We suppose that the user is risk-neutral and attempts to select m so as to minimise $\mathbf{E}_G f(m; M)$, the expected cost per unit time: call a minimising choice of m, $\hat{m}$ say, an *optimal* declaration for the user. What properties would the network like the optimal declaration $\hat{m}$ to have? Well, first of all the network would like to be able to deduce from $\hat{m}$ the user's expected mean rate $\mathbf{E}_G M$, and hence the effective bandwidth (A.12) of the connection. A second desirable property would be that the expected cost per unit time under the optimal declaration $\hat{m}$ be proportional to the effective bandwidth of the connection (or, equivalently, *equal* to the effective bandwidth under a choice of units). In [81] it is shown that these two requirements essentially characterise the tariff $f(m; M)$ as

$$f(m; M) = a(m) + b(m)M, \tag{A.13}$$

defined as the tangent to the curve $B(h, M)$ at the point $M = m$ (see Figure A.1), where $B(h, M)$ is the effective bandwidth of the on/off source

$$B(h, m) = \frac{1}{s} \log \left[1 + \frac{m}{h} \left(e^{sh} - 1 \right) \right]. \tag{A.14}$$

The key property used in the proof [81] is the strict concavity of $B(h, M)$ as a function of M. By a simple differentiation of the function (A.14), the coefficients in expression (A.13) are given by

$$b(h, m) = \frac{e^{sh} - 1}{s[h + m(e^{sh} - 1)]}, \qquad a(h, m) = B(h, m) - mb(h, m) \qquad \text{(A.15)}$$

where we now make explicit the dependence of the coefficients on the peak rate h.

Note that a very simple interpretation is available for the tariff f: the user is free to declare a value m, and then incurs a charge $a(m)$ per unit time and a charge $b(m)$ per unit of volume carried. If the user's connection has actual mean rate $M = m$ then the user is charged for the bounding effective bandwidth $B(h, m)$. If the user's connection has a different mean rate then the charge (determined by the tangent $a(h, m) + b(h, m)M$) is greater than the effective bandwidth.

The properties characterising the tariff f have many interesting and desirable consequences. For example, suppose that a user can, with some effort, improve its prediction of the statistical properties of a connection. A crude method of deciding upon the declaration m might be to take the average of the measured means for the last n connections, but more sophisticated methods are possible. If the user is an organisation containing many individuals, the user might observe the identity of the individual making the connection, the applications active on that individual's desktop computer, as well as the called party, and utilise elaborate regression aids to make the prediction m. Is it worth the effort? In [81] it is shown that improved prediction reduces the expected cost per unit time of the connection by exactly the expected reduction in the effective bandwidth required from the network. This is an important property: users should not be expected to do more work determining the statistical properties of their connections than is justified by the benefit to the network of better characterisation.

A.4   Charges that are linear in general measurements

In this section we investigate more general charging schemes in which the *per unit time* charge for a connection of type j can be expressed as a linear function of the form

$$f(X) = a_0 + a_1 g_1(X) + \cdots + a_L g_L(X) = a_0 + \mathbf{a}^\top \mathbf{g}(X), \qquad \text{(A.16)}$$

where $g_1(X), \ldots, g_L(X)$ are measurements taken from the observation of $X = (X_1, \ldots, X_T)$, or some functions of those measurements. Here X and $a_0, \ldots, a_L$ depend on j, and hence perhaps on policing parameters for sources of type j, but we suppress the dependence on j for convenience.

Note that by making the charge a linear function of specified statistics the user's expected charge is a function only of the expected values of those statistics. The expected value of the charge per unit time is just

$$\mathbf{E}f(X) = a_0 + \mathbf{a}^\top \mathbf{E}\mathbf{g}(X).$$

Our aim is to construct linear functions of the form (A.16) so that the expected charge bounds the effective bandwidth. The analysis is described in [48] and is analogous to the discussion of charges linear in time and volume in section 2.2. We define $\bar{\alpha}(\mathbf{m}, \mathbf{h})$ to be an upper bound on the effective bandwidth subject to the appropriate constraints. We are now able to define a family of charging functions of the form,

$$f_{\mathbf{m},\mathbf{h}}(X) = \bar{\alpha}(\mathbf{m}, \mathbf{h}) + \lambda_{\mathbf{m}}^{\top}(\mathbf{g}(X) - \mathbf{m}) \tag{A.17}$$

parameterised by $\mathbf{m}$ and $\mathbf{h}$. Here $\mathbf{h}$ is fixed by the type of connection, but the user is permitted to choose $\mathbf{m}$. These charging functions are of the form $a_0 + \mathbf{a}^{\top}\mathbf{g}(X)$, where

$$
\begin{aligned}
a_0[\mathbf{m}, \mathbf{h}] &= \bar{\alpha}(\mathbf{m}, \mathbf{h}) - \lambda_{\mathbf{m}}^{\top}\mathbf{m}\,, \\
(a_1[\mathbf{m}, \mathbf{h}], \dots, a_k[\mathbf{m}]) &= \lambda_{\mathbf{m}}^{\top} = \left(\tfrac{\partial}{\partial \mathbf{m}_1}\bar{\alpha}(\mathbf{m}, \mathbf{h}), \dots, \tfrac{\partial}{\partial \mathbf{m}_k}\bar{\alpha}(\mathbf{m}, \mathbf{h})\right).
\end{aligned}
$$

For any given choice of $\mathbf{m}$ the expected value of the charging rate satisfies

$$\mathbf{E}f_{\mathbf{m},\mathbf{h}}(X) \geq \bar{\alpha}(\mathbf{E}\mathbf{g}(X), \mathbf{h})\,,$$

with equality if $\mathbf{m} = \mathbf{E}\mathbf{g}(X)$. As we intended, the coefficients $a_i[\mathbf{m}, \mathbf{h}]$ depend upon both static information, such as knowledge of a policed peak rate, as well as the user's expectations about measurements that will be taken during the duration of the call.

A taxband charging scheme

An important issue for a charging scheme is its complexity. We expect that by taking more measurements the charge can be made to more faithfully reflect the effective bandwidth. In this section we develop a refinement to the simple time and volume scheme in which separate time and volume measurements are made for periods during which the source rate lies in either a higher or lower band. We divide the time interval $[0, T]$ into T/t intervals of length t. For notational ease let $X_i = X[(i-1)t, it]$, $i = 1, \dots, T/t$. Taking $L = 4$, let us define for a chosen threshold h_1,

$$I_1 = \{i : X[(i-1)t, it] \leq h_1\} \text{ and } I_2 = \{i : X[(i-1)t, it] > h_1\}.$$

and

$$
\begin{aligned}
g_1(\mathbf{X}) &= \tfrac{1}{T/t} \textstyle\sum_{i \in I_1} 1 \\
g_2(\mathbf{X}) &= \tfrac{1}{T/t} \textstyle\sum_{i \in I_2} 1 \\
g_3(\mathbf{X}) &= \tfrac{1}{T/t} \textstyle\sum_{i \in I_1} X[(i-1)t, it] \\
g_4(\mathbf{X}) &= \tfrac{1}{T/t} \textstyle\sum_{i \in I_2} X[(i-1)t, it]
\end{aligned}
$$

One might generalise this further to ℓ bands by choosing thresholds, $h_0, \ldots, h_t$, such that $-1 = h_0 < h_1 < \cdots < h_\ell = ht$, and define,

$$I_k = \{i : h_{k-1} < X_i \leq h_k\}$$

and

$$g_k(X) = \frac{1}{T/t} \sum_{i \in I_k} 1, \quad g_{\ell+k}(X) = \frac{1}{T/t} \sum_{i \in I_k} X_i, \quad k = 1, \ldots, \ell.$$

So then

$$\mathbf{E} g_k(X) = \sum_{j \in I_k} \theta_j, \quad \mathbf{E} g_{\ell+k}(X) = \sum_{j \in I_k} j\theta_j, \quad k = 1, \ldots, \ell.$$

The bounding effective bandwidth function can then be found from the following linear program:

$$\text{maximise } \sum_{j=0}^{h} \theta_j e^{sj}$$

subject to $\quad \sum_{j=0}^{h} \theta_j = 1, \quad \sum_{j \in I_k} \theta_j = m_k, \quad \sum_{j \in I_k} j\theta_j = m_{\ell+k}, \quad k = 1, \ldots, \ell.$

This is easily solved to give

$$\bar{\alpha}(\mathbf{m}, \mathbf{h}) = \frac{1}{st} \log \sum_{k=1}^{\ell} \left[\frac{m_{\ell+k} - m_k h_{k-1} - m_k}{h_k - h_{k-1} - 1} e^{sh_k} + \frac{m_k h_k - m_{\ell+k}}{h_k - h_{k-1} - 1} e^{s(h_{k-1}+1)} \right]$$

It follows from $a_k = \partial \bar{\alpha}(\mathbf{m}, \mathbf{h})/\partial m_k$ that

$$a_1 > a_2 > \cdots > a_\ell \quad \text{and} \quad a_{\ell+1} < a_{\ell+2} \cdots < a_{2\ell}.$$

Furthermore

$$a_k + (h_{k-1} + 1)a_{\ell+k} = \beta e^{s(h_{k-1}+1)} \quad \text{and} \quad a_k + h_k a_{\ell+k} = \beta e^{sh_k},$$

where $\beta = \frac{1}{st} e^{-st\bar{\alpha}(\mathbf{m}, \mathbf{h})}$. The total charge takes the form

$$a_0 T + \sum_{i=1}^{T} \max_k \{a_k + a_{\ell+k} X_i\}.$$

The maximum occurs for k if $i \in I_k$, i.e. $h_{k-1} < X_i \leq h_k$. This corresponds to a 'tax-band charging scheme', in that cells incur a cost per cell that depends on which of ℓ bands into which X_i falls. If $h_{k-1} < X_i \leq h_k$, then the charge for those cells is

$$a_k + (h_{k-1} + 1)a_{\ell+k} + (X_i - h_{k-1} - 1)a_{\ell+k} = \beta e^{s(h_{k-1}+1)} + (X_i - h_{k-1} - 1)a_{\ell+k}.$$

Note that since we are maximising over a more restricted set, the expected charge which results under this tax-band scheme is less than the one based on only T and V in section 3 (which is actually the case $\ell = 1$). It also makes more distinction between sources that differ, but at the price of gathering a greater amount of data.

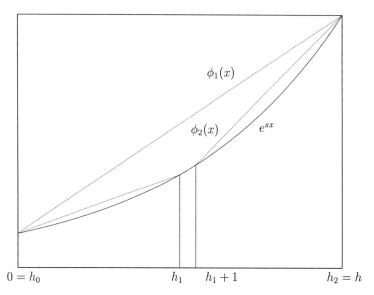

$$0 = h_0 \qquad\qquad\qquad h_1 \quad h_1 + 1 \qquad\qquad\qquad h_2 = h$$

Figure A.2: The tax band scheme - using two chords to bound the effective bandwidth

Discussion of the tax band scheme

The schemes described above and in section 3 effectively correspond to bounding the effective bandwidth by using $\mathbf{E}e^{sX[0,t]} \le \mathbf{E}\phi(sX[0,t])$, where $\phi = \phi_1$ is either a single chord lying above e^{sx} (the case $\ell = 1$), or two chords $\phi = \phi_2$ lying above e^{sx} (the case $\ell = 2$), as depicted in Figure A.2.

We have called the second scheme a 'tax-band scheme' because of its similarity to the system of graduated (or banded) income tax which is operated in most countries. In such countries there is a charging period for income tax calculation, t, which is usually one year. Suppose for simplicity that there are only two tax bands, and that the tax for a year's income I is computed from the following table, in which $0 < a_3 < a_4 < 1$ and $h_1 > 0$.

income band	tax
$0 \le I \le h_1$	$a_0 + Ia_3$
$h_1 < I$	$a_0 + h_1a_3 + (I - h_1)a_4$

One can think of a_0 as a fixed 'poll' tax which is paid equally by all taxpayers, irrespective of income. This leads to total tax over T years that can be written in the form

$$a_0T + a_1T_1 + a_2T_2 + a_3I_1 + a_4I_2,$$

where T_1 and T_2 are respectively the numbers of these years in which the taxpayer does not or does pay higher rate tax, I_1 and I_2 are respectively his total income, summed over years of these types, and $a_1 = 0$, $a_2 = a_0 + h_1(a_3 - a_4)$.

Notice that a taxpayer who has a constant income in each of 40 years will pay less tax than a taxpayer who has the same total income over those 40 years but whose income varies above and below h_1 from year to year. While this anomaly is not desirable in a tax system (and indeed some countries allow taxpayers to average their income over several years to reduce this effect), it is precisely what we want, in the context of charging for variable rate traffic, so that a source that is more bursty will pay a greater charge.

Our analogous charging scheme for a connection is to divide the duration of the connection, T, into T/t intervals of length t, where its value is determined from the parameters of the system. In the examples we consider, the critical parameter t ranges from about 50ms to 1500ms. Each such interval will be our *charging* interval for the traffic stream.

Let us classify a charging interval as being of type I or II as the total volume of cells the source produces during that interval is either $\leq h_1$ or $> h_1$. The charging function takes the form

$$a_1[\ldots]T_1 + a_2[\ldots]T_2 + a_3[\ldots]V_1 + a_4[\ldots]V_2. \tag{A.18}$$

Recall that T_1 and T_2 are the total durations of intervals of types I and II respectively; so $T_1 + T_2 = T$. Similarly, V_1 and V_2 are the total volumes of cells generated by the source during intervals of types I and II respectively; so $V_1 + V_2 = V$. Then the charge is equivalent to

$$\sum_{i=1}^{T/t} \max\{a_1 t + a_3 v_i,\ a_2 t + a_4 v_i\},$$

where v_i is the number of cells which the source generates during the ith charging interval. Notice that the charge is an increasing and convex function of v_i.

Numerical comparison of two charging schemes

To illustrate these ideas, we give some numerical results for a theoretical model of a video telephone source that has been a popular testbed in other studies. This source alternates between on and off states according to a two-state Markov process. The mean duration of an on phase is 350 ms and the mean duration of an off phase is 650 ms. In the on phase the source produces cells at a constant rate of 64 kbps, and in the off phase it is silent. Thus these sources have mean rate $.35(64) = 22.4$ kbps. Suppose the total bandwidth available to a number of such calls is 155 Mbps. On the basis of peak rate allocation, the switch could carry just $155,000/64 = 2,420$ connections. If there were an infinite buffer then it would be possible to carry $155,000/22.4 = 6,920$ connections.

Suppose the switch has a buffer of 200 ATM cells ($= 84.4$k bits, since a cell is 53 bytes.) This is a typical size in practice. Solving so that A.3 gives about 17.75 (which we take as a target value as $e^{-17.75} \doteq 2 \times 10^{-8}$), we find $n = 6,350$ and the extremising values in equation A.3 of $t = 95$ms and $s = 0.027$. Similar calculations are shown when the bandwidth which is available to these sources is reduced to 50% and 25% of the maximum (perhaps because some of the bandwidth is being used by constant bit rate sources). Other lines in the table show results for buffers of smaller and larger sizes.

B (cells)	C (kbps)	n	γ	t ms	s (kb)$^{-1}$
50	155,000	6,315	17.6	46	0.054
	155,000	6,350	17.6	95	0.027
200	77,500	3,075	17.6	116	0.032
	37,750	1,430	17.7	143	0.039
2000	155,000	6,505	17.5	359	0.008
10000	155,000	6,705	17.9	1332	0.003

The following tables show values of

$$(a) \ \frac{1}{st} \log \mathbf{E} e^{sX[0,t]} \quad (b) \ \frac{1}{st} \log \mathbf{E} \phi(sX[0,t]) \quad (c) \ \frac{1}{st} \log \left[\left(1 - \frac{m}{h} \right) + \frac{m}{h} e^{sht} \right]$$

for $t = 150$ ms and $t = 1000$ ms. Here $\phi(x)$ denotes the piecewise linear function that bounds e^x for a tax-band scheme with two bands, where the point at which the two bands are divided is chosen to minimise (b). The data for $t = 150$ demonstrates that there is not much difference for typical values of t and s. The data for $t = 1000$ demonstrates that the tax-band scheme can give a substantially better approximation to the effective bandwidth when t is large. However, as we have seen, the circumstance in which it is appropriate to take t large (relative to the mean durations of on and off phases of a source) is when there is a large buffer; in this case s is small and there is not much difference between the two charging schemes.

	$t = 150$ ms				$t = 1000$ ms		
s	(a)	(b)	(c)	s	(a)	(b)	(c)
0	22.4	22.4	22.4	0	22.4	22.4	22.4
0.001	22.46	22.46	22.47	0.001	22.56	22.63	22.87
0.01	22.97	23.00	23.11	0.01	24.04	24.73	27.29
0.05	25.34	25.51	26.03	0.05	31.05	34.34	44.46
0.1	28.42	28.75	29.82	0.1	38.80	42.75	53.53
0.2	34.48	35.09	37.03	0.2	47.94	50.49	58.75
0.5	47.04	47.74	50.20	0.5	56.61	57.36	61.90
1	54.79	55.18	57.00	1	60.15	60.36	62.95
2	59.23	59.38	60.50	2	62.04	62.09	63.48
5	62.05	62.08	62.60	5	63.21	63.21	63.79
∞	64	64	64	∞	64	64	64

However, we do expect to see more marked differences when there is a mixture of sources of different types and whose burstiness differs widely. For example, if there are also a small number of sources for which the mean on and off phases are 35 and 65 ms then the extremising values of t and s in equation (A.3) will be much as before (since the proportion of these sources is small). For these sources (and also for a source with even shorter on and off phases) the values of (a)–(c) at $t = 95$ and $s = 0.027$ are

mean on, off	(a)	(b)	(c)
350, 650	23.47	23.51 (+ 0.2%)	23.62 (+ 0.6%)
35, 65	22.84	23.01 (+ 0.7%)	24.62 (+ 3.4%)
3.5, 6.5	22.44	22.57 (+ 0.6%)	24.62 (+ 5.3%)

Thus to charge for these sources simply on the basis of T and V results in 3.4% over-charging relative to their effective bandwidths, even when the most favorable tariff of this type is used. Users whose sources are of this type will prefer to be charged according to the tax-band scheme or to smooth their traffic in a small buffer so that it has a smaller peak rate.

For this model of Markov modulated on-off sources we can conclude that

1. typical values of t are 100–200 ms;

2. typical values of s are 0.01–0.04 per kb;

3. the quantities of interest change slowly in s, t, so it is not important that these be determined very accurately;

4. as buffer or bandwidth increases, t increases and s decreases;

5. the charge based on T and V over-charges, as compared to a charge which is simply the effective bandwidth, by about 0.6%;

6. the charge based on a tax-band scheme using two bands over-charges by about 0.1%.

A.5 Accuracy and fairness

There are many considerations that will influence the price of network services, such as marketing and regulation. The theory presented in the previous sections focuses on an important part of the charging activity: the part which aims to assess a connection's relative resource usage. This raises the interesting question of when one charging scheme is more accurate than another, where accuracy is measured not in terms of the absolute value of charges, but in terms of their correspondence to actual network usage.

Let $\tilde{\alpha}$ be some approximation of the bound of the effective bandwidth $\alpha(x)$. The three different approximations we consider are the simple bound, the peak/mean bound, and the inverted T approximation. The "simple" bound is given by the following equation:

$$\tilde{\alpha}_{sb}(m, \mathbf{h}) = \frac{1}{st} \log \left[1 + \frac{tm}{H(t)} \left(e^{sH(t)} - 1 \right) \right] , \qquad (A.19)$$

where

$$H(t) := \min_{k \in K} \{ \rho_k t + \beta_k \} . \qquad (A.20)$$

If t=1, then the bound (A.19) reduces to

$$\tilde{\alpha}_{pm}(m, \mathbf{h}) = \frac{1}{s} \log \left[1 + \frac{m}{h} (e^{sh} - 1) \right] , \qquad (A.21)$$

which is appropriate when the buffers are small and the argument minimising expression (A.20) corresponds to the peak rate h. We refer to this as the "peak/mean" bound. Charges based on this bound were discussed above.

When the time parameter and the leaky bucket parameters are rational, and the amount of workload produced by a source is integral, then the worst case traffic (for given values of the link operating parameters s, t) consists of blocks of an inverted T pattern repeating periodically or with random gaps. We consider here the periodic pattern shown in Figure A.3, which gives the following effective bandwidth approximation (referred to as the "inverted T " approximation):

$$\tilde{\alpha}_\perp(m, \mathbf{h}) = \frac{1}{st} \log E \left[e^{sX_\perp[0,t]} \right] , \qquad (A.22)$$

where $X_\perp[0, t]$ denotes the amount of load produced by the inverted T pattern in a time interval of length t. The expected value in the right-hand side of (A.22) can be computed analytically.

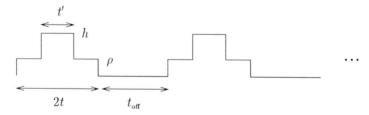

Figure A.3: Periodic pattern for the inverted T approximation. $t' = \frac{\beta}{h-\rho}$, $t_{off} = \frac{(2t-t')\rho+t'h}{m} - 2t$

Ideally we would like the relative charges using the approximation of the bound of the effective bandwidth $\tilde{\alpha}$ to be as close as possible to those using the actual effective bandwidth

α. Hence, if (with a slight abuse of notation) we denote by $\tilde{\alpha}(x)$ and $\alpha(x)$ the corresponding charges for a connection x, then we would like to have $\tilde{\alpha}(y)/\tilde{\alpha}(x) \approx \alpha(y)/\alpha(x)$, for any two connections x, y. A reasonable measure of the *unfairness* of an approximation for a set of connections is the standard deviation of $\tilde{\alpha}(x)/(\mu\alpha(x))$, where μ is the average of $\tilde{\alpha}(x)/\alpha(x)$ as x ranges over the connection set. We will refer to this as the *unfairness index* $\mathcal{U}$. For example, an approximation that consistently overestimates the true effective bandwidth by some constant factor will have $\mathcal{U} = 0$, hence would be preferable than some other approximation which, on the average, is closer to the true effective bandwidth, but whose ratio $\tilde{\alpha}(x)/\alpha(x)$ varies (hence $\mathcal{U} > 0$).

Recall that the parameters s, t characterise the link's operating point. The results we present are for s, t values that are typical for the specific capacity and buffer size. These are computed using relations (A.1) and (A.3), where the expectation in (A.1) is replaced by the empirical mean, which is estimated from the traces [50] (related software is available at [110]). We assume that specific pairs (s, t), which are computed off-line, will characterise different periods of day.

Finally, we assume that users are rational and that they know their traffic profile, hence they can compute their actual mean rates and select the optimal leaky bucket parameters for the whole duration of the call.

Internet WAN traffic

We first consider Internet Wide Area Network (WAN) traffic using the Bellcore Ethernet trace BC-Oct89Ext[5] [87], which has a duration of 122797 seconds. We assume that a customer is policed by two leaky buckets $\mathbf{h} = \{(h, 0), (\rho, \beta)\}$, and assume that traffic is shaped in a 200 ms buffer. This reduces the peak rate to $h = 0.88$ Mbps. The pairs (ρ, β) for which no traffic is discarded by the policer form a curve, which we call the indifference curve G (Figure A.4).

From the initial Bellcore trace we created a set of 15 non-overlapping trace segments, each with duration 8186 seconds (approximately 2.5 hours). For this set, we wish to compare the three different charging schemes based on approximations (A.19), (A.21) and (A.22) according to the unfairness index $\mathcal{U}$ defined above.

We consider values of s, t which are typical for link capacity $C = 34$ Mbps , buffer size $B = 0.25 \times 10^6$ bytes and $B = 1 \times 10^6$ bytes, and target overflow probability equal to 10^{-6}.

Figure A.5 shows that the unfairness for the simple bound and inverted T approximations is close, and much smaller than that for the peak/mean bound. Furthermore, while the unfairness for the former two approximations decreases when the buffer size increases, this is not the case for the peak/mean bound. This is expected because the peak/mean bound becomes accurate for small values of t, which are realised for small buffer sizes.

---

[5]Obtained from The Internet Traffic Archive, <http://www.acm.org/sigcomm/ITA/>.

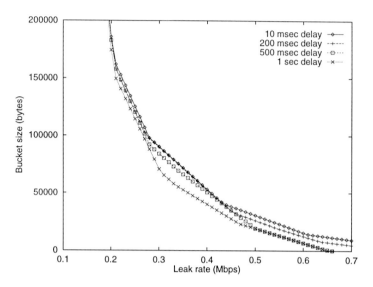

Figure A.4: Indifference curve $G(d)$ for theBellcore trace.

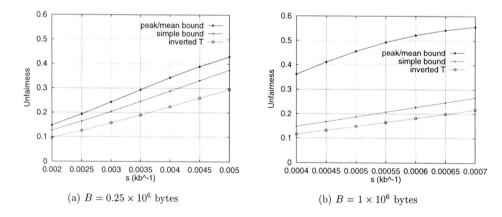

(a) $B = 0.25 \times 10^6$ bytes

(b) $B = 1 \times 10^6$ bytes

Figure A.5: Unfairness for $C = 34$ Mbps and two buffer sizes.

MPEG-1 compressed video traffic

In this section we consider the two pricing schemes based on the simple bound (A.19) and the inverted T approximation (A.22). Because the peak/mean bound is a special case of the simple bound for $t = 1$, it will always be less accurate than it. For this reason we do not consider it further. The specific issue we investigate is how the fairness of the effective bandwidth bounds is affected by the link parameters (capacity and buffer) and traffic smoothing.

Our investigations involve the MPEG-1 [61] compressed video traces[6] shown in Table A.1. Three sets of video traffic are used in our experiments: *movies, news* and *talk shows.* These were created by breaking the cell streams containing the MPEG-1 traffic into non-overlapping segments, each with a duration of approximately 3 minutes (4500 frames). The resulting *movies* set contained 54 segments, the *news* set contained 16 segments, and the *talk shows* set contained 18 segments.

Unfairness for various link capacities and buffer sizes

Figure A.6 compares the fairness of the effective bandwidth bounds for various link capacities and buffer sizes. Observe that the fairness of the simple bound and inverted T pricing schemes, in general, increases when the link capacity and buffer size increases. However, this depends on the time scale t of the system (link and multiplexed traffic). For example, at a link with capacity 155 Mbps (Figure A.6(b)), the fairness of the simple charging schemes does not change significantly when the buffer is increased from 1 msec (≈ 351 cells) to 8 msec (≈ 2811 cells). However, it does increase when the buffer increases to 16 msec (≈ 5622 cells). This can be explained as follows. For small values of t, which are typical for buffer sizes up to 8 msec, the leaky bucket does not produce a tight bound. On the other hand, for the larger time scales which are typical for a 16 msec buffer, the leaky bucket produces a tighter bound.

Effects of traffic smoothing on unfairness

In the results shown in Figure A.7, the traces are smoothed such that cells produced during two consecutive frames are evenly spaced throughout the duration of the two frames. Comparing Figure A.7 with Figure A.6, we observe that traffic smoothing has an effect on pricing up to a certain buffer size: 8 msec (≈ 2811 cells) for capacity 155 Mbps, and 4 msec (≈ 5660 cells) for capacity 622 Mbps. Again, this is related to the time scale of the system. For large buffer sizes, the time scale t is large, and smoothing traffic in a smaller time scale has no effect.

---

[6]Made available by O. Rose [103], at ftp://ftp-info3.informatik.uni-wuerzburg.de/pub/

Movies	
bond	James Bond: Goldfinger
dino	Jurassic Park
lambs	The Silence of the Lambs
movieprev	Movie Preview
star	Star Wars
terminator	Terminator II
News	
news1	News
news2	News
Talk Shows	
talk1	Talk show
talk2	Talk show

Table A.1: MPEG-1 sequences. The frame pattern of the sequences is IBBPBBPBBPBB and their frame rate is 25 frames per second.

A.6   Charging and acceptance control

In this section we outline how the framework of section 3 allows the development of measurement-based connection acceptance mechanisms sympathetic to statistical sharing (for a fuller development see [63]). Again our emphasis will be on the case where statistical sharing is important over short timescales, comparable or less than round-trip delay times across the network.

Suppose that a resource has accepted connections $1, 2, \dots, J$, and write (a_j, b_j) for the coefficients $(a(h, m), b(h, m))$ describing the choice of a tangent to the effective bandwidth function of connection j (see equation (A.15) and Figure A.1). Suppose that the resource measures the arriving workload $A_j[t]$ from connection j over a period of length t (the same length t as appears in the definition (A.1)), and let $M_j = A_j[t]/t$. Define the *effective load* on the resource to be

$$\sum_{j=1}^{J}(a_j + b_j M_j). \tag{A.23}$$

Then a connection acceptance control may be defined as follows. A new request for a connection should be accepted or rejected according as the most recently calculated effective load lies below or above a threshold value, with the proviso that if a request is rejected then later requests are also rejected until either a short interval has elapsed or an existing connection has terminated.

If admitted calls have high peak-to-mean ratios then the above control may amount to

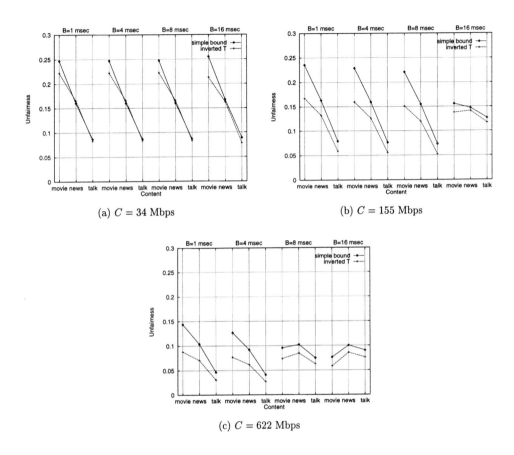

(a) $C = 34$ Mbps

(b) $C = 155$ Mbps

(c) $C = 622$ Mbps

Figure A.6: The fairness of the effective bandwidth bounds increases in general as the link capacity and buffer size increase. [MPEG-1 video traffic (each segment has duration $\approx$ 3 minutes)]

comparison of $\sum_j b_j M_j$ with a threshold, where b_j is the variable charge for call j. It may seem that such a call admission control is naively straightforward: after all, the measurements M_j will be highly variable, according to whether the source is on, off or somewhere in between. In [66] it is shown that such a simple call admission control can be both robust and efficient: an example is analysed where a 1 in 10^9 condition on loss rates is combined with a utilisation at least 97% of that achievable when mean rates are known.

Both the charging mechanism of section 3 and the connection acceptance control described above use bounding tangents to the effective bandwidth function. If the same tangents are used for both purposes then the effective load has a natural interpretation as an aggregate charge at the resource over a recent short period. But there is no necessity for identical

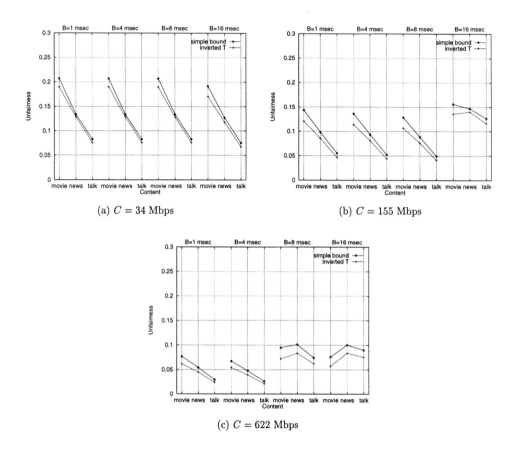

(a) $C = 34$ Mbps

(b) $C = 155$ Mbps

(c) $C = 622$ Mbps

Figure A.7: Comparison of this figure with Figure A.6 shows that traffic smoothing increases the fairness of the effective bandwidth bounds up to a certain buffer size, which depends on the link capacity. The buffer sizes for which smoothing has a very small effect are such that the time parameter t is larger than the smoothing interval which is two frame times (=80 msec). [MPEG-1 video traffic (each segment has duration $\approx$ 3 minutes)]

tangents to be used for charging and for connection acceptance. Thus users choosing a small peak rate might be offered no further choice of tariff, so that for charging purposes the effective bandwidth function is bounded by a single tangent. In contrast, the resource might choose its tangent to the effective bandwidth function at the point where the mean rate is the long-term observed average for traffic with that peak rate. Or, if distinct effective bandwidth functions are used for charging and connection acceptance control, then the resource might still choose its tangent according to the user's declaration of expected mean rate.

Distinct effective bandwidth functions might be appropriate for charging and connection acceptance control, since the two areas have quite different timescales and requirements for precision. Connection acceptance control must use accurately calculated effective bandwidths, based on the buffer sizes, port speeds and other features of current hardware to make decisions on connections as they request connection, otherwise quality of service guarantees on loss rates may be compromised. While charges need to be precisely defined, they influence users' behaviour and software application design over much longer timescales, where features of hardware may evolve. Thus tariff design might include consideration of the possible effective bandwidth functions appropriate to future hardware and network scale.

A fuller discussion of connection acceptance control would consider multiple constraints of the form (A.4), (A.5), network routing, and the shadow prices associated with different physical and logical resources (cf. [80]). The analysis and implementation of dynamic routing schemes often use Lagrange multipliers or shadow prices for each of the internal resources of the network, but only certain aggregates of this network detail might usefully influence charges to users. For example, competition between network providers might appear to users as a choice between routes, and averaged congestion measures might motivate a predictable time-of-day element to charges for delay-sensitive connections. We shall see in Appendix B that there are other ways of providing dynamic feedback on congestion, for users able to respond to such feedback.

Appendix B

Pricing for elastic services

B.1 Overview

The Available Bit Rate (ABR) transfer capability of ATM networks, and TCP traffic over the Internet, are examples of *elastic* traffic services which use applications that are able to modify their data transfer rates according to the available bandwidth within the network. How should this available bandwidth be shared between competing streams of elastic traffic?

There is a substantial literature on rate control algorithms, reviewed by Hernandez-Valencia et al. [74]. Key early papers of Jacobson [76] and Chiu and Jain [42] identified the advantages of adaptive schemes that either increase flows linearly or decrease flows multiplicatively, depending on the absence or presence of congestion. Important papers of Bolot and Shankar [33], Fendick et al. [56] and Bonomi et al. [35] have analysed the stability of networks with a single bottleneck resource, where congestion is signalled by the build-up of a queue at the bottleneck's buffer, and where propagation delays are significant. (In wide-area networks propagation times may be significant in comparison with queueing times: for a transatlantic link of 600 Megabits per second, ten million bits may be in flight between queues). The framework we adopt in this Appendix is simpler than that analysed by these authors in that we directly model only rates and not queue lengths, but more complex in that we model a network with an arbitrary number of bottleneck resources. Theoretical work [52], [82] on queues serving the superposition of a large number of streams indicates circumstances when the busy period preceding a buffer overflow may be relatively short, and several authors have argued the advantages of preventing queue build-up through the bounding of rates (see, for example, Charny et al. [41]).

Any discussion of the performance of a rate control scheme must address the issue of fairness, since there exist situations where a given scheme might maximise network throughput, for example, while denying access to some users. The most commonly discussed fairness criterion is that of max-min fairness: loosely, a set of rates is max-min fair if no rate may be increased without simultaneously decreasing another rate which is already smaller. In a network with a single bottleneck resource max-min fairness implies an equal share of the resource for each flow through it. Mazumdar et al. [94] have pointed out that from a game-theoretic standpoint such an allocation is not special, and have advocated instead the Nash bargaining solution, from cooperative game theory, as capturing natural assumptions as to what constitutes fairness.

The need for networks to operate in a public (and therefore potentially non-cooperative) environment has stimulated work on charging schemes for broadband networks: see MacKie-Mason and Varian [90] for a description of a 'smart market' based on a per-packet charge when the network is congested, and the collection edited by McKnight and Bailey [95] for several further papers and references. Kelly [84] describes a model for elastic traffic in which a user chooses the charge per unit time that the user is willing to pay; thereafter the user's rate is determined by the network according to a proportional fairness criterion applied to the rate per unit charge. It was shown that a system optimum is achieved when users' choices of charges and the network's choice of allocated rates are in equilibrium. There remained the question of how the proportional fairness criterion could be implemented in a large-scale network. In section 2 of this Appendix we show that simple rate control algorithms, using additive increase/multiplicative decrease rules or explicit rates based on resource shadow prices, can provide stable convergence to proportional fairness per unit charge, even in the presence of random effects and delays.

The processes by which supply and demand reach equilibrium have, of course, long been a central concern of economists, and there exists a substantial body of theory on the stability of various auction mechanisms [27], [73], [115]. The rate control algorithms described in this paper may be viewed as distributed implementations of an auction mechanism (or 'smart market' of [90]), searching for market clearing prices. We show that the structure of a communication network provides a natural context within which to investigate the consequences for a distributed auction mechanism of stochastic perturbations and time lags.

The organisation of this Appendix is as follows. In section 2 we review the work of Kelly et al. [85] and present an approach to pricing based on a proportional fairness criterion. In section 3 we describe a model based on the work of Courcoubetis et al. [51] and present two possible ABR implementations of proportionally fair pricing. In section 4 we review the work of Courcoubetis et al. [49], which proposes a pricing scheme based on the sharing of effective usage rather than the sharing of simple rates.

B.2   Proportionally fair pricing

The basic model

Consider a network with a set J of *resources*, and let C_j be the finite capacity of resource j, for $j \in J$. Let a *route* r be a non-empty subset of J, and write R for the set of possible routes. Set $A_{jr} = 1$ if $j \in r$, so that resource j lies on route r, and set $A_{jr} = 0$ otherwise. This defines a $0 - 1$ matrix $A = (A_{jr}, j \in J, r \in R)$.

Associate a route r with a user, and suppose that if a rate x_r is allocated to user r then this has utility $U_r(x_r)$ to the user.

Assume that the utility $U_r(x_r)$ is an increasing, strictly concave and continuously differentiable function of x_r over the range $x_r \geq 0$ (following Shenker [106], we call traffic that leads to such a utility function *elastic* traffic). Assume further that utilities are additive, so that the aggregate utility of rates $x = (x_r, r \in R)$ is $\sum_{r \in R} U_r(x_r)$. Let $U = (U_r(\cdot), r \in R)$ and $C = (C_j, j \in J)$. Under this model the system optimal rates solve the following problem.

$SYSTEM(U, A, C)$:

$$\text{maximise} \quad \sum_{r \in R} U_r(x_r)$$
$$\text{subject to} \quad Ax \leq C$$
$$\text{over} \quad x \geq 0.$$

While this optimisation problem is mathematically fairly tractable (with a strictly concave objective function and a convex feasible region), it involves utilities U that are unlikely to be known by the network. We are thus led to consider two simpler problems.

Suppose that user r may choose an amount to pay per unit time, w_r, and receives in return a flow x_r proportional to w_r, say $x_r = w_r/\lambda_r$, where λ_r could be regarded as a charge per unit flow for user r. Then the utility maximisation problem for user r is as follows.

$USER_r(U_r; \lambda_r)$:

$$\text{maximise} \quad U_r\left(\frac{w_r}{\lambda_r}\right) - w_r$$
$$\text{over} \quad w_r \geq 0.$$

Suppose next that the network knows the vector $w = (w_r, r \in R)$, and attempts to maximise the function $\sum_r w_r \log x_r$. The network's optimisation problem is then as follows.

$NETWORK(A, C; w)$:

$$\text{maximise} \quad \sum_{r \in R} w_r \log x_r$$
$$\text{subject to} \quad Ax \leq C$$
$$\text{over} \quad x \geq 0.$$

It is known [84] that there always exist vectors $\lambda = (\lambda_r, r \in R)$, $w = (w_r, r \in R)$ and $x = (x_r, r \in R)$, satisfying $w_r = \lambda_r x_r$ for $r \in R$, such that w_r solves $USER_r(U_r; \lambda_r)$ for $r \in R$ and x solves $NETWORK(A, C; w)$; further, the vector x is the unique solution to $SYSTEM(U, A, C)$.

A vector of rates $x = (x_r, r \in R)$ is *proportionally fair* if it is feasible, that is $x \geq 0$ and $Ax \leq C$, and if for any other feasible vector x^*, the aggregate of proportional changes is zero or negative:

$$\sum_{r \in R} \frac{x_r^* - x_r}{x_r} \leq 0. \tag{B.1}$$

If $w_r = 1, r \in R$, then a vector of rates x solves $NETWORK(A, C; w)$ if and only if it is proportionally fair. Such a vector is also the Nash bargaining solution (satisfying certain axioms of fairness [62]), and, as such, has been advocated in the context of telecommunications by Mazumdar et al. [94].

A vector x is such that the *rates per unit charge* are proportionally fair if x is feasible, and if for any other feasible vector x^*

$$\sum_{r \in R} w_r \frac{x_r^* - x_r}{x_r} \leq 0. \tag{B.2}$$

The relationship between the conditions (B.1) and (B.2) is well illustrated when $w_r, r \in R$, are all integral. For each $r \in R$, replace the single user r by w_r identical sub-users, construct the proportionally fair allocation over the resulting $\sum_r w_r$ users, and provide to user r the aggregate rate allocated to its w_r sub-users; then the resulting rates *per unit charge* are proportionally fair. This construction also illustrates the need to adapt the notion of fairness to a non-cooperative context, where it is possible for a single user to represent itself as several distinct users. It is straightforward to check [84] that a vector of rates x solves $NETWORK(A, C; w)$ if and only if the rates per unit charge are proportionally fair.

We note in passing that if, for a fixed set of users and arbitrary parameters $w = (w_r, r \in R)$, the network solves $NETWORK(A, C; w)$, then the resulting rates $x = (x_r, r \in R)$ solve a variant of the problem $SYSTEM(U, A, C)$, with a weighted objective function $\sum_r \alpha_r U_r(x_r)$ where $\alpha_r = w_r/(x_r U_r'(x_r))$ for $r \in R$. Thus a choice of the parameters $w = (w_r, r \in R)$ by the network (rather than by users) corresponds to an implicit weighting by the network of the relative utilities of different users, with weights related to the users' various marginal utilities.

Under the decomposition of the problem $SYSTEM(U, A, C)$ into the problems $NETWORK(A, C; w)$ and $USER_r(U_r; \lambda_r)$, $r \in R$, the utility function $U_r(x_r)$ is not required by the network, and only appears in the optimisation problem faced by user r. The Lagrangian [117] for the problem $NETWORK(A, C; w)$ is

$$L(x, z; \mu) = \sum_{r \in R} w_r \log x_r + \mu^T (C - Ax - z)$$

where $z \geq 0$ is a vector of slack variables and μ is a vector of Lagrange multipliers (or shadow prices). Then

$$\frac{\partial L}{\partial x_r} = \frac{w_r}{x_r} - \sum_{j \in r} \mu_j,$$

and so the unique optimum to the primal problem is given by

$$x_r = \frac{w_r}{\sum_{j \in r} \mu_j} \tag{B.3}$$

where $(x_r, r \in R)$, $(\mu_j, j \in J)$ solve

$$\mu \geq 0, \quad Ax \leq C, \quad \mu^T (C - Ax) = 0 \tag{B.4}$$

and relation (B.3). Furthermore the associated dual problem quickly reduces, after elision of terms not dependent on the shadow prices μ, to the following problem:

$DUAL(A, C; w)$:

$$\text{maximise} \quad \sum_{r \in R} w_r \log(\sum_{j \in r} \mu_j) - \sum_{j \in J} \mu_j C_j$$
$$\text{over} \quad \mu \geq 0.$$

While the problems $NETWORK(A, C; w)$ and $DUAL(A, C; w)$ are mathematically tractable, it would be difficult to implement a solution in any centralised manner. A centralised processor, even if it were itself completely reliable and could cope with the complexity of the computational task involved, would have its lines of communication through the network vulnerable to delays and failures. Rather, interest focuses on algorithms which are decentralised and of a simple form: the challenge is to understand how such algorithms can be designed so that the network as a whole reacts intelligently to perturbations. Next we describe two simple classes of decentralised algorithm, designed to implement solutions to relaxations of the problems $NETWORK(A, C; w)$ and $DUAL(A, C; w)$.

A primal algorithm

Consider the system of differential equations

$$\frac{d}{dt} x_r(t) = \kappa \left(w_r - x_r(t) \sum_{j \in r} \mu_j(t) \right) \tag{B.5}$$

where

$$\mu_j(t) = p_j \left(\sum_{s: j \in s} x_s(t) \right). \tag{B.6}$$

(Here and throughout we assume that, unless otherwise specified, r ranges over the set R and j ranges over the set J). We may motivate the relations (B.5)–(B.6) in several ways. For example, suppose that $p_j(y)$ is a price charged by resource j, per unit flow through resource j, when the total flow through resource j is y. Then by adjusting the flow on route r, $x_r(t)$, in accordance with equations (B.5)–(B.6), the network attempts to equalise the aggregate cost of this flow, $x_r(t) \sum_{j \in r} \mu_j(t)$, with a target value w_r, for every $r \in R$. In section 3 we shall describe how such algorithms may be implemented in an ATM network.

For an alternative motivation, suppose that resource j generates a continuous stream of feedback signals at rate $p_j(y)$ when the total flow through resource j is y. Suppose further that when resource j generates a feedback signal, a copy is sent to each user r whose route passes through resource j, where it is interpreted as a congestion indicator requiring some reduction in the flow x_r. Then equation (B.5) corresponds to a response by user r that comprises two components: a steady increase at rate proportional to w_r, and a multiplicative decrease at rate proportional to the stream of feedback signals received. (For early discussions of algorithms with additive increase and multiplicative decrease see Chiu and Jain [42] and Jacobson [76]; Hernandez-Valencia et al. [74] review several algorithms based on congestion indication feedback.)

We establish that under mild regularity conditions on the functions p_j, $j \in J$, the expression

$$\mathcal{U}(x) = \sum_{r \in R} w_r \log x_r - \sum_{j \in J} \int_0^{\sum_{s: j \in s} x_s} p_j(y) dy \tag{B.7}$$

provides a Lyapunov function for the system of differential equations (B.5)–(B.6), that is, a function which steadily increases towards its maximimum as the system evolves in time ([96], Chapter 5). We can deduce that the vector x maximising $\mathcal{U}(x)$ is a stable point of the system, to which all trajectories converge.

The functions p_j, $j \in J$, may be chosen so that the maximisation of the Lyapunov function $\mathcal{U}(x)$ arbitrarily closely approximates the optimisation problem $NETWORK(A, C; w)$, and, in this sense, is a relaxation of the network problem. We show that certain relaxations correspond naturally to a system objective which takes into account loss or delays, as well as flow rates.

The Lyapunov function (B.7) thus provides an enlightening analysis of the global stability of the system (B.5)–(B.6), and of the relationship between this system and the problem $NETWORK(A, C; w)$. However, the system (B.5)–(B.6) has omitted to model two important aspects of decentralised systems, namely stochastic perturbations and time lags. We analyse these aspects by considering small perturbations to the stable point x.

Stochastic perturbations within the network may well arise from a resource's method of sensing its load. Equation (B.6) represents the response $\mu_j(t)$ of resource j as a continuous function of a load, $y = \sum_{s:j \in s} x_s$, which is assumed known. In practice a resource may assess its load by an error-prone measurement mechanism, and then choose a feedback signal from a small set of possible signals. (See Hernandez-Valencia et al. [74] and Bonomi et al. [35] for more detailed descriptions of binary feedback and congestion indication rate control algorithms). We describe how such mechanisms motivate various stochastic models of the network. One particular model takes the form

$$dx_r(t) = \kappa \left(w_r dt - x_r(t) \sum_{j \in r} \left(\mu_j(t) dt + \mu_j(t)^{1/2} \varepsilon_j^{1/2} dB_j(t) \right) \right) \qquad (B.8)$$

where $B_j(t)$ is a standard Brownian motion, representing stochastic effects at resource j, and ε_j is a scaling parameter for these effects. If the scaling parameters $\varepsilon_j, j \in J$, are small then the stochastic differential equation (B.8) has a solution of a particularly tractable form (called a multidimensional Ornstein–Uhlenbeck process), centred on the stable point x of the differential equations (B.5)–(B.6). The stationary distribution for $(x_r(t), r \in R)$ is then a multivariate normal distribution, with covariance matrix that can be explicitly calculated in terms of the parameters of the network.

Similarly we describe a model incorporating time lags that generalises equations (B.5)–(B.6), and shall analyse its behaviour close to the stable point x. Our models of stochastic effects and of time-lags provide important insights into the behaviour of the network, and provide a theoretical framework within which to examine the various relationships and trade-offs between speed of convergence, the magnitude of fluctuations about the equilibrium point, and the stability of the network.

A dual algorithm

The equations (B.5)–(B.6) represent a system where rates vary gradually, and shadow prices are given as functions of the rates. Next we consider a system where shadow prices vary gradually, with rates given as functions of the shadow prices. Let

$$\frac{d}{dt} \mu_j(t) = \kappa \left(\sum_{r:j \in r} x_r(t) - q_j\left(\mu_j(t)\right) \right) \qquad (B.9)$$

where

$$x_r(t) = \frac{w_r}{\sum_{k \in r} \mu_k(t)}. \qquad (B.10)$$

The relationship between the algorithm (B.9)–(B.10) and the problem $DUAL(A, C; w)$ parallels that between the primal algorithm (B.5)–(B.6) and the problem $NETWORK(A, C; w)$, and, again, we may motivate the algorithm in several ways. For example, suppose that $q_j(\eta)$ is the flow through resource j which generates a price at resource j of η. Then an economist would describe the right hand side of equation (B.9) as the vector of excess demand at prices $(\mu_j(t), j \in J)$, and would recognise equations (B.9)–(B.10) as a tatonnement process by which prices adjust according to supply and demand (Varian [115], Chapter 21).

We establish that under mild regularity conditions on the functions q_j, $j \in J$, the expression

$$\mathcal{V}(\mu) = \sum_{r \in R} w_r \log \left(\sum_{j \in r} \mu_j \right) - \sum_{j \in J} \int_0^{\mu_j} q_j(\eta) d\eta \tag{B.11}$$

provides a Lyapunov function for the system of differential equations (B.9)–(B.10), and we deduce that the vector μ maximising $\mathcal{V}(\mu)$ is a stable point of the system, to which all trajectories converge. Further, by appropriate choice of the functions $q_j, j \in J$, the maximisation of the function $\mathcal{V}(\mu)$ can arbitrarily approximate the problem $DUAL(A, C; w)$.

We consider stochastic perturbations of system (B.9)–(B.10), with a typical example taking the form

$$d\mu_j(t) = \kappa \left(\sum_{r:j \in r} \left(x_r(t) dt + x_r(t)^{1/2} \varepsilon_r^{1/2} dB_r(t) \right) - q_j \left(\mu_j(t) \right) dt \right) \tag{B.12}$$

where $B_r(t)$ is a standard Brownian motion, representing stochastic effects associated with the flow on route r. If the scaling parameters $\varepsilon_r, r \in R$, are small then the stationary distribution for $(\mu_j(t), j \in J)$ is centred on the stable point μ of the differential equations (B.9)–(B.10), with a covariance matrix that can be explicitly calculated in terms of the parameters of the network. Also it is possible to analyse the stability of the model (B.9)–(B.10) when time-lags are introduced.

User adaptation

Our analyses of the primal algorithm (B.5)–(B.6) and the dual algorithm (B.9)–(B.10) assume that the parameters $(w_r, r \in R)$ chosen by the users are fixed, at least on the time scales concerned in the analyses. With increasing intelligence embedded in end-systems, users may in the future be able to vary the parameters $(w_r, r \in R)$ even within these short time scales. Both the algorithms may be extended to this situation.

Suppose that user r is able to monitor its rate $x_r(t)$ continuously, and to vary smoothly the parameter $w_r(t)$ so as to track accurately the optimum to $USER_r(U_r; \lambda_r(t))$, where $\lambda_r(t) = w_r(t)/x_r(t)$ is the charge per unit flow to user r at time t. Then, using revised Lyapunov functions, stability of both the primal and dual algorithms may again be established.

In [85] we provide detailed proofs of the various results outlined above, together with some numerical illustrations. We also extend the discussion to include routing control.

Concluding remarks

In this section we have addressed the issue of how available bandwidth within a large-scale broadband network should be shared between competing streams of elastic traffic. An optimisation framework leads to a decomposition of the overall system problem into a separate problem for each user, in which the user chooses a rate per unit time that the user is willing to pay, and one for the network; we have shown that two classes of rate control algorithm are naturally associated with the objective functions appearing in, respectively, the primal and dual formulations of the network's problem. In consequence the algorithms provide natural implementations of proportionally fair pricing.

B.3 Dynamic pricing for ABR services

In this section we discuss how the pricing schemes discussed in section B.2 can be implemented using the closed loop rate-based congestion control framework of the Available Bit Rate (ABR) service category. The ABR service is one of the five service categories identified by the ATM Forum [60] and is intended for "elastic" traffic which has no strict requirements on delay or delay variance. Applications using this service are assumed to respond appropriately to congestion control messages they receive from the network. In addition, they may specify some Minimum Cell Rate (MCR), below which they will not be asked to fall.

Because our approach utilises mechanisms provided by ABR's rate-based flow control, it imposes no additional communication overhead, while the added complexity at the switches and end-systems is small. According to the approach, prices depend on the demand for bandwidth and are adjusted in a decentralised and iterative manner. When the system (network and users) reaches equilibrium, the demand will equal the supply of bandwidth. In the implementation based on the distributed and iterative solution of the System and User Problems of section B.2, the network posts the price per unit of bandwidth to each user. Based on this price, the user selects the bandwidth he wishes to send with. In the implementation based on the dual algorithm of section B.2, the explicit rate that the network sends back to the user, which is the maximum rate the user is allowed to send with, is a function of the user's willingness-to-pay (price per unit of time) and the current price per unit of bandwidth. The latter is adjusted, as before, in a decentralised and iterative manner.

Implementation of dynamic prices

The solution to the System and User Problems can be computed in a decentralised manner if at each link l, the price per unit of rate μ_l is increased or decreased if $C_l < \sum_{i:l\in R_i} x_i$ or $C_l > \sum_{i:l\in R_i} x_i$, respectively, where C_l is the bandwidth for ABR connections, x_i is the rate of connection i, and R_i is the set of links connection i traverses. The update of μ_l can be written as

$$\frac{d}{dt}\mu_l(t) = \kappa \left(\sum_{i:l\in R_i} x_i(t) - C_l \right), \tag{B.13}$$

where κ is some small constant. Prices are updated in time intervals (we will assume that they all have the same length) whose duration depends on how fast the aggregate demand $\sum_i x_i(t)$ changes. This interval (price update interval) should not be less than the interval from the time new prices are posted until the time the users' responses to these prices are received by the network, i.e. one round-trip delay.

Next we discuss how to implement dynamic prices within the framework of ABR congestion control.

According to ABR rate-based congestion control [60], every source sends special control cells, called Resource Management (RM) cells, either periodically or after a specific number of data cells carrying user information (Figure B.1). When the destination receives an RM cell (called *forward RM* cell), it copies its information to a *backward RM* cell which it sends back to the source. When an intermediate switch detects congestion on one of its links, it sets a congestion indication bit and (optionally) places a rate in the Explicit Rate (ER) field of all backward RM cells traversing that link.[1] While the source does not receive RM cells, or while it receives RM cells with the congestion bit set, it decreases its cell rate by some percentage (multiplicative decrease). Furthermore, its cell rate must always be smaller than the explicit rate in the received RM cell. If the source receives an RM cell with the congestion indication bit cleared, it is allowed to increase its cell rate by some additive quantity (additive increase).

To implement the dynamic pricing scheme, switches adjust the price of bandwidth for each of their output links using a discrete version of equation (B.13). This equation requires that the total demand is known to the switches. The latter can be achieved by having every source place its demand in the ER field of the forward RM cells.

Finally, (B.13) requires the price $\lambda_i = \sum_{l\in R_i} \mu_l$ for each connection i. This sum can be created by adding a new price field P in the RM cell. When a backward RM cell is sent by the destination, the value of P is zero. Each switch adds the price μ_l to the amount contained in the price field P of the backward RM cells that traverse link l. When a backward RM cell reaches the source, P will contain the value $\lambda_i = \sum_{l\in R_i} \mu_l$.

Based on the price λ_i in the received RM cell, user i selects an amount of bandwidth based

---

[1]In ATM networks, the forward and backward RM cells follow the same route.

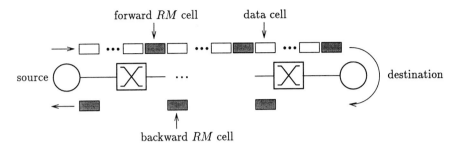

forward RM cell   data cell

source   destination

backward RM cell

Figure B.1: ABR congestion control loop

on some demand function $D_i(\lambda_i)$. The relationship between the demand function and the utility functions U of Section B.2 is the following. Let $D_i(\lambda) = x_i$, where x_i is the solution to $\lambda = U_i'(x_i)$, with $D_i(\lambda) = 0$ if $\lambda \geq U_i'(0)$ and $D_i(\lambda) = \infty$ if $\lambda \leq U_i'(\infty)$. Hence, $D_i(\lambda)$ can be interpreted as the demand of user i when confronted with a price per unit flow of λ.

Simulation results

The goal of our simulation experiments was to study the convergence properties and transient behaviour of the dynamic prices. Rather than simulating the network at the cell level, we have modelled the propagation of rate changes and the propagation of resource management cells, thus achieving considerably smaller simulation times. The simulated network is shown in Figure B.2. All link rates are 155 Mbps. In the three experiments we present here, interswitch distances were 1 km, 100 km, and 1000 km, respectively. Hence we can observe the transient behaviour in both a local and wide area environment.

We assume that switches update the prices $\mu_l(t)$ in discrete time intervals using the following discrete time version of (B.13):

$$\mu_l(t) = \mu_l(t-1) + \kappa \left(\sum_{i:l \in R_i} x_i(t-1) - C_l \right) , \qquad (B.14)$$

where C_l is the capacity of link l used by ABR services and $x_i(t-1)$ is the demand for bandwidth by connection i during the price update interval $t-1$. We assume that $\mu_l(0) = 0$ for all $l \in L$. In [51] we have experimented with a price update function where κ is a function of $\mu_l(t-1)$.

For simplicity, we assume that sources send RM cells in fixed time intervals, equal to $200\mu s$ (interval-based behaviour), rather than after a specific number of data cells (counter-based behaviour). Furthermore, we assume that all sources i have a demand for bandwidth D_i

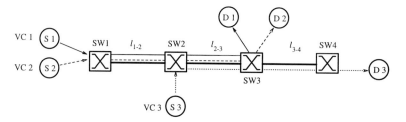

Figure B.2: Simulated network

which decreases exponentially with the price per unit of rate λ_i, i.e., $D_i(\lambda_i) = v_i e^{-\lambda_i}$, where $v_i =155$ Mbps.

In the first experiment, the distance between switches was 1 km and the price update interval was 200μs. The value of parameter κ in (B.14) was set to 0.0005 Mbps^{-1}. This parameter determines the number of round-trip times needed for prices to converge (the number of round-trips is independent of the round-trip delay). Larger values of κ could lead to oscillations. In general, the selection of κ depends on the number of multiplexed Virtual Connections (VCs), the magnitude of changes relative to link capacity, the network topology, and the sources' demands. Figure B.3 shows that prices converge quickly after changes of the input traffic.

In the second experiment, the distance between switches was 100 km and the price update interval was 2.5 msec. Parameter κ in equation (B.14) was 0.001 Mbps^{-1}. From Figure B.4(a), we see that convergence times ($\approx$ 30 msec) are greater than the case of 1 km links ($\approx$ 5-10 msec). In practice, this will not be a problem since in wide area networks, due to the high aggregation of traffic, changes are expected to be smaller and less frequent.

Finally, Figure B.4(b) shows the dynamic behaviour of prices when the distance between switches was 1000 km. The price update interval in this case was 21 msec. In the experiments of Figures B.4(a) and B.4(b) the network reached the equilibrium state after the same number of iterations (approximately 15). However, the convergence time is longer when the distance between switches is larger. This is due to the larger pricing interval (21 msec for 1000 km links compared to 2.5 msec for 100 km links) which is required because of the longer round-trip delay.

An alternative user-network interaction

In order to implement the willingness-to-pay scheme given by the dual algorithm in section B.2, we introduce a new field W in the RM cells which stores the value of the willingness-to-pay w_i of each connection i. Furthermore, as discussed above, we introduce a price field P which stores the sum of the prices per unit of bandwidth on all links which a connection

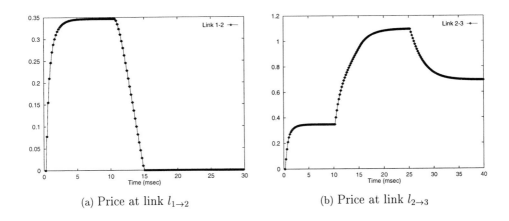

(a) Price at link $l_{1\to2}$ (b) Price at link $l_{2\to3}$

Figure B.3: Results for 1 km switch distances. VC 1 started at 0 msec and terminated at 25 msec, VC 2 started at 0 msec, and VC 3 at 10 msec. Convergence time is approximately 5-10 msec.

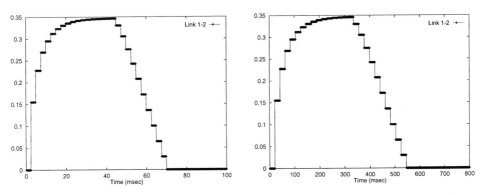

(a) Results for 100 km switch distances. Convergence time is approximately 30 msec.

(b) Results for 1000 km switch distances. Convergence time is approximately 300 msec.

Figure B.4: Price at link $l_{1\to2}$ when the distance between switches is 100 km and 1000 km, respectively. VC 1 and VC 2 started at 0 msec, and VC 3 at 40 msec (for 100 km switch distances) or 300 msec (for 1000 km switch distances).

traverses, i.e. the value $\sum_{l \in R_i} \mu_l$. This sum is created by having each switch add the price μ_l to the price field P in the backward RM cells (refer to Figure B.1). When the first switch connected to the source receives the backward RM cell, it computes $x_i = w_i / \sum_{l \in R_i} \mu_l$ by dividing the two fields W and P, and sets the ER field of the backward RM cells of connection i equal to x_i.

From the received value of $ER = x_i$, the source can compute the current price λ_i $(= w_i/x_i)$. Based on the value of λ_i, the source can select a new willingness-to-pay which it inserts in the forward RM cells.

B.4   Sharing effective usage

It would be advantageous for a network operator that offers elastic traffic services to have a simple way to reason about resource usage and fairness, in order to charge its users while achieving a stable and economically efficient operation of the network. Such an operator would greatly benefit from the existence of a simple but accurate unifying measure of the information transfer capability that the network provides to its users, which could also be used as a basis for charging. How to define such a measure is not at all obvious since different users value the quality of a network service differently. For example, for some users the delay might be the important aspect, whereas for others it might be the average rate of data transfer or the probability of not losing cells.

Traditional measures of resource usage are the average bit rate, and minimum or maximum throughput; these measures do not capture the requirements on network resources by bursty users which value *combinations* of properties, such as the average bit rate *and* the amount of distortion the network will apply to their traffic by delaying its entry into the network. To understand why this is important, consider a charging scheme that charges solely based on the maximum rate, or explicit rate (ER) in ABR terminology, that a user is allowed to send traffic. Also consider two users, one bursty and one smooth. If both users are charged the same amount, both are entitled to the same explicit rate. However, the bursty user, who does not use his explicit rate at all times, is actually using less resources compared to the non-bursty user. Hence, the pricing scheme is unfair to him. Facing such a pricing scheme, the bursty user does not have the incentive to use less than his explicit rate at all times, even though he actually needs less. As a result, network resources will not be used according to the actual needs of users; such incentive incompatibility will induce a non-economically optimal operation of the network.

We propose that a user's information transfer capability, or "effective rate", is measured in terms of the effective bandwidth of the traffic that the user is allowed to send through the network. Users bid for effective bandwidth and the network controls the effective bandwidth of the users' traffic streams by adjusting their explicit rates (ER) in order to achieve the economically fair sharing of resources. Since the effective bandwidth is an adequate measure of resource usage and burstiness, bidding for effective bandwidth allows users to reveal their true preference for network usage, and results in charges that reflect actual resource usage. The approach relies on heavy multiplexing, due to the large capacity of the links, which provides for the accuracy of the effective bandwidth definitions, and on the bursty nature of the traffic, which allows simple effective bandwidth approximations to be used. Since effective bandwidths are naturally defined over long time scales compared to round trip delays, the above control loop is a natural candidate to be implemented on long WAN links.

Sharing bandwidth according to effective usage

Next we discuss how the effective usage resource-sharing scheme, whose mathematical underpinnings are based on the price mechanism described by equations (B.9-B.10) and on the notion of effective bandwidths, can be implemented using ABR's flow control loop. The procedures that we describe refer solely to the operation of switches. The source behaviour is the same as that of a normal ABR source [60]. The user is only required to declare at connection setup (or during renegotiation) his willingness-to-pay w_r (price per unit of time).

We first define the following notation. Let $\tilde{\alpha}_j(m, h)$ be the effective bandwidth using the on/off approximation (B.15) of a connection with mean m and peak h at link j (hence j captures the link's operating point parameters s, t).

$$\tilde{\alpha}_k(s, t) = \frac{1}{st} \log \left[1 + \frac{m}{h} (e^{sht} - 1) \right]. \tag{B.15}$$

Let $\tilde{\alpha}_j^{-1}(m, a)$ be the value of the peak rate h for which $\tilde{\alpha}_j(m, h) = a$, for some positive value a.

The network can control a bursty source so that its effective rate through link j becomes equal to a by measuring the source's mean rate m and limiting the source's peak rate to the value $\tilde{\alpha}_j^{-1}(m, a)$. This can be achieved with ABR rate-based flow control by setting the explicit rate ER of the source equal to $\tilde{\alpha}_j^{-1}(m, a)$. To allow for efficient implementation, simple tables can be used for computing $\tilde{\alpha}_j^{-1}(m, a)$. An accurate estimate of the short term mean for each source is not necessary, since ABR users are more interested in their average explicit rate over a large time interval. Furthermore, the mean rate can be measured once at the first switch of the network and circulated to the intermediate switches via RM cells.

We start by defining the simplest version of our effective flow control implementation where all links of the network have similar operating characteristics, and hence the values of s, t are identical throughout the network[2]. Under the above simplification, we can drop the link subscript from the effective bandwidth formula, which becomes $\tilde{\alpha}(m, h)$ for all links.

---

[2]There is an economic argument based on marginal costs of buffer and bandwidth which supports this argument [48].

The implementation of the scheme is now straightforward. In the RM cells we introduce a new field W storing the value of the willingness-to-pay w_r[3], and a new field P storing the sum of the unit prices for effective bandwidth as posted by the links the connection traverses, i.e., the value $\sum_{k \in r} \mu_k(t)$. This sum is created by having each link add the price $\mu_j(t)$ to the price field P in the backward RM cells. (We assume that the price field P has an initial value zero when the backward RM cell is sent by the destination). The prices $\mu_j(t)$ are computed using a discrete version of (B.9), with the right hand side replaced by the expression

$$\kappa \left(\sum_{r:j \in r} \frac{w_r}{\sum_{k \in r} \mu_k(t)} - C_j \right) , \tag{B.16}$$

where C_j is the effective capacity of link j. When the first switch connected to the source receives the backward RM cell, it computes the value of the effective rate $a_r = w_r / \sum_{k \in r} \mu_k$ (equation (B.10)) by dividing the two fields W, P, and sets the ER field of the RM cells of connection r equal to

$$ER = \tilde{\alpha}^{-1}(m_r, a_r) , \tag{B.17}$$

where m_r is the mean rate of connection r. Such a procedure will provably converge to a fair allocation of the effective rates (as defined by formula (B.15)) which solve the optimisation problem $NETWORK(A, C; w)$.

Now we discuss the general situation where the operating conditions of the various links are different, and hence $\tilde{\alpha}_j(m, h)$ possibly differs for different links j. In this case, the prices at each link are computed as before, but every link j must compute for each connection r the value of its explicit rate $ER' = \tilde{\alpha}_j^{-1}(m_r, a_r)$, where $a_r = w_r / \sum_{k \in r} \mu_k$. The latter requires that all switches know the sum $\sum_{k \in r} \mu_k$. This can be achieved by having the first switch connected to the source copy the value of the price field P of the backward RM cells to the price field P of the forward RM cells, thus making the sum available to all the switches along the route of connection r. After computing ER', the switch sets the value of the ER field of the backward RM cells belonging to connection r equal to the minimum of its current value and ER'.

The achievable utilisation using the above procedures relies on one hand on the degree of multiplexing that takes place, and on the other hand on the accuracy of the effective bandwidth approximation (B.15). However, this formula tends to be conservative [47]. A simple way to remedy this inefficiency, while keeping the essential merits of the approach, is to couple it with direct measurements of the cell loss probability (or equivalently, of the probability that cells are delayed more than some target value). Hence, while the operating point (link prices) is defined as above, we slowly perturb it in order to increase the

---

[3]Either the source can insert its willingness-to-pay w_r in the W field of every RM cell it sends, or declare it at connection setup and have the first switch to which it is connected to insert it in the W field of the RM cells belonging to that connection.

efficiency. This can be done by having each link j measure the buffer overflow probability (or some "proxy" of it), and compute a load factor z_j reflecting the under-utilisation or over-utilisation of the link resources. The effective capacity C_j in (B.16) is replaced by the product $z_j C_j$. While the cell loss probability is higher or lower than the pre-specified maximum value, the value of z_j is decreased or increased, respectively. One anticipates that changing the load factor z_j at a slower time scale compared to the time it takes for prices to converge will eventually stabilise the system at an operating point where all links have the desired maximum utilisation.

The procedures that we have described in this section for implementing the effective usage resource sharing scheme are summarised in Table B.1. Note that these procedures refer solely to the operation of switches. The source behaviour is the same as that of a normal ABR source [60]. The user is only required to declare at connection setup (or during renegotiation) the price per unit of time w_r.

/* Link parameters */
κ : price update parameter
T_p : price update interval
T_m : mean rate measurement interval
C_j : link capacity available for ABR connections

/* Link variables */
μ_j : price per unit of bandwidth
z_j : link load factor

/* Connection variables */
w_r : price per unit of time for connection r
λ_r : price per unit of bandwidth for connection r
V_r : total number of cells of connection r since last mean rate measurement

/* RM cell fields */
ER : Explicit Rate field
P : Price field
W : Willingness-to-pay field

/* functions performed for each link j */

if (forward RM cell received for connection r)
        $\lambda_r = P$
        $w_r = W$

if (backward RM cell received for connection r)
        $P = P + \mu_j$
        $x_r = w_r/\lambda_r$
        $ER' = \tilde{\alpha}^{-1}(m_r, x_r)$
        $ER = \min(ER', ER)$

if (time to perform price update) /* performed once every T_p */
        $\mu_j = \mu_j + \kappa \left(\sum_{r:j \in r} w_r/\lambda_r - z_j C_j \right)$

if (time to measure mean rate) /* performed once every T_m */
        $m_r = V_r/T_\mathrm{p}$

Table B.1: **Switch operation for the effective usage resource sharing scheme.** The first switch to which a source is connected to, in addition to the above, copies the value of the price field P of the backward RM cells (i.e., the value $\lambda_r = \sum_{k \in r} \mu_k$) to the price field P of the forward RM cells. The link load factor z_j changes in a smaller time scale (compared to the price updates), based on whether the loss probability (or probability that the queue length becomes greater than some threshold) is higher or lower than some target value.

Appendix C

CA$hMAN participants

Ascom Monetel, France

Damien Artiges, Michel Besson, Karim Traore

ATecoM GMBH, Germany

Thomas Kusch, Joachim Noll, Frank Winzen

Ericsson AS, Norway

Øyvind Breivik, Snorre Corneliussen, Kevin Kliland, Nina Kloster, Olaf Moe, Trond Borgen Mork, Jon Skandssen, Ngyen Hoi Thanh

ICS-FORTH, Greece

Fotis Charmantzis, Costas Courcoubetis, Stelios Sartzetakis, Vasilios A. Siris, Georgios Stamoulis

Intrasoft, Greece

Nikolaos Antoniu, Vangelis Baltatzis, Georgios Manos, Yannis Markopoulos, Georgios Matinopolous, George Memenios, Gerasimos Tinios

ISS University of Aachen, Germany

Thorsten Groetker, Andrea Mueller

Lucent Technologies (previously Bell Laboratories), USA

Martin Reiman

Lyndewode Research, UK

Frank Kelly, Jackie Pullin, David Songhurst

Royal KPN, Netherlands

Jacob de Bie, Nicky van Foreest, Peter de Graaff, Cor Lavrijsen, Jeroen van Lierop, Michel Mandjes, Marion Schreinemachers, Jan Gerard Snip, Kees van der Wal, Ingrid Zevenbergen

Telenor Research, Norway

Ragnar Andreassen, Einar Edvardsen, Thor Eskedal, Terje Jensen, Terje Ormhaug, Olav Østerbø, Mechthild Stoer

Telscom AG, Switzerland

Rajko Porobic, Sathya Rao

University of California Berkeley, USA

Pravin Varaiya, Jean Walrand

University of Cambridge, UK

Richard Gibbens, Richard Weber

Glossary

AA ABR agent

AAL ATM adaptation layer

ABR Available bit rate

ABT ATM block transfer

ACTS Advanced Communication Technologies and Services

AFS & PCF ATM fault supervision and parameter control function

ALPU ATM layer processing unit

AoC Advice of charge

ASEP Access session end-point

ATC ATM Layer Transfer Capability

ATM Asynchronous Transfer Mode

BISDN Broadband Integrated Services Digital Network

CAC Connection admission control

CA$hMAN Charging and Accounting Schemes in Multiservice ATM Networks

CBR Constant bit rate

CCR Chargeable cell rate

CCU CA$hMAN charging unit

CCUA CA$hMAN charging unit agent

CDR Call detail record

CDV Cell delay variation

CLP Cell loss priority

CMIP Common management information protocol

CO Computational object

CORBA Common object request broker architecture

CPN Customer premises network

CSM Communication session manager

DARPA Defense Advanced Research Projects Agency

DAVIC Digital Audio Visual Council

DBR Deterministic bit rate

DP Device processor

DPE Distributed processing environment

DSP Digital signal processor

EPCU Ericsson Policing and Charging Unit

ER Explicit rate

ET Exchange Terminal

FPGA Field-programmable gate array

GIOP General inter-ORB protocol

GUI Graphical user interface

IA Initial agent

IETF Internet Engineering Task Force

IN Intelligent network

INDEX Internet Demand Experiment

IP Internet Protocol

ITU International Telecommunications Union

LAN Local area network

LEO Low earth orbit

MBONE IP Multicast backbone

Mbps Megabits per second

MBS Maximum burst size

MCR Minimum cell rate

MM Metering manager

MPEG Motion Picture Experts Group

NE Network element

NFC Network flow connection

NFEP Network flow end-point

NMF Network Management Forum

NMSE Normalised mean square error

NNI Network-network interface

OMG Object Management Group

ORB Object request broker

PA Provider agent

PCR Peak cell rate

PDH Plesiochronous digital hierarchy

PNO Public network operator

PSTN Public switched telephone network

PuA Purchasing agent

PVC Permanent virtual circuit

QoS Quality of service

RM Resource management

RSVP Resource reservation setup protocol

RTT Round trip time

SAPU Stand-Alone Policing Unit

SBR Statistical bit rate

SCP Service control point

SCR Sustainable cell rate

SDH Synchronous digital hierarchy

SFC Stream flow connection

SIB Service-independent building block

SNMP Simple network management protocol

SP Service provider

SSEP Service session end-point

TCP Transmission control protocol

TINA Telecommunications Information Network Architecture

TMN Telecommunications Management Network

UA User agent

UAP User application

UBM User billing manager

UBR Unspecified bit rate

UDP User datagram protocol

UMC Usage metering control

UMDF Usage metering data function

UMR Usage metering record

UNI User-network interface

UPC Usage parameter control

USM User session manager

UTM User tariffing manager

VBR Variable bit rate

VC Virtual circuit

VCI Virtual channel identifier

VPI Virtual path identifier

WAN Wide area network

WWW World Wide Web

Bibliography

[1] Accounting Management Architecture, TINA-C Deliverable, Version 1.3.

[2] DAVIC 1.2 Specification, Digital Audio-Visual Council, Geneva, Switzerland.

[3] *Recommendation I.321: B-ISDN protocol reference model and its application.* International Telecommunications Union.

[4] *Recommendation M.3010: Principles for a Telecommunication Management Network.* International Telecommunications Union.

[5] *Recommendation X.734: Event Management Function.* International Telecommunications Union.

[6] B-ISDN Inter Carrier Interface Specification, Usage Measurement Chapter of the B-ICI Specification version 2.0, af-bici-0013.003, December 1995.

[7] *Draft Recommendation M.3400: TMN Management Functions.* International Telecommunications Union, October 1995.

[8] Effective Competition: a Framework for Action, 1995. Oftel statement.

[9] *Recommendation X.742: Usage Metering Function for Accounting Purposes.* International Telecommunications Union, April 1995.

[10] The Common Object Request Broker: Architecture and Specification, July 1995. Object Management Group.

[11] CORBA: Architecture and Specification, OMG, 1996.

[12] *Recommendation I.356: B-ISDN ATM layer cell transfer performance.* International Telecommunications Union, 1996.

[13] *Recommendation I.371: Traffic control and congestion control in B-ISDN.* International Telecommunications Union, 1996.

[14] TMN; Functional Specification of the usage Metering Information Management on the Operation System to Network Element Interface, I-ETS draft, December 1996.

217

[15] Broadband Billing - Equipment to Service Provider Interface, NMF 505 Issue 1, October 1997.

[16] CORBA services: Common Object Services Specification, OMG, 1997.

[17] Micropayments: Are they finally real? *MicroTimes Magazine*, (166), June 1997.

[18] Network Resource Architecture, TINA-C Deliverable, Version 3.0, February 1997.

[19] Promoting Competition in Services over Telecommunication Networks, 1997. Oftel statement.

[20] *Recommendation I.371.1: Traffic Control and Congestion Control in B-ISDN: conformance definitions for ABR and ABT.* International Telecommunications Union, 1997.

[21] *Recommendation X.711: Information technology - Open Systems Interconnection - Common management information protocol: Specification.* International Telecommunications Union, October 1997.

[22] Service Architecture, TINA-C Deliverable, Version 5.0, June 1997.

[23] TINA Business Model and Reference Points, TINA-C Deliverable, Version 4.0, May 1997.

[24] L. Anania and R.J.Solomon. Flat - the minimalist rate. In L.W. McKnight and J.P. Bailey, editors, *Internet Economics*. MIT Press, Cambridge, MA, 1997.

[25] R. Andreassen and M. Stoer. On-line traffic contract renegotiation for aggregated traffic. In P. B. Key and D. G. Smith, editors, *Teletraffic Engineering in a Competitive World: Proceedings of the 16th International Teletraffic Congress*, Edinburgh, 1999. Elsevier, Amsterdam.

[26] R. Andreassen, M. Stoer, and O. Østerbø. Charging ATM internet access, an experiment of usage based ATM charging. In *Colloquium on Charging for ATM - the Reality Arrives*. IEE, London, November 1997.

[27] K. J. Arrow and F. H. Hahn. *General Competitive Analysis*. Oliver and Boyd, Edinburgh, 1971.

[28] R. Baeza-Yates, J. M. Piquer, and P. V. Poblete. The Chilean Internet Connection or I Never Promised You a Rose Garden. In *INET 93 Proceedings*, 1993.

[29] J. P. Bailey and L. W. McKnight. Internet Economics: What Happens When Constituencies Collide. In *INET 95 Proceedings*, 1995.

[30] V. Baltatzis, S. Sartzetakis, and K. Traore. Advanced software systems for usage based charging in broadband multi-service networks. In *Interworking 98*, 1998.

[31] R.E. Barlow, D.J. Bartholomew, J.M. Bremner, and H.D. Brunk. *Statistical Inference under Order Restrictions: the Theory and Application of Isotonic Regression*. John Wiley & Sons, 1972.

[32] R. Bohn, H.-W. Braun, K. C. Claffy, and S. Wolff. Mitigating the coming Internet crunch: multiple service levels via Precedence. Technical report, UCSD, San Diego Supercomputer Center, and NSF, March 1994.

[33] J.-C. Bolot and A.U. Shankar. Dynamic behavior of rate-based flow control mechanisms. *ACM SIGCOMM Computer Commun. Review*, 20:35–49, 1990.

[34] J.-C. Bolot and T. Turletti. Experience with control mechanisms for packet video in the internet. In *SIGCOMM Computer Communication Review*, vol.28, No 1, January 1998.

[35] F. Bonomi, D. Mitra, and J.B. Seery. Adaptive algorithms for feedback-based flow control in high-speed wide-area networks. *IEEE J. Selected Areas in Comm.*, 13:1267–1283, 1995.

[36] D. D. Botvich and N. Duffield. Large deviations, the shape of the loss curve, and economies of scale in large multiplexers. *Queueing Systems*, 20:293–320, 1995.

[37] R. Braden, D. Clark, and S. Shenker. Integrated services in the Internet architecture: an overview. RFC 1633. ISI, MIT, and Xerox PARC, June 1994.

[38] N. Brownlee. New Zealand Experiences with Network Traffic Charging. *Connexions*.

[39] B. Carpenter. Metrics for Internet Settlements. Draft RFC:draft-carpenter-metrics-00.txt. CERN, May 1996.

[40] J. Case, M. Fedor, M. Schoffstall, and J. Davin. Simple network management protocol. Technical Report STD15, RFC 1157, May 1990.

[41] A. Charny, K.K. Ramakrishnan, and A. Lauck. Time scale analysis and scalability issues for explicit rate allocation in ATM networks. *IEEE/ACM Trans. Networking*, 4:569–581, 1996.

[42] D.-M. Chiu and R. Jain. Analysis of the increase and decrease algorithms for congestion avoidance in computer networks. *Comput. Networks ISDN Systems*, 17:1–14, 1989.

[43] D. D. Clark. Adding service discrimination to the Internet. *Telecommunications Policy*, 20:169–181, 1996. Also available at <http://ana-www.lcs.mit.edu/anaweb/papers.html>.

[44] D. D. Clark. A model for cost allocation and pricing in the Internet. In L. W. McKnight and J. P. Bailey, editors, *Internet Economics*. MIT Press, Cambridge, MA, 1997.

[45] D. D. Clark, S. Shenker, and L. Zhang. Supporting real-time application in an integrated services packet network: Architecture and mechanism. In *ACM SIGCOM 92 Proceedings*, August 1992.

[46] National Research Council. *Realizing the Information Future*. National Academy Press, Washington, D.C., 1994.

[47] C. Courcoubetis, F. P. Kelly, V. A. Siris, and R. Weber. A study of simple usage-based charging schemes for broadband networks. In *Proceedings of IFIP International Conference on Broadband Communications (BC98)*, 1998.

[48] C. Courcoubetis, F. P. Kelly, and R. Weber. Measurement-based usage charges in communication networks. http://www.statslab.cam.ac.uk/reports/1997/1997-19.html. To appear, Operations Research.

[49] C. Courcoubetis and V. A. Siris. An approach to pricing and resource sharing for Available Bit Rate (ABR) services. In *IEEE Globecom 98 Proceedings*, 1998.

[50] C. Courcoubetis, V.A. Siris, and G.D. Stamoulis. Application of the many sources asymptotic and effective bandwidths to traffic engineering. http://www.ics.forth.gr/netgroup/publications/. To appear, Telecommunication Systems. A shorter version appeared in Proceedings of ACM SIGMETRICS'98/PERFORMANCE'98.

[51] C. Courcoubetis, V.A. Siris, and G.D. Stamoulis. Integration of pricing and flow control for available bit rate services in ATM networks. In *IEEE Globecom 96 Proceedings*, 1996.

[52] C. Courcoubetis and R.R. Weber. Buffer overflow asymptotics for a switch handling many traffic sources. *J. Appl. Probab.*, 33:886–903, 1996.

[53] J. Crowcroft and P. Oechslin. Differentiated end-to-end Internet services using a weighted proportional fair sharing TCP. *Computer Communications Review*, 28(3):53–67, July 1998.

[54] J.W. Roberts (ed.). *Performance Evaluation and Design of Multiservice Networks*. Office for Official Publications of the European Communities, Luxembourg, 1992.

[55] R.J. Edell, N. McKeown, and P.P. Varaiya. Billing users and pricing for TCP. *IEEE J. Selected Areas in Comm.*, 13(7):1162–1175, 1995.

[56] K.W. Fendick, M.A. Rodrigues, and A. Weiss. Analysis of a rate-based feedback control strategy for long-haul data transport. *Performance Evaluation*, 16:67–84, 1992.

[57] S. Floyd. Tcp and explicit congestion notification. *ACM Computer Communications Review*, 24:10–23, 1994.

[58] S. Floyd and K. Fall. Promoting the use of end-to-end congestion control in the internet. http://www-nrg.ee.lbl.gov/floyd/end2end-paper.html, 1998.

[59] S. Floyd and V. Jacobson. Random early detection gateways for congestion avoidance. *IEEE/ACM Trans. Networking*, 1:397–413, 1993.

[60] ATM Forum. Traffic Management Specification v4.0, ATM Forum document af-95-0013R12, March 1996.

[61] D. Le Gall. MPEG: A video compression standard for multimedia applications. *Comm. ACM*, 34(4):46–58, April 1991.

[62] R. Gardner. *Games for Business and Economics*. John Wiley & Sons, 1995.

[63] R. J. Gibbens and F. P. Kelly. Measurement-based connection admission control. In V. Ramaswami and P.E. Wirth, editors, *Teletraffic Contributions for the Information Age: Proceedings of the 15th International Teletraffic Congress*, pages 879–888, Washington DC, 1997. Elsevier, Amsterdam.

[64] R. J. Gibbens, R. Mason, and R. Steinberg. An economic analysis of Paris Metro Pricing. Preprint, 1998.

[65] R.J. Gibbens and F.P. Kelly. Resource pricing and the evolution of congestion control. http://www.statslab.cam.ac.uk/~frank/evol.html, 1998.

[66] R.J. Gibbens, F.P. Kelly, and P.B. Key. A decision-theoretic approach to call admission control in ATM networks. *IEEE J. Selected Areas in Comm.*, 13:1101–1114, 1995.

[67] A. Gokhale and D. Schmidt. Measuring and optimizing corba latency and scalability over high speed networks. *IEEE Trans. Comp.*, 47, April 1998.

[68] M. Grossglauser, S. Keshav, and D. Tse. RCBR: A simple and efficient service for multiple time-scale traffic. *IEEE/ACM Trans. Networking*, 5(6):741–755, 1997.

[69] IETF Working Group. Differential Services for the Internet. URL: <http://diffserv.lcs.mit.edu/>.

[70] IETF Working Group. IP Performance Metrics (ippm). URL: <http://www.ietf.org/html.charters/ippm-charter.html>.

[71] A. Gupta, A. O. Stahl, and A. B. Whinston. Priority pricing of integrated services networks. In L. W. McKnight and J. P. Bailey, editors, *Internet Economics*. MIT Press, Cambridge, MA, 1997.

[72] A. Gupta, D. O. Stahl, and A. B. Whinston. Pricing of Services on the Internet. Technical report, University of Texas, Austin, Texas, 1995.

[73] F. Hahn. Stability. In K.J. Arrow and M.D. Intriligator, editors, *Handbook of Mathematical Economics*, pages 745–793. North Holland-Elsevier Science Publishers, Amsterdam, 1982.

[74] E.J. Hernandez-Valencia, L. Benmohamed, R. Nagarajan, and S. Chong. Rate control algorithms for the ATM ABR service. *European Transactions on Telecommunications*, 8:7–20, 1997.

[75] S. Herzog, S. Shenker, and D. Estrin. Sharing the "cost" of multicast trees: An axiomatic analysis. In *ACM SIGCOM 95 Proceedings*, Cambridge, Massachusetts, USA, August 1995.

[76] V. Jacobson. Congestion avoidance and control. In *ACM SIGCOM 88 Proceedings*, pages 314–329, 1988.

[77] W. W. Barns Jr. Defense Data Network Usage Accounting Enhancement Approaches. Technical Report MTR-89W00022, April 1989.

[78] U. Mocci J.W. Roberts and J. Virtamo (eds). *Broadband Network Traffic: Final Report of Action COST 242*. Lecture Notes in Computer Science 1155, Springer, Berlin, 1996.

[79] F.P. Kelly. Tariffs and effective bandwidths in multiservice networks. In *14th Int. Teletraffic Congress Proceedings*, Antibes Juan-les-Pins.

[80] F.P. Kelly. Routing in circuit-switched networks: optimization, shadow prices and decentralization. *Adv. in Appl. Probab.*, 20:112–144, 1988.

[81] F.P. Kelly. On tariffs, policing and admission control for multiservice networks. *Oper. Res. Lett.*, 15:1–9, 1994.

[82] F.P. Kelly. Notes on effective bandwidths. In F.P. Kelly, S. Zachary, and I. Ziedins, editors, *Stochastic Networks: Theory and Applications, Volume 4 of Royal Statistical Society Lecture Notes Series*, pages 141–168. Oxford University Press, Oxford, 1996.

[83] F.P. Kelly. Charging and accounting for bursty connections. In L.W. McKnight and J.P. Bailey, editors, *Internet Economics*, pages 253–278. MIT Press, Cambridge, MA, 1997.

[84] F.P. Kelly. Charging and rate control for elastic traffic. *European Transactions on Telecommunications*, 8:33–37, 1997.

[85] F.P. Kelly, A. Maulloo, and D. Tan. Rate control for communication networks: shadow prices, proportional fairness and stability. *Journal of the Operational Research Society*, 49:237–252, 1998.

[86] Barry M. Leiner, Vinton G. Cerf, David D. Clark, Robert E. Kahn, Leonard Klein-rock, Daniel C. Lynch, Jon Postel, Larry G. Roberts, and Stephen Wolff. URL: <http://info.isoc.org:80/internet/history/brief.html>.

[87] W.E. Leland and D.V. Wilson. High time-resolution measurement and analysis of LAN traffic: Implications for LAN interconnection. In *Proceedings of IEEE INFO-COM'91*, pages 1360–1366, 1991.

[88] K. Lindberger. Cost based charging principles in ATM networks. In *Teletraffic Con-tributions for the Information Age: Proceedings of the 15th International Teletraffic Congress*, pages 771–780, Washington DC, 1997. Elsevier, Amsterdam.

[89] S.H. Low and P.P. Varayia. A new approach to service provisioning in ATM networks. *IEEE Transactions on Networking*, 1:547–553, 1993.

[90] J.K. MacKie-Mason and H.R. Varian. Pricing the internet. In B. Kahin and J. Keller, editors, *Public Access to the Internet*. Prentice-Hall, Englewood Cliffs, New Jersey, 1994.

[91] J.K. MacKie-Mason and H.R. Varian. Pricing congestible network resources. *IEEE J. Selected Areas in Comm.*, 13:1141–1149, 1995.

[92] T. Magedanz, K. Rothermel, and S. Krause. Intelligent agents: An emerging tech-nology for next generation telecommunications? In *Infocom96*, 1996.

[93] M. Mandjes and A. Ridder. Optimal trajectory to overflow in a queue fed by a large number of sources. To appear, Queueing Systems.

[94] R. Mazumdar, L.G. Mason, and C. Douligeris. Fairness in network optimal flow control: optimality of product forms. *IEEE Trans. Comm.*, 39:775–782, 1991.

[95] L. W. McKnight and J. P. Bailey. *Internet Economics*. MIT Press, Cambridge, MA, 1997.

[96] R.K. Miller and A.N. Michell. *Ordinary Differential Equations*. Academic Press, 1982.

[97] J. Murphy, L. Murphy, and E.C. Posner. Distributed pricing for embedded ATM networks. In *14th Int. Teletraffic Congress Proceedings*, Antibes Juan-les-Pins.

[98] K. Nichols, V. Jacobson, and L. Zang. A two-bit differentiated service architecture for the internet. Draft RFC:draft-nichols-diff-svc-arch-00.txt., November 1997.

[99] NSF. Internet Statistics Measurement and Analysis. San Diego Supercomputer Center, February 1996.

[100] A. Odlyzko. A modest proposal for preventing Internet conges-
      tion. Preprint, September 1997. AT&T Labs - Research. Available at
      <http://www.research.att.com/~amo>.

[101] OECD. *Information Infrastructure Convergence and Pricing: the Internet*. Organi-
      sation for Economic Co-operation and Development, Paris, 1996.

[102] V. Paxson. Towards a framework for defining Internet Performance Metrics. In *INET
      95 Proceedings*, Montreal, Canada, June 1996.

[103] O. Rose. Statistical properties of MPEG video traffic and their impact on traffic
      modeling in ATM systems. Technical Report 101, February 1995.

[104] B.K. Ryu and A. Elwalid. The importance of the long-range dependence of VBR
      video traffic in ATM traffic engineering. In *ACM SIGCOM 96 Proceedings*. Stanford,
      CA, USA, 1996.

[105] R. Sessions. *COM and DCOM; Microsoft's Vision for Distributed Objects*. John
      Wiley & Sons, 1997.

[106] S. Shenker. Fundamental design issues for the future internet. *IEEE J. Selected
      Areas in Comm.*, 13:1176–1188, 1995.

[107] S. Shenker, D. Clark, D. Estrin, and S. Herzog. Pricing in computer networks:
      Reshaping the research agenda. *ACM Computer Communication Review*, pages 19–
      43, 1996.

[108] S. Shenker, C. Partridge, and R. Guérin. Specification of guaranteed quality of
      service. RFC 2211. MIT-LCS, September 1997.

[109] A. Simonian and J. Guibert. Large deviations approximations for fluid queues fed by
      a large number of on-off sources. *IEEE J. Selected Areas in Comm.*, 13(7):1017–1027,
      September 1995.

[110] V.A. Siris. Large deviation techniques for traffic engineering.
      http://www.ics.forth.gr/netgroup/msa/.

[111] V.A. Siris, D.J. Songhurst, G.D. Stamoulis, and M. Stoer. Usage-based charging
      using effective bandwidths: studies and reality. In P. B. Key and D. G. Smith,
      editors, *Teletraffic Engineering in a Competitive World: Proceedings of the 16th
      International Teletraffic Congress*, Edinburgh, 1999. Elsevier, Amsterdam.

[112] D.J. Songhurst. Charging mechanism and policy: Adapting to the commercial envi-
      ronment. In *Colloquium on Charging for ATM - the Reality Arrives*. IEE, London,
      November 1997.

[113] D.J. Songhurst and F.P. Kelly. Charging schemes for multiservice networks. In V. Ramaswami and P.E. Wirth, editors, *Teletraffic Contributions for the Information Age: Proceedings of the 15th International Teletraffic Congress*, pages 781–790, Washington DC, 1997. Elsevier, Amsterdam.

[114] University of California, Berkeley. The Internet Demand Experiment (INDEX). URL: <http://www.index.berkeley.edu>.

[115] H.R. Varian. *Microeconomic Analysis*. Norton, 1992.

[116] D. Walker, F. P. Kelly, and J. Solomon. Tariffing in the new IP/ATM environment. *Telecommunications Policy*, May 1997.

[117] P. Whittle. *Optimization Under Constraints*. John Wiley & Sons, 1971.

[118] D. Wischik. The output of a switch, or, effective bandwidths for networks. To appear, Queueing Systems.

[119] D. Wischik. Sample path large deviations for queues with many inputs. To appear, Annals of Applied Probability.

[120] J. Wroclawski. Specification of the controlled-load network element service. RFC 2212. Xerox PARC, BBN, IBM, September 1997.

Index